S0-CBF-310

CHABOT COLLEGE-HAYWARD
2 555 000 034180 X

Men, Money, and Markets

To Shaw ... who helped, as always.

Men, Money, and Markets

AN INTRODUCTION TO ECONOMIC REASONING

by

Robert B. Bangs

Distributed by

THE BOXWOOD PRESS
183 Ocean View Boulevard
Pacific Grove, California 93950

Phone: 408–375-9110

Library of Congress Card
No. 72-81139

Standard Book Number: 910286-17-5

Printed in U.S.A.

PREFACE

This is a textbook for younger readers and others who have not previously had formal instruction in the subject. It is perhaps a little informal compared to the usual textbook. This is because of my view that economics should be a living and changing subject rather than a rigid discipline such as mathematics.

This book is by no means a complete introduction to all the topics that economics includes. Rather it is a sampling that I hope will encourage the student to read more. The daily paper, many magazines, the financial press, and many other sources are filled with articles and discussions of economic problems. What one needs to read this material perceptively is a little formal background; the current issues need to be seen in systematic context and in relation to received economic thinking. This book, in a word, is strictly an introduction to a larger volume of literature. I hope that as such it will be both interesting and helpful.

Robert B. Bangs

Bethesda, Maryland

CONTENTS

Page	Chapter	
1	1	THE NAME OF THE GAME—Some Economic Concepts
20	2	BUSINESS REARS ITS HEAD—The Individual Firm
40	3	THE PAST IS PROLOGUE—Economics as an Historical Process
57	4	NOT TO BUY TOO DEAR—Prices and the Price System
72	5	IT'S SYSTEMATIC—The Price System, continued
85	6	CHARGED WITH A PUBLIC INTEREST—Public Utilities
99	7	THE WHOLE IS GREATER THAN THE SUM—Macroeconomics
115	8	THE ROOT OF ALL EVIL— Money and Banking
131	9	THE PROMISES MEN LIVE BY—The Credit System
148	10	A FOOL AND HIS MONEY—Personal Finance and Investments
163	11	IT'S IN THE BAG—Budgets
183	12	THE POWER TO DESTROY—Taxation
199	13	TO WHOM SHALL BE GIVEN—Distribution of Income
214	14	WORTHY OF HIS HIRE—Labor Problems and Labor History
233	15	STOP MAKING THOSE WAVES—Business Cycles
248	16	THE SILKS OF CATHAY—International Trade and Finance
268	17	ALWAYS TO BE TOPICAL—Current Topics in Economics
283	18	FOR WANT OF A POLICY—Economic Policies
302		Index

Chapter 1

THE NAME OF THE GAME—Some Economic Concepts

George Bernard Shaw, a celebrated wit and playwright, wrote that a highwayman should be rewarded more generously than a railroad shareholder because the former ran a greater risk. He also wrote that we defend capitalists because they are large employers of labor. "In other words we praise a man for giving a great deal of trouble to other people, and the more trouble he gives, the more we praise him."

Shaw was a Fabian socialist. He thought the arrangements of this world could be improved by pure logic, particularly if the logic applied was his own. As an economist he was more interested in ideology than explanation, more concerned about how things should be than how they are. He treated economics as a huge, rather pathetic joke—an attitude he held toward other subjects as well. H. G. Wells, a contemporary of Shaw, once wrote that Mr. Shaw is "one of those perpetual children who live in a dream of make believe, and the make believe of Mr. Shaw is that he is a person of incredible brilliance and subtlety, running the world, when he is an elderly adolescent, still at play."

Whether Shaw was a good or a bad economist, an adult or an adolescent is hardly the point. One cannot hope to prescribe until one understands. We each need to know how the economy works before we can hope to improve it. The pages that follow are an attempt to tell what the economy is and how it works.

Why is New Bedford, Massachusetts, a distressed area with high unemployment while Tulsa, Oklahoma, has a labor shortage? Why are food prices rising (or falling) now, when only a few months ago they were falling (or rising)? What does it mean when the United States has a deficit in its balance of payments, and how may this affect me? Why do stock prices fluctuate?

Have you ever wondered about questions like these and wished you could find some answers? You can by studying the ebb and flow of economic forces, and by getting some knowledge about economic principles. All these issues and many others like them are a result of the operation of economic trends, which are tides and crosscurrents in the world at work. Economics is about work and its product, wealth. It is also about the use of this wealth to support and enrich human life, to give it dignity and meaning, to enhance the welfare of people.

R. H. Tawney has said ours is an acquisitive society, while J. K. Galbraith has called it affluent. Each is right in his way. Our society *is* acquisitive in that the desire to acquire—goods, money, status—provides much of the drive to work and produce that makes the economic machine go. Ours is also an affluent society because, as a result of work and saving in the past, we have reached a level of affluence undreamed of 100 years ago, and also far above that of many other countries. As a result of this affluence, which is relative and not absolute (since many Americans do not share in it), we are rethinking some established ideas about work and leisure, and about private and public goods.

Art or Science?

Economics is a subject that is continually evolving and changing because it is about the world as it is and not as it used to be or ought to be. Economics is about people—in their workaday activities, as wage earners, as consumers, as investors, as business managers, and as public officials concerned with the formulation or implementation of public policy. It is not about people in the particular but in the mass—people as interest groups, as residents of a particular country or area, as sets of political and social attitudes, whether liberal or conservative, free traders or protectionists, work or leisure oriented, and so on.

Early in the present century it was fashionable among professional economists to debate whether economics was art or science. There have always been economists who wanted to be scientific; they desired to formulate laws as precise as Boyle's law of gases or Newton's law of gravity—on the theory that knowledge should consist primarily of eternal verities, immutable and unchanging.

Other economists have been eminently practical men who studied their subject primarily to determine why certain problems arose, persisted, and how they might be cured.

Thus, Robert Malthus, a compassionate clergyman living in early 19th century England, sought to analyze why people were chronically poor; the answer he found was that population tended to outrun the means of subsistence. But because he wrote in a period before modern birth control techniques and before the spectacular advances in agricultural productivity, Malthus' explanation is questioned in today's world. In Malthus' time the lack of knowledge of birth control was balanced by lack of modern medicine. Discovery of the New World and the Industrial Revolution put off Malthus' dilemma. The problem remains.

I have always found those practical economists who were passionately interested in current human problems, and who considered political economy to be more art than science, to be more interesting than those more rigorous thinkers who wanted all of economics to be scientific and divorced from policy problems. For one thing, most of the economic scientists' so-called "immutable laws" have proved, over time, to be neither immutable nor even laws; they have proved instead to be principles of some generality, particularly adapted to a certain set of historical circumstances or a given constellation of institutions. The *iron law of wages,* for example, which held that wages could never rise much above the level of subsistence, has proved to be neither iron nor worthy of being called a law analogous to the laws of physics or biology.

Most modern economists now see the old controversy about whether economics was art *or* science to be fundamentally sterile and largely beside the point. Actually, economics is both art *and* science; the proportions of each can be varied to suit the exigencies of the problem and the temperament of the applier. This is true also of certain fields of biology, such as ecology which involves human values. Marriage counselors say that a major cause of divorce is the differing values on how to spend the family income.

Thomas Robert Malthus, 1766-1834. Economist, sociologist, and clergyman. Best known for his principle of population published in 1798. He also did important work in economics including criticizing, as a pamphleteer, many of the prevalent economic doctrines of his time.

The scientific element in economics concerns the discovery and description of general principles which are applicable over a broad range of different environments. For example, it is a general principle of economic science that a complex economy needs a price system in order to function; this holds true whether its organization is along capitalist, free enterprise, or socialist, state-owned lines.

The art of economics consists largely in devising policies to deal with emerging problems. For example, should an incipient recession with rising unemployment be dealt with by tax reduction, by supplying more abundant or "easier" money as it is often called, or in some other way? The more one is concerned with policy, the greater the tendency to emphasize the *art* of economics. But, unfortunately, until a problem has been both analyzed and understood, one cannot devise policies to cope with or to overcome it. Both art *and* science are necessary elements of economics.

What is Economics?

Perhaps the easiest way to answer this question is first to specify what economics is not. It is not home economics, cooking and sewing; these are separate and useful arts. It is not how to make a million in the stock market, although a good knowledge of economics is an aid in understanding how and why the market moves. Nor is it how to run a business successfully; that is another useful art called management.

Rather, economics is the systematic study of the processes of producing, distributing, and consuming goods and services; of the creation, distribution, and use of incomes arising from that productive process; of financing business and government activities; of problems and policies that relate to work, wealth, and welfare.

Economics is about business in the large, not about a particular business. It is about how people earn their living, and the factors which determine how good or poor that living is. It is about organizations that relate to production and work—corporations, labor unions, associations of manufacturers, regulatory commissions, bank clearinghouses, and the like.

Above all, economics tries to see the whole rather than merely a part—the whole business system, the whole banking system, the whole picture of international trade. It is an effort to understand and to analyze a complex society at work.

To grasp all these things takes a long time and a great deal of study. You will not learn all of it from this book or any other single book. What you can learn from this and other books is enough to whet your appetite for more learning and perhaps some comprehension of the range and scope of economics as an intellectual discipline. You can also learn to think a little more broadly and constructively about economic problems and policies. You will be dealing with these matters all the rest of your life, whether you wish it or not. Doesn't it seem reasonable, therefore, to be prepared as well as possible for what is inevitable?

Economics is a practical art, like swimming, driving a car, or baking a cake. It is also an intellectual discipline, like philosophy, psychiatry, or history. Someone once said that those who do not study history are doomed to relive it; it might equally be said that those who don't study economics are doomed to muddle through it the rest of their days.

Why study economics?

A good question, deserving of a no-nonsense answer. Perhaps the first reason is that, since economic problems are inevitable, why not have a systematic framework for dealing with them, instead of trying to cope in a hit-or-miss, haphazard manner?

Basically, economics is about the allocation of scarce resources to alternative uses. The money in your pocket, for example, is a scarce resource; if you are like most of us it is never enough to cover all your needs, wants, and caprices. The $5 in your pocket or purse might be spent for food, for records, for movies, for stockings, or whatever else may be your desire at the moment. Alternatively it may be saved because no more will be coming in until next week, and you might want something tomorrow or Friday more than you do today.

These are economic decisions—deciding to buy this instead of that, or to buy nothing today in order to buy something else tomorrow. They are consumer decisions about how to apply a scarce resource, the money in your pocket, to a myriad of different wants or desires.

Suppose you get a summer job. The pay is $50 per week of which $10 is withheld for taxes and social security, leaving you a net of $40. What do you do with this income? If you live at home with food and shelter provided, the whole $40 is discretionary income, to be used as you wish. But if you have to provide your own food and shelter, that might take $25 per week, leaving you with a discretionary income of only $15. Manifestly, with only $15, you have less discretion—your range of choice, your options, are more limited.

We are not just consumers. We are also workers, or employers, or investors—perhaps all three. Suppose you decide to go into business for yourself. You are good at fixing things and you have heard people complain about how hard it is to get appliances and other durable goods repaired and back in service. You decide to set up a repair shop.

That in itself is an economic decision. But it leads in turn to numerous other economic decisions. Where should the shop be located? How much space and equipment will you need? What kind of help will you require, and where will you find them? Who are your potential customers? What kind of advertising will best notify these potential customers of the services you are equipped to provide? How is the venture to be financed? How much capital can you provide yourself? How much can you borrow, and from what sources? All these are economic questions which require economic decisions for their resolution.

In the end your business may fail because you have misjudged your market or underestimated your capital requirements—in a word because you have miscalculated the economics of the situation or made some wrong economic decisions. Or your shop may succeed because you have sensed a need and moved appropriately to satisfy it.

A businessman spends most of his working life making economic decisions; to expand here or there, to push this product or that one, to modernize his facilities or make do with what he has already, to establish a branch in this shopping center or that one, to import from Japan or buy at home—these are the questions he faces daily; in the end they determine whether or not he prospers.

In the United States we operate under the free enterprise system. If you want to set up a repair shop, you are free to do so. You need no permission from the government, no licenses, and no bothersome formalities. You cannot, of course, establish your shop in the midst of a residential area; you must honor the local zoning laws. But, aside from that, you are free to operate your business as you wish. No one guarantees you customers, of course. It is strictly up to you to find them, to serve them well, and to charge them reasonable prices.

If you do all these things, your business may grow and prosper. If you don't, if your service is poor and your prices too high or too low, you will get into trouble. Then, you can expect no rescue—no government salvage operation to straighten out your business. You may end in failure and bankruptcy.

This is what the free enterprise system means. It is founded on initiative in judging what the public wants, needs, and is willing to pay for; on filling that want; on charging prices that will cover your costs and leave a little over for profit.

We call a businessman who organizes and develops a business an entrepreneur—a French word meaning undertaker, but in the sense of a "take charge person" rather than a mortician. The entrepreneur is very important to the free enterprise system; it is he who sees an opportunity and moves to meet it; he puts the pieces together so that a new business actually comes into being—repairing shoes, mining coal, transporting merchandise, or doing any of the thousand and one things required to be done in a complex interrelated society. The entrepreneur takes a risk, which is usually considerable. If he is successful, his reward is profit; if not, he may try some other venture, some other place, some other time.

The entrepreneur is more a psychological type than a product of any particular training. He may have little or no formal education, but great native shrewdness. He may be a highly trained engineer, or merely a mechanic who has a flair for organization. He may be almost anything; but if he is a success, he will have vision, great capacity for taking pains, a belief in what he is doing, and the persistence to stick with it in spite of many difficulties and obstacles.

As a general rule, individual entrepreneurs today start only small businesses, such as retail stores, or service establishments, or small specialty manufacturing operations. The bulk of American business is dominated by large corporations, each having thousands of employees and assets in millions or even billions of dollars. General Motors, for example, produces half of all the automobiles made in this country, and is also active in weapons production, aircraft, and other lines as well.

It would not be easy for an individual entrepreneur to start manufacturing automobiles in competition with General Motors, but it is possible; to do so the entrepreneur has to see something GM doesn't do or some-

Typical of modern business establishments is this relatively large pulp and paper mill located in New Zealand. Paper is made from softwood logs which are first reduced to pulp and then reconstituted as paper. Paper use per capita is a good indication of a country's stage of economic development.

thing he can do better than the corporative giant—perhaps it is racing cars, or golf carts, or some other specialty. Part of the genius of the free enterprise system is that it is possible for giants and pygmies to coexist and to cooperate in harmony.

The tyranny of words.

One of the problems with economists is that, when they use commonplace terms—like *demand, cost, capital,* and *income tax*—their meaning is often a highly technical one. D. H. Robertson, a British economist with a puckish sense of humor, used to say that all economists should be compelled to translate their technical terms into Latin, so it would be clear that the ordinary, commonsense meaning was not intended.

Needless to say, Robertson did not carry his point; we still have terminological confusion. One aspect of this is that many of the terms in economics are multifaceted.

An example is the term *capital.* This means different things depending on context. If we are talking of production and ways to increase it, capital goods are *produced means of production*—machinery, tools, etc. If we are talking of invested capital, we mean past savings embodied in securities or put to work in some similar way to finance business. The capital of a business may mean its *net worth* or sometimes its *total assets.* Another accounting concept is the *working capital* of a business, usually taken to mean the excess of current assets over current liabilities.

Working capital thus measures the potential uncommitted cash flow of a business over a reasonably short period, such as a year.

There are many other senses to the term capital as used in economics; but perhaps the essential point has been made. One reason economics is difficult (and it is) is that its terminology is difficult. Many familiar words are used in an unfamiliar sense. Also many terms have numerous senses or meanings which cannot always be determined from context. It is important, then, in writing about economics, to specify the sense intended, when this is not entirely clear from the context. Economics is difficult enough, without adding semantic confusion to it.

We escape from the tyranny of words not by using them loosely, but by using them precisely. Economics is full of technical terms; the fact that the words may also have a common meaning does not make them any less technical.

Wealth.

Wealth is another of those terms in economics with manifold meanings. To an individual it means simply assets or net worth with a monetary valuation. Thus a man is a millionaire because he controls $1 million in assets or has a net worth equal to that figure. His assets may be land, stocks and bonds, or control of a business—even gold or postage stamps. Ordinarily, wealth is not kept as money because money is unproductive; it earns income only when invested in some way.

Passing from the private or individual concept of wealth as assets to more social concepts, we are told that the wealth of a country is its natural resources, its capital embodied in buildings, roads, mines, and factories, and in human capital—the skill, ability, and enterprise of its people. Underdeveloped countries are underdeveloped because they lack the physical and human capital that is the product of a long, sustained accumulation. They may also be poor in natural resources, as Egypt is poor, for example.

Some years ago when the author was in Burma, trying with a few others to help the Burmese government realize some of its aspirations for economic development, we advisers used to remark among ourselves that Burma was one of the richest poor countries we knew. It was extremely rich in natural resources, in fertile land, in forests, in water-power sites, and in many other respects. But it was extremely poor in accumulated physical

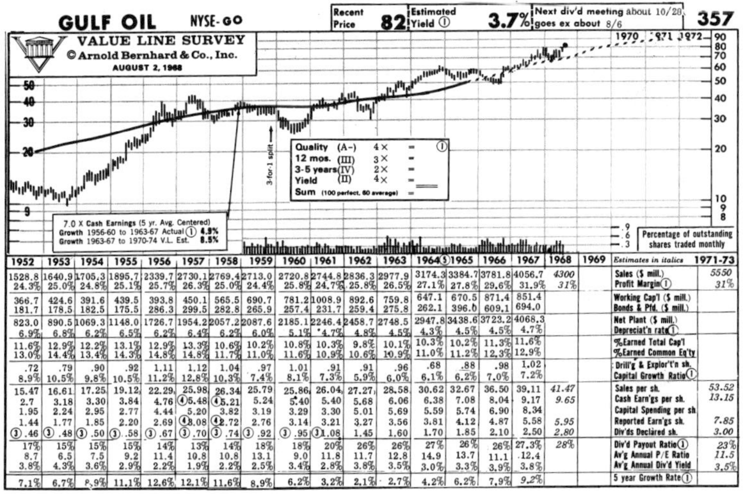

Estimates in italics	1952	1953	1954	1955	1956	1957	1958	1959	1960	1961	1962	1963	1964⑤	1965	1966	1967	1968	1969	1971-73
Sales ($ mill.)	1528.8	1640.9	1705.3	1895.7	2339.7	2730.1	2769.4	2713.0	2720.8	2744.8	2836.3	2977.9	3174.3	3384.7	3781.8	4056.7	*4300*		*5550*
Profit Margin ①	24.3%	25.0%	24.8%	25.1%	25.7%	26.3%	25.0%	24.4%	25.8%	24.7%	25.8%	26.5%	27.1%	27.8%	29.6%	31.9%	*31%*		*31%*
Working Cap'l ($ mill.)	366.7	424.6	391.6	439.5	393.8	450.1	565.5	690.7	781.2	1008.9	892.6	759.8	647.1	670.5	871.4	851.4			
Bonds & Pfd. ($ mill.)	181.7	178.5	182.5	175.5	286.3	299.5	282.8	265.9	257.4	231.7	259.4	275.8	262.1	396.0	609.1	694.0			
Net Plant ($ mill.)	823.0	890.5	1069.3	1148.0	1726.7	1954.2	2057.2	2087.6	2185.1	2246.4	2458.7	2748.5	2947.8	3438.6	3723.2	4068.3			
Depreciat'n rate ①	6.9%	6.8%	6.2%	6.5%	6.2%	6.4%	6.2%	6.0%	5.1%	4.7%	4.8%	4.5%	4.3%	4.5%	4.5%	4.7%			
%Earned Total Cap'l	11.6%	12.9%	12.2%	13.1%	12.9%	13.3%	10.6%	10.2%	10.8%	10.3%	9.8%	10.1%	10.3%	10.2%	11.3%	11.6%			
%Earned Common Eq'ty	13.0%	14.4%	13.4%	14.3%	14.8%	14.8%	11.7%	11.0%	11.6%	10.9%	10.6%	10.9%	11.0%	11.2%	12.3%	12.9%			
Drill'g & Explor't'n sh.	.72	.79	.90	.92	1.11	1.12	1.04	.97	1.01	.91	.91	.96	.68	.88	.98	1.02			
Capital Growth Ratio ①	8.9%	10.5%	9.8%	10.5%	11.2%	12.8%	10.3%	7.4%	8.1%	7.3%	5.9%	6.0%	6.1%	6.2%	7.0%	7.2%			
Sales per sh.	15.47	16.61	17.25	19.12	22.29	25.98	26.34	25.79	25.86	26.04	27.27	28.58	30.62	32.67	36.50	39.11	*41.47*		*53.52*
Cash Earn'gs per sh.	2.7	3.18	3.30	3.84	4.76	④5.48	④5.21	5.24	5.40	5.40	5.68	6.06	6.38	7.08	8.04	9.17	*9.65*		*13.15*
Capital Spending per sh.	1.95	2.24	2.95	2.77	4.44	5.20	3.82	3.19	3.29	3.30	5.01	5.69	5.59	5.74	6.90	8.34			
Reported Earn'gs sh.	1.44	1.77	1.85	2.20	2.69	④3.08	④2.72	2.76	3.14	3.21	3.27	3.56	3.81	4.12	4.87	5.58	*5.95*		*7.85*
Div'ds Declared sh.	③.46	③.48	③.50	③.58	③.67	③.70	③.74	③.92	③.95	③1.08	1.45	1.60	1.70	1.85	2.10	2.50	*2.80*		*3.00*
Div'd Payout Ratio ①	17%	15%	15%	15%	14%	13%	14%	18%	18%	20%	26%	26%	27%	26%	26%	27.3%	*28%*		*23%*
Av'g Annual P/E Ratio	8.7	6.5	7.5	9.2	11.4	10.8	10.8	13.1	9.0	11.8	11.7	12.8	14.9	13.7	11.1	12.4			*11.5*
Av'g Annual Div'd Yield	3.8%	4.3%	3.6%	2.9%	2.2%	1.9%	2.2%	2.5%	3.4%	2.8%	3.8%	3.5%	3.0%	3.3%	3.9%	3.8%			*3.5%*
5 year Growth Rate ①	7.1%	6.7%	8.9%	11.1%	12.6%	12.1%	11.6%	8.9%	6.2%	3.2%	2.1%	2.7%	4.2%	6.2%	7.9%	9.2%			

Price history of a stock. The chart shows the monthly high and low prices, in dollars per share, of this oil company issue. The solid black line is a trend line fitted mathematically. Courtesy Arnold Bernhard & Co.

capital such as roads, factories, and functioning harbors, and even poorer in the training and enterprise of its people. Human capital was the most backward feature of the country; this backwardness limited all possibilities and all efforts at economic growth. What Burma needed above all else was education and training for its people. This by no means meant sending them all to college; they needed to be educated in plumbing, in farming, in shopkeeping, and as machinists as well as in philosophy, or economics, or law.

Economists used to call their subject the "science of wealth," or the "study of the production, distribution, and consumption of wealth." By wealth they meant goods and services (the content of current production) as well as the accumulations from past output (the produced means of production). Wealth was seen simply as an enormous and diverse pile of commodities, to be added to, shared in some way, and partially used up. It was, if you will, a kind of national stockpile of everything, constantly turning over from additions and subtractions.

To social critics and socialists wealth means ostentation, because some wealthy people have always engaged in conspicuous consumption of housing, yachts, lavish entertainment, and expensive motor cars. These social critics have concentrated on inequality in the distribution of wealth—the contrast between affluence and poverty, the waste in the midst of near starvation—and have been preoccupied with the development of systems for taking from the rich and giving to the poor. What they fail to see is that, because the rich are few and the poor many, taking from the rich will provide too little to make much difference to the poor. At best, the poor will get an extra dollar or an extra crust of bread. What these social critics also fail to see clearly is that the economic system runs because of incentives, and that money, distinctions, and other inequalities may be necessary to provide these incentives.

In Russia after the revolution following World War I, the dominant Bolshevik party set out to build a new economic order, on Marxian lines. Marxian economics taught that equality was a great thing, that a workman was as worthy as his employer, and one should not exploit another. What the Communists discovered, after many false starts, and a great deal of inefficiency, and plain bureaucratic confusion, was that to get production rolling there had to be managers and other supervisors; they had to have authority; and they had to be rewarded. Equality may be a great philosophic ideal but, when applied to a group activity, it results in a chaotic mob scene instead of a disciplined and functioning working unit. The result is that in Russia today managers, technicians, and other specialists who make the economy go are highly rewarded in money, perquisites, and other ways. Inequality under Communism is in some ways greater than it is under Capitalism. Incentives or rewards are necessary, whatever one's philosophy.

The relevance of theory.

A theory is an explanation of how or why something works—an effort to make a complex process comprehensible. From this it follows that the relevance of a theory in economics is not to be found in the elegance of its internal logic, but in whether it accurately explains what happens. There are many theories of the business cycle, for example. Some of these attribute the cycle primarily to overinvestment, others to underinvestment; some find the devil in underconsumption, others in undersaving. Now it is obvious to anyone that, since certain of these categories are mutually exclusive, they all cannot be true. We cannot as root causes have both over and underinvestment; it must be one or the other, or something else.

The differences arise primarily from the things which spinners of different theories leave out, or choose to abstract from. One analyst may think the monetary process unimportant, that it merely conceals the real forces at work underneath. Another may think the monetary process is the very essence of maladjustments that fuel the cyclical process. A third may think price determination and price setting are the central processes around which all else pivots. Because economics is such an extensive subject, there is room under the umbrella of the discipline for all shades of both opinion and emphasis; but all who study economics (and especially those who teach it) share the common need to simplify and thereby to understand the complex process.

You will ask, why bother with theory when it is all partial and may leave out the most important matter? The answer is that without theory we could make little sense of the whole business. We should be lost in the middle of a dense jungle with no paths leading out.

Economic theories are paths which generations of economists have constructed in their individual efforts to get out of the jungle. Sometimes their paths lead nowhere. Sometimes, when it seems daylight is about to be seen, a new impenetrable wall of vegetation will appear, making further progress impossible. Moreover, the old paths get forgotten and overgrown, and the jungle itself is constantly changing, shrinking here and growing there.

Theory, then, is the alternative, imperfect though it may be, to being permanently lost in the jungle. In studying theory we have different optional paths pointed out to us; more importantly we are handed a machete fashioned by others and thus armed are equipped to find our own way out.

You have all heard the expression "something is all right in theory, but not in practice." If theory is a simplified explanation of how something works, there cannot be a gulf between theory and practice, but only between good and bad theory. Either a theory explains how and why a process works, in which case it is good theory, or it doesn't, in which case it is bad theory.

John Gardner, formerly Secretary of Health, Education, and Welfare, once made the point rather neatly when he wrote, "an excellent plumber is infinitely more admirable than an incompetent philosopher. The society which scorns excellence in plumbing because plumbing is a humble activity and tolerates shoddiness in philosophy because it is an exalted activity will have neither good plumbing nor good philosophy. Neither its pipes nor its theories will hold water."

Good theory is an excellent plumber; bad theory is a shoddy philosopher. The often mentioned gulf between theory and practice is an ancient illusion, unfortunately still cherished in many quarters.

A systematic approach to the resolution of an economic issue is illustrated by the diagram below. You will notice that the central part of the process is labeled analysis and that the inputs into this analytical process are the lessons from past experience, the general principles involved, and the dimensions of the problem as disclosed by statistical or other measures. From the analytical process will issue a purely economic conclusion, which may require modification by other considerations, such as political or human ones. These non-economic considerations feed back into the analytical process, from which then issues a policy recommendation or policy action.

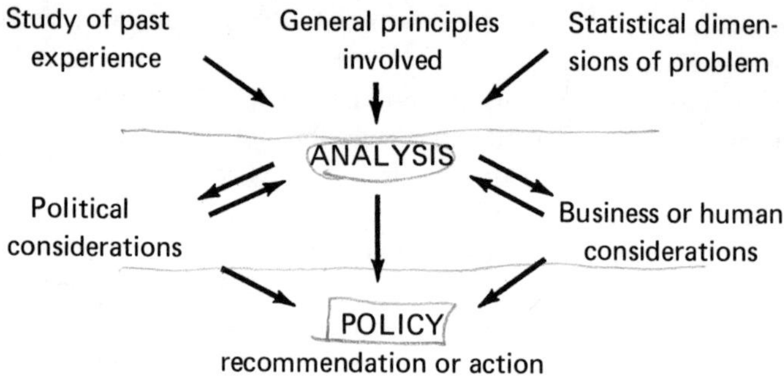

Model of the process involved in studying and resolving an economic issue. The analytical study is central. Into it feed inputs from past experience, applications of the general principles involved, and statistical or other measurements of the problem's dimensions. Economic analysis interacts with other considerations to produce the final policy recommendation or action.

Such a policy should be both an efficient and a practical one if the analytical process has been correctly carried out and the noneconomic considerations properly weighed. However, even the most carefully considered policies may be inappropriate or ineffective because of failure to consider properly some strategic aspect of the problem.

Macro and micro economics.

This distinction is simply between studying the economy as a whole (macro) vs. studying some part (micro). Thus, the economics of the individual firm or of the coal industry is microeconomics, whereas studying aggregate personal saving or the total level of employment is macroeconomics.

Perhaps the most interesting thing about this dichotomy is the relative attention paid to the respective sides of the coin at different times. Thus, the 19th century was a long period of ascendancy for microeconomics. Partial analysis made great strides and occupied most of the attention of virtually all economists, save a few in Switzerland and Italy.

In the last 30 years, on the contrary, macroeconomics has held the center of the stage, while only a handful of economists have been concerned with micro problems. Unemployment, inflation, and economic growth have all been concerned primarily with aggregates for the whole national economy. Only specialized economists have been engaged with the steel industry, problems of basing point pricing, functioning of the capital markets, and other micro problems of this nature.

In part, the shift to macroeconomics has reflected the growing role of economists in economic policy formulation. It would never have occurred to President Harding in 1921 to have on his staff or to listen to an economic adviser. No recent President has been able to function without one or more, however much he may deplore on occasion the kind of advice he gets from them.

The Federal government today accepts far more responsibility for maintaining a satisfactory general level of economic activity, and for intervening in economic problems, such as a sharply rising level of shoe imports, or a wage dispute between truckdrivers and their employers, than it did some years ago. The great depression of the 1930's marked a real watershed in political opinion concerning the role of government in economic affairs. A whole generation said to itself that this kind of catastrophic event must not be allowed to happen again.

For the study of economics, a few tools, such as a slight knowledge of accounting and statistics, are necessary. Let us turn to these now.

Accounting.

Today's accounting is simply an elaboration of the system of double entry bookkeeping invented by an Italian monk, Pacoli, in the 16th century. It utilizes the simple principle that every transaction has two sides, thus involving a double entry. If you pay a bill, you charge or *debit* some expense item on your books and *credit* cash. *Assets* are things you own, *liabilities* are items you owe. Increases in assets are debits; decreases in assets are credits. Decreases in liabilities are debits and increases in liabilities are credits.

In a rudimentary bookkeeping system all transactions are first recorded in a *journal* or daybook. Then they are posted to a *ledger* which, when summarized, gives the status of each account. A summary of all ledger accounts is called a *trial balance.* It shows merely that double entries have been made for all transactions so that the accounts are "in balance." This does not mean that they are correct.

If all asset and liability accounts are assembled, we have what is known as a *balance sheet.* In American practice, assets appear on the left and liabilities on the right. The British reverse this. Let us follow the American convention, for that is all it is.

If you were to construct a personal balance sheet it might look like this:

ASSETS		LIABILITIES	
Cash in pocket	$ 5.	Borrowed from friend	$ 10.
Cash in bank	100.	Bills unpaid	15.
Clothing and books	150.		
Automobile	200.	Net worth	$430.
Total assets	$455.	Total liabilities	$455.

You will notice that the accounts "balance" because the net worth item is a residual or difference between what you own and what you owe. In effect, you owe this to yourself if you are treating your personal business as an entity.

If you were in business you would set up the business accounts as an entity apart from your personal accounts. To draw up a balance sheet for the business you would list all assets used in the business and all obligations of the business. The difference would be the business' net worth or your investment in the business. In effect, you are treating the business as an entity apart from the proprietor.

Accounting also involves the systematic recording of income and expense items. Under American convention expenses are debits, while income items are credits. When a merchant records his sales for the day, he debits cash or accounts receivable and credits sales income. When he pays his help for the week, he debits or charges labor expense and credits cash.

A balance sheet always records status at a particular point in time, for example Dec. 31, 1970. An income statement always records income and expense for a particular period, for example the month of December, 1970.

One other distinction is of some importance in accounting, namely that between *cash* items and *accrual* items. When you buy something for cash you have acquired an asset or incurred an expense (debit items) and you match this by an immediate decrease (credit) to cash. When you charge a purchase at a store you have acquired an asset (new dress) and incurred a liability (account payable at the store). You may not pay the bill until next month, so this month's accounts should show the accrual of a liability.

When a merchant casts up his accounts for a month he figures total sales as income, whether matched by cash or merely by receivables, and expenses attributable to the month, whether or not matched by cash outgo. He is thus calculating his income statement on an accrual rather than on a cash basis. Accrual accounting is generally considered more accurate than cash accounting, especially where many transactions are on a credit basis. Most personal income tax returns, however, are on a cash basis.

One other concept important in accounting is that of depreciation. Suppose you operate a repair shop and use a truck to pick up and deliver your work. The truck cost $2000, but you calculate it will last for 5 years. Each year you should charge the business with 1/5th the cost of the truck or $400. This is known as *depreciation* and is merely prorating the cost of the truck over its probable useful life. Depreciation is merely the loss in value of long-lived assets with use or over time. If you own a car you know it depreciates each year whether you use it or not.

The purpose of these few pages is not to make accountants of you. That is the function of another course. However, to discuss many topics in economics intelligently, it is necessary to have a rudimentary knowledge of accounting. You need to know, for example, that deposits are liabilities of a bank and that the net worth of a corporation is what its stockholders own. Each share is a proportionate claim to that net worth.

Uses and abuses of statistics.

If you progress beyond first base in economics, you will find yourself surrounded by statistics—on employment, exports and imports, national income, steel production, freight carloadings, and many other matters. Statistics are numbers, the raw material for much of economic analysis, and for many of the policy issues that inevitably arise.

Suppose the question is whether or not the minimum wage should be raised. To appraise this question rationally one should know how many workers are now at the minimum wage, and how many just above; in what industries are they concentrated; what is the profit position in these industries? These questions by no means exhaust the facts that would bear on the minimum wage issue; but they typify the varieties of statistical material that would be relevant.

One reason economics is so difficult is that everything is related to nearly everything else. Steel workers' wages depend on steel imports, on wages paid in other industries, on living costs, and on many other factors. Since things are so interrelated it is necessary to simplify them by building models which treat only the most significant relationships while neglecting or put-

Assets	(thousands of dollars)		December 31 1970	196
Current Assets				
Cash			$ 11,441	$ 21,3
Receivable from				
Customers, less reserves for discounts and doubtful items of $2,656—1970; $2,595—1969			62,403	64,2
Others			9,250	8,9
Inventories, at lower of cost (principally latest production or purchase cost) or market	1970	1969		
Finished products	$ 53,837	$ 40,196		
Work in process	17,705	15,231		
Pulp, logs and pulpwood	29,762	22,412		
Other materials and supplies	31,616	29,836	132,920	107,6
Prepaid items			7,692	5,4
			223,706	207,6
Plant Assets, at cost				
Land	9,844	9,455		
Buildings	147,713	133,599		
Machinery and equipment	710,871	667,966		
	868,428	811,020		
Accumulated depreciation	(384,672)	(353,786)	483,756	457,2
Timber Resources, at cost less depletion			57,665	57,9
Investments in Affiliates, at cost ($56,157—1970; $50,387—1969) plus equity in undistributed earnings				
International	62,585	52,769		
Domestic	32,343	30,075	94,928	82,8
Other Investments, at cost			1,434	1,5
Patents, Trademarks and Goodwill				
Other Assets			5,329	4,7
Total Assets			$866,818	$811,9

Balance sheet of a corporation (Scott Paper Company) taken from its annual report. Notice that the balance sheet is comparative since it covers two years. It is consolidated because it covers both the parent company and its subsidiaries. It balances because shareholders' investment is the residual item. (Courtesy Scott Paper Co.)

ilities and Shareholders' Investment	(thousands of dollars)		December 31 1970	1969
rent Liabilities				
ayable to suppliers and others			**$ 65,966**	$ 66,452
oans and current maturities of long term debt			**54,020**	90,022
ividend declared on preferred shares			**64**	64
stimated taxes on income			**8,362**	10,566
			128,412	167,104
g Term Debt			**180,781**	106,060
erred Income Taxes			**36,864**	33,690
reholders' Investment				
umulative preferred shares without par value				
Authorized—110,640 shares				
Outstanding	**1970**	1969		
$3.40 series—46,205 shares	**$ 4,684**	$ 4,684		
$4.00 series—24,435 shares	**2,444**	2,444		
Investment of preferred shareholders			**7,128**	7,128
oting preferred shares				
Authorized—1,000,000 shares				
Issued—none				
ommon shares without par value				
Authorized—80,000,000 shares				
Issued—35,102,062 shares—1970; 35,044,750 shares—1969	**212,493**	210,983		
Reinvested earnings	**320,104**	305,539		
	532,597	516,522		
Common shares in treasury, at cost 630,038 shares—1970; 616,750 shares—1969	**(18,964)**	(18,546)		
Investment of common shareholders			**513,633**	497,976
al Liabilities and Shareholders' Investment			**$866,818**	$811,958

ting aside the others. This is why economists are always saying "other things being equal, such and such will follow from so and so." Of course "other things" are not necessarily equal, but the economist is trying to simplify relationships down to the few he deems most important.

Alfred Marshall, a great English teacher of economics in the late 19th century, used to describe economic interrelationships as a dish filled with marbles. If one marble was picked out of the dish, all the remaining ones would shift slightly; those nearest the one removed would shift most; those farther removed would shift less and less; but all would be affected to some degree. Marshall used this to illustrate what he called *states of equilibrium.* Before being touched the marbles in the bowl would be at rest or in equilibrium. When the one was removed, the remaining ones would shift and come to a new posture of rest or a new equilibrium. Marshall taught that economic adjustments were always working from a change to a new equilibrium position; even if this equilibrium were never reached or reached only momentarily, motion would always be in that direction. For example, if someone were to shake the dish of marbles every few seconds, it would seek a new equilibrium position after each shaking, only to lose this equilibrium at the next shaking. The concept of equilibrium is an important one in formal economic analysis. If you are puzzled by this concept or have difficulty in remembering what it signifies, remember Alfred Marshall, a grandfatherly looking man, and his bowl of marbles.

Since statistics are the raw material for much of economic analysis, we must be concerned with their coverage, their completeness, their accuracy, and their relevance to the problem at hand. An old saw, regularly mentioned by teachers of statistics in their first lecture, is that figures don't lie but liars will figure. The sense of this proverb is that statistical materials can be rearranged or combined or interpreted to try to prove a point that is no point at all.

For example, suppose figures show the average age of women at marriage in Ireland to be 23 and in the United States 21. One might be tempted to conclude that American women marry younger; actually, if one looked more closely, it might be found that 25 percent of American women are age 20–25, whereas only 20 percent of Irish women fall into this age bracket. Do American women really marry younger, or are there merely more younger American women? Does looking at the figures in this light change your conclusion in any way?

Most statistical compilations are either arrays or time series. An *array* would be the population figures for each county in the United States, more than 3,000 of them, from the 1970 census of population. This means as of April 1, 1970. A *time series* would be the price of General Motors stock daily over the past two months.

Arrays are averaged, measured for dispersion, and treated in other ways. Time series have trends fitted and seasonal variations observed. They are also associated and correlated with other time series in various ways.

Stock market analysts have noted for a long time that the market is related to ladies' hemlines. When the market falls, hemlines will, after some delay, fall also; when the market rises, skirts, also after some delay, will get shorter. Hemlines, in other words, are a lagging indicator of stock market prices. The analysts wish they were a leading indicator. Fashion designers are less concerned to predict the future than are speculators.

Because the purpose here is not to give a capsule course in statistics, let us merely remember to collect them, to study them for the dimensions of an economic problem, to relate them when the relationship is direct and significant, and to take them with a grain of salt and skepticism.

Sir William Petty, who invented economic statistics, wrote in 1672 that, "instead of using only comparative and superlative words and intellectual arguments, I have taken the course to express myself in terms of number, weight, and measure; to use only arguments of sense, and to consider only such causes as have visible foundations in nature."

These rules are still worth following.

Chapter 2

BUSINESS REARS ITS HEAD—The Individual Firm

In *Alice in Wonderland* the Duchess at one point remarks that "if everybody minded his own business, the world would go round a deal faster than it does." Her point was more profound than it might appear. Our economy is built on business and on the belief that, in general, the common welfare is best advanced by each sticking to his own business; this leads to a result which, as Adam Smith said, was no part of everyman's intention.

In its beginnings, economics was virtually identical with household management; later its horizons expanded to encompass businesses organized and operated for profit. When at a later date economics came to include statecraft, it maintained a business orientation. Some people still believe governments can be run on business principles. This is a fallacy, but to expose the fallacy we need to know what business principles are. Some of them are treated briefly in this chapter.

A basic building block in our complex economic society is the individual business firm. There are nearly five million of them in this country, ranging from one-man shops to giant corporations; the great majority of people who work are employed by business establishments.

People engage in business to supply goods and services the public wants, or can be induced to want; and they hope in the process of supplying these goods and services to make a profit.

Businesses come in great variety, because of the diversity of commodities and services which members of a relatively affluent society want to consume. They provide every commodity from tropical fish for aquariums to steel plates for shipbuilding; every service from cutting hair to medical and hospital treatment. We have businesses selling Bibles and others selling shoes; we have farmers selling wheat and city dwellers selling women's apparel; businesses selling transportation, such as airlines and truckers; and businesses selling storage, such as warehousemen; business supplying tangibles such as meat and potatoes, and intangibles such as insurance; business selling only to consumers, and those selling only to other businesses.

Most of you will make your living at one time or another (and perhaps permanently) by being part of a business. You should, therefore, have an understanding of how a business functions, and of some of the problems it must face. We call this study the economics of the individual firm; it is the subject of this chapter.

As noted in the first chapter, a person who starts a new business is known as an entrepreneur. He combines what economists call the factors of production—namely, land, labor, capital, and technology—in the best proportions he can in search of profit. His concerns are with the quality and marketability of his product, and with its cost of production; these determine whether or not he will actually make a profit. He is also concerned with competition, both actual and potential. Competition will limit his market and the selling prices he can charge.

Adam Smith, 1723-1790. Professor of Moral Philosophy at Glasgow. He wrote the *Theory of Moral Sentiments* in 1759, traveled for two years in France as tutor to the young Duke of Buccleuch, and wrote *The Wealth of Nations,* published in 1776, after many years of work. For the last twelve years of his life he was Commissioner of Customs.

Suppose you have decided to open a repair shop, for television and radio sets primarily. How do you combine the factors of production to best advantage? The land, the business premises, you will presumably rent. You need a proper location, with sufficient space but not an excess of it. The location is important, but so is its cost, which will vary considerably.

Suppose you find that a store building on the main street costs $300 per month, but that a former garage on a side street can be had for $100. You reason that, once you are established, most of your orders will be by telephone, and therefore that a main street location, aside from its advertising value, is not too important for your purposes. So you opt for the side-street location at the lower rent. This may or may not be a wise decision; only time will tell.

The labor for the repair shop will be partly your own, but you decide you must have a helper. So you arrange to hire a friend, who is also experienced in fixing televisions and radios, as you are; you can hire him for $75 per week. This is the going wage for repairmen in your area, and your friend could get this much working for another shop; but he decides to take a chance with you because you promise to pay him more later if the business prospers. So much for the labor factor.

Now for the capital factor. This has two aspects, requirements and capital available. Let us look at requirements first. So far, you have agreed to rent a building and to hire a helper. In addition, you figure you will need about $1000 for benches, tools, and test equipment. You will also need about $2,000 for an inventory of spare parts, tubes, condensers, capacitors, etc. Finally, you need a truck, costing $2,000, to pick up and deliver work; plus some money for advertising, business cards, a sign, etc.

Adding up the capital requirements for your first two months of operation, you come out with a result like this:

Rent	$ 200
Wages for helper	600
Equipment	1,000
Spare parts	2,000
Payments on truck (to be financed)	150
Advertising, etc.	400
Total	$4,350

You have saved $2,500, so you take the above statement to your banker and ask to borrow $2,000. The banker, knowing you are hard working and a good credit risk, agrees to lend you this amount on the security of your equipment and your spare parts.

He points out that in your calculations you have provided no wages for yourself. You reply you will draw only $50 per week for living expenses until the business is established. So much for the capital factor.

It may be noted, in passing, that you have made no provisions for contingencies and that your capital resources are very slender compared to your requirements. But many businesses begin on a shoestring.

Finally, the technology. This is the skill which both you and your helper have as repairmen. On this skill the business will largely be based. If you can repair effectively, can deliver the work when promised, and if your charges are reasonable, you can expect to meet competition and gradually to build up a volume of business. While technology is not a tangible factor of production, it is the catalyst that will make the business succeed or fail.

So with all the necessary factors of production assembled, you open your repair business. The first month you take in $600. Against this you have the following expenses:

Rent	$100
Wages for your helper	300
Wages for yourself	200
Advertising	50
Parts used	40
Depreciation	100
Total	$790

Obviously you have sustained a loss for this first month and have impaired your working capital slightly. Put another way, you need to do about $800 worth of repair work each month to break even. Call this your break-even point. Every business has one. Beyond this point you get into the profit area and your profits will increase more than proportionately to the volume of your business. If in the second month you do $1,000 worth of repair work, you are in the profit area.

A small repair shop. This one is for minor repair work on automobiles. Repair shops are typical of the small businesses that can be started by one or two people with limited capital. Such a business will depend on the owner's skill as a mechanic and his ability to operate the business economically.

An optimum combination of the factors of production must obviously be related to the volume of business being done. It will be different for a small repair shop than for a large corporation with thousands of employees and hundreds of different products. Moreover, alternative technology defines different combinations of factors that are optimal depending on the relative cost of the different factors.

If labor is cheap, in the sense that wages are low while productivity of labor is high, labor intensive methods, those using much labor and relatively little capital equipment, will tend to be used. In India, for example, we would probably not find expensive materials handling equipment because human labor can be hired cheaply to move materials about by hand. Building the great pyramids in Egypt was a classic example of labor intensive methods.

Wheat farming in Canada. Because land is abundant and labor relatively expensive, the method of farming uses large scale mechanical equipment like this seeder. If land were less abundant and more expensive, more labor could be applied without encountering diminishing returns.

On the other hand, if land is cheap and labor relatively expensive, as in Canadian wheat farming, for example, we find extensive methods of cultivation using relatively sophisticated equipment, such as combines, gang plows, etc. By contrast, in Japanese rice farming, where land is scarce and consequently very expensive, we find very different methods, using much labor and obtaining higher yields per acre. The idea in each of these cases is to use as much as possible of the cheap factor or factors of production and to economize on use of the expensive factors.

We have remarked that an entrepreneur seeks always to make the most efficient combination of factors of production. This is merely the economist's way of saying he seeks to keep costs as low as possible. If the business premises are too large and elaborate for the business being done, costs will be high because too much land has been combined with the other factors.

If you hire two helpers when there is work for only one, your wage costs will be excessive, or too much labor is being combined with other factors. If you have $5,000 invested in tools and equipment when all you actually need and use is $1,000, then too much capital has been combined with other factors for the most efficient mix. If you are a skilled electronics engineer who could be designing test equipment, but you prefer to be a repairman, you have brought too much technology to the business.

Just as it is possible to have too much of any factor in a combination, so there can be too little—too little capital, too little labor, and too little technology. Any of these deficiencies can prevent the business from functioning properly.

The right combination of factors of production is thus the mix that gives the lowest possible cost for the scale of operations being carried on. If the operation is a small repair shop, the right combination may be fairly easy to find. If the operation is a large corporation, producing, say, 1,000 different styles, colors, and sizes of shoes, the minimum cost combination may be extremely difficult to establish. Actually, it is reached primarily by trial and error and by what economists call marginal adjustments. Let us see what these are.

The marginal concept

A central idea in economic analysis is that of an incremental change—a little more or a little less—minor adjustments to reach the best possible or optimum position. Thus, a businessman seeks to maximize his profits by producing a little more of whatever it is he sells—ships or shoes or sealing wax—and by observing the effect of this incremental expansion in production upon his total intake or revenue and his total outlay or costs.

Professional economists call this addition to revenue from the sale of one more unit of product the *marginal revenue* and the addition to cost of producing this additional item the *marginal cost.* It can be demonstrated by elementary calculus or by simple geometry that profit will be at a maximum when marginal revenue and marginal cost are equal. So long as marginal revenue is greater than marginal cost, total profit may be increased by producing and selling a little more; when marginal cost exceeds marginal revenue, additional production reduces total profit; the best thing to do is to then cut back production a little. Equality of marginal revenue and marginal cost therefore defines the maximum profit or optimum position.

If you were to talk to a businessman and ask him how he goes about equating marginal revenue and cost, he would say he doesn't do any such thing; but though he may not recognize the language, this is precisely the sort of calculation he is continually making. He is concerned about growth, about his share of the market and how it may be increased, and what it will cost him to expand his sales. He is therefore vitally concerned with both incremental or marginal revenues and costs, as his endeavor is continually to maximize his profit within the available constraints.

The marginal concept is not limited to revenues and costs but runs throughout economic analysis. We speak, for example, of the marginal product of labor, meaning the increase in total output from adding one additional worker to the payroll. It follows from the theorem just developed that, unless the marginal product of the additional worker is at least equal to or greater than the marginal cost of his employment, the firm will not gain from putting this additional person on the payroll.

The marginal concept may be made a little clearer by an example. Consider, if you will, a baseball player and his batting average. Midway through the season, Slugger O'Neal, of the Giants, is batting .300 which means he is hitting safely in 30% of his trips to the plate. This .300 average may be termed his average product as a batsman during the current season.

Marginal revenue is the increase in total revenue as output increases. Marginal cost is the change in total cost as output increases. Typically, as output expands, total revenue increases at a diminishing rate. The marginal revenue curve slopes downward and to the right. Total cost typically increases at an increasing rate, giving a marginal cost curve that slopes upward and to the right. The point where marginal revenue and marginal cost intersect, and therefore are equal, defines the most profitable price and the optimum quantity to be sold.

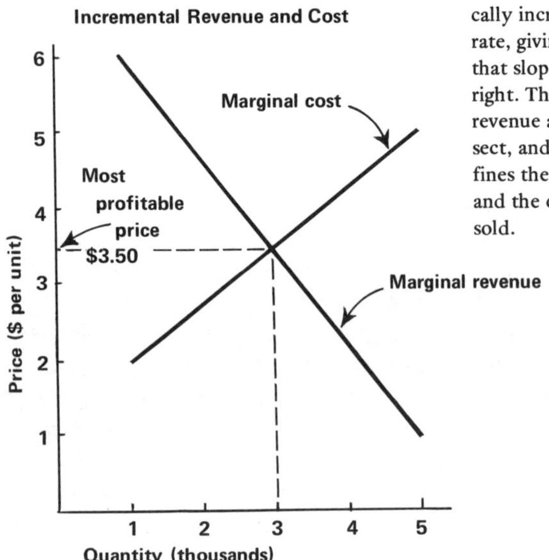

In yesterday's game against the Cubs, O'Neal got two hits in five trips. This was his marginal product as a batsman for that day—incidentally, it raised his batting average from .299 to .300. Today, against a southpaw with a sneaky slider, O'Neal goes 0 to 5; his marginal product as a batsman is zero and his average for the season declines to .298.

Slugger O'Neal and his batting average have illustrated some important mathematical principles about the relations of average and marginal products, or costs, or revenues, or whatever aggregates are changing incrementally. For example, when an average is increasing, the corresponding marginal must be greater than the average. O'Neal can only raise his average by doing better than the average on a given day. When he does worse, when his average falls, it is because the marginal effort or product is less than the average. It follows, then, that when the marginal effort is just equal to the average, the average will not change. If O'Neal had made one hit in the second game, his marginal product for the two games would have been 3 for 10 and his batting average would have been unchanged at .300.

Now if you can tear yourself away, let us leave the baseball diamond and return to the businessman trying to maximize his profits. Mr. Applebaum sells phonograph records for $1.50 each; they cost him, including overhead, $1.35 each. He realizes his profits are not a maximum, so he decides to expand. He modernizes his store and advertises more. His volume rises, but so do his costs. He now calculates he is selling more records but his profit per record is only 10 cents instead of 15 cents. Nevertheless, his total profit may be larger than before, provided the additional or marginal revenue is greater than the additional or marginal cost. If the cost increase should prove greater than the revenue gain, his decision to expand would have proved uneconomic, since it effectively reduced rather than expanded his profit. What Mr. Applebaum the merchant is trying to do is to equate marginal revenue and marginal cost; to do so means to maximize his profit.

The marginal concept in economics is important because individuals, business firms, and governments are continually adjusting to a changing environment. In this process, they must expand and contract sales and purchases, increase and diminish employment, invest more or less in plant and equipment. Decisions of this type are based on marginal calculations. They may not be formal calculations expressed in these terms, but that is what they are in effect. Thus, adjustments at the margin, or marginal adjustments, are continually being made—by consumers, businessmen, investors, and other economic interest groups. A large part of formal economics is simply the study of the little more or the little less—adjustments at the margin.

The function of competition.

The free enterprise system is largely self-regulating, with competition being the chief instrument of this self-regulation. If you start a shop on a particular corner and it proves to be highly profitable, someone else is likely to start another one close by, in competition with you. Competition may take many forms—lower prices, better service, easier credit terms, delivery as opposed to cash and carry, and so on. Competition may reduce the variation in prices from store to store, may force all firms to advertise more, improve the appearance of their business premises, and make other efforts to attract and hold customers.

Nor is competition limited to retailing, although there we see it most frequently. Manufacturers compete in price, in product design, in performance characteristics, and in service. For example, in this country, competition among manufacturers of motor cars is intense, although these manufacturers are in the main extremely large corporations.

When suppliers of a given product are few, competition is less apt to take the form of reducing prices, and more apt to appear in product design, in service, or in some other non-price form. For example, in household durable goods such as washing machines, the prices for medium grade models of uniform quality tend to be fairly well-standardized; competition is in design, in convenience features, in durability, or in installation and service.

Competition which takes the form of making one product seem quite different from its competitors is known as *product differentiation.* A Ford is different from a Chevrolet because each manufacturer feels that by building in unique designs and unique features he can attract and hold customers that would otherwise stray to other products. Design and appearance may be very important in this kind of competition. For example, the Edsel automobile, designed and developed by the Ford Motor Company at great expense some years ago, was a commercial failure largely because the design did not appeal strongly to consumers.

Although competition has many dimensions, it is primarily competition among suppliers within an industry that concerns many economists, and also the Antitrust Division of the Department of Justice. This agency is charged with administering the Federal statutes requiring the maintenance of competition. When the number of suppliers in an industry is small, there is always concern about price rigging, agreements to divide the market, and other practices that limit or control competition. In contrast, when the number of suppliers is many, competition, in price at least, is apt to be more aggressive, because each supplier has more to gain by offering more than his competitors. If a supplier's market share is only 1 percent, he has a better chance of doubling it by reducing prices than when it is 25 percent.

When the number of suppliers is so large that any one supplier is unable significantly to affect the selling price, the industry is said to be characterized by "pure" or nearly pure competition. Wheat farmers are very numerous, for example, and each produces a fairly uniform product. No wheat farmer can successfully differentiate his product from that of any other supplier.

Wheat therefore sells at a uniform price over broad areas because any individual wheat farmer is unable significantly to affect that price. If he thinks the price too low, he may plant less next year, or store some of his harvest in the expectation that prices will rise enough to cover storage charges and loss of interest on the proceeds he would have received from selling his crop. Essentially, he takes the price of wheat as determined and calculates his gain or loss from the prevailing market price.

An industry characterized by pure or relatively pure competition is one which is comparatively easy to enter. It is not too difficult, for example, to set up a retail store. The capital requirements, although they may be substantial, are still low compared to other types of business; no special training is required, although it may be highly desirable; no complex technology is needed.

A steel mill. Steelmaking is a capital intensive business requiring a large investment in plant and equipment. It also requires handling large tonnages of iron ore, coking coal, and limestone. As the photo shows only too clearly, steelmaking is a major industrial polluter of the environment.

On the other hand, basic steel manufacturing is a difficult business to enter; capital requirements are extremely high, transportation is very important, and complex technology is involved. Competitition in steel manufacturing is therefore less pure than in retailing. The difference, however, is not so great as might appear at first glance. Retailers compete only within a limited geographical area, such as within one town, or within a metropolitan marketing area. Steelmakers, on the other hand, compete nationally and even internationally. It is the number of suppliers serving a given conventional market that determines how pure competition actually is.

Competition is important not only as a regulator of price, quality, and service to the consumer, but also as a regulator of business profits. If a firm is making very high profits, this is likely to draw competitors. In meeting this competition, the original high profit firm may have to face additional costs for more advertising, better service, or improvements to its products. The additional costs may reduce its profits from outstanding to a level more nearly comparable to what is earned by other firms. Thus, if competitition within an industry is intense, the level of profits will tend to be reduced.

This tendency for profits to fall can only be defeated by efficiencies that reduce costs, by developing better products that will command premium prices, or by beating the competition in some other way. Thus competition helps to keep business efficient and to work against poor quality, obsolete methods, and lack of progress. Many an old firm has declined and even been forced out of business by failure to meet its competition.

Fair and unfair competition.

The difference between fair and unfair competition is very unclear and very dependent on the point of view. One of the basic ideas behind the free enterprise system is that competition is healthy and a good regulator of prices; therefore, competition needs to be maintained, by positive action if necessary. On the other hand, one of the realities of the marketplace is that competition is destructive; among the things it destroys is itself. In economic competition, as in any contest, one party eventually proves the stronger. Pushed to its ultimate conclusion, competition can become a duel to the death, in which one or more of the competitors is totally destroyed.

The idea of unfair competition arose from a wish that business competition should not be a series of mortal duels, but should have limits beyond which it would be unethical or illegal to go. If competition should be preserved but actually may be self-destructive, it needs to be limited to prevent its ultimate consequences. Thus, there has arisen, in administration of the antitrust laws of this country, a vague judicial doctrine of certain competitive practices being unfair and therefore being enjoined or restricted in some way; while other practices are seen as fair and therefore in no need of being hindered.

The doctrine is vague because business practice is continually changing and developing. If a practice is judged unfair, some alternative method of achieving substantially the same result can usually be invented. In the last century when John D. Rockefeller, Sr., was putting together the Standard Oil Company, he obtained rebates of part of the freight rates paid to the railroads. A railroad would charge Standard $5 a ton for hauling oil, but would later and secretly return $1 per ton as a rebate. Naturally this gave Standard an edge over its competitors who were not able to wring these rate concessions from the reluctant rails. Eventually, the United States courts declared the rebate technique illegal as a restraint of trade or an unfair competitive practice.

Yet railroads to this day have negotiated special freight rates for favored customers in an effort to develop traffic or to meet competition from trucks and inland waterways. The point seems to be that overt rate concessions are fair but secret ones are unfair.

Another practice that has caused much trouble involves state resale price maintenance laws. If a state has such a law, a manufacturer can dictate to wholesalers and retailers what their selling prices will be. The objective is to prevent discounting of nationally advertised brands of cosmetics, etc., by retailers in their efforts to compete with one another.

Retailers have always used the technique of "loss leaders" to draw people to their stores. They advertise some well-known product at cost or at a loss, underselling their competition in this item but counting on people who come for the loss leader buying other items as well. Under the resale price maintenance laws, use of nationally advertised brands as loss leaders is effectively outlawed, on the ground that this is an unfair competitive practice.

This is somewhat analogous to making a rule for a boxing match that jabs, hooks, and crosses will be legal, but uppercuts will not. In either business or a boxing match, such rules are complex and difficult to enforce.

It will be apparent by now that competition, far from being a simple notion in economics, actually has many dimensions. We have noted earlier that competition is pure or impure depending on whether a single seller is able significantly to affect selling prices. It is perfect or imperfect depending on how rapidly firms adjust to changes in demand or in cost. It is now also fair or unfair depending on whether the business practices employed have or lack the sanction of courts. For a single word like competition to be so many-valued is, to say the least, slightly confusing.

Business is, in many respects, like war. Both employ strategies and tactics to reach objectives. The object in each is to win, in one case money and power, and in the other territory and dominion. Since both are competitive games in which wits and strength are matched against opponents, it is not surprising that both business and war appeal strongly to aggressive temperaments. In legislating rules to place limits on the forms competition may properly take, we are in effect trying to make business resemble more the gentlemanly warfare of the Middle Ages than the total warfare of World War II.

Forms of business organization.

Only three are important, although there are some variations on the more complex forms. Basically these are legal forms, although their economic significance is to be found chiefly in the aggregations of capital each can bring together and in their suitability for different situations.

Simplest is the sole proprietorship in which one person is both owner and manager. This form of organization has the advantage of greatest flexibility because there are no committees or groups to make decisions. What the proprietor decides is what is done. Decisions can be made quickly or as quickly as the proprietor's personality will permit.

Legally this form is characterized by unlimited liability; there is no distinction between business and personal property; all may be reached by creditors to satisfy debts. The proprietorship is found today mainly in small businesses, because the capital available is only what the proprietor owns or can borrow. Some proprietorships which were once small become quite large with success; often, with increased size, they are changed into either partnerships or corporations.

A partnership is, as the name implies, founded on an agreement among two or more persons to pool their assets and often their services for a common business purpose. The agreement, which may be expressed or implied, covers such points as who will make what decisions, what capital and services each partner will contribute to the venture, and how profits will be divided.

A partnership ceases with the death or withdrawal of one partner and may also be terminated by a disagreement among the partners over expansion, location of business premises, or some other major issue of policy. Sometimes a partnership will be terminated by one partner buying out the interests of the other partners, thus changing the business back to a sole proprietorship.

A partnership is also characterized by unlimited liability in the sense that both personal and business property of the partners may be reached by creditors. One partner can also bind the others by contracts he makes in the name of the partnership, even though the other partners are ignorant of these contracts. Each partner is, in effect, general agent for all the others, unless they advertise a specific division of labor.

You have probably heard of a "silent partner," one who takes no part in the management of day-to-day conduct of business, although he contributes or has contributed capital to it. Less common is the limited partner who may or may not be active in the business. Since his liability is limited by agreement with the other partners, it is necessary for the partnership to inform the public that he is not a general or unlimited partner.

The advantages of a partnership over a proprietorship are the pooling of capital, experience, and judgment it makes possible. Many investment banking firms and most brokerage houses are partnerships; sometimes with partners numbering up to 100. In these cases the partnership succession will be secured by standing arrangements to liquidate or acquire the interest of any partner desiring to withdraw or removed by death or inability to operate.

The corporation is the third form of business organization. A corporation is a creature of a state, brought into being by a charter. Formerly, charters were special acts of a state legislature; now they are issued under general incorporation laws which merely require a purpose to be stated, officers and directors named, and fees paid.

Justice John Marshall wrote many years ago in the Dartmouth College case that, "a corporation is a person, invisible, intangible, and existing only in contemplation of the law." As a legal person, a corporation can own property and sue and be sued in its own name. It thus has a legal existence apart from its founders, owners, etc.

From this legal separation comes limited liability for those who invest in a corporation. If the corporation becomes insolvent or bankrupt, creditors have no security except the assets of the corporation itself.

Corporations raise capital by selling stock; that is, ownership claims to fractional parts of their net worths. Stock is usually offered in convenient denominations so that one may own one, ten, 100, 1000 or more shares. Once issued, the value of a corporation's stock fluctuates with its fortunes and the general state of the economy. A corporation is said to be closely held if it has few stockholders and widely held if it has many stockholders. American Telephone and Telegraph is the most widely held stock in the United States today.

In addition to the capital it raises by selling stock, a corporation also borrows by issuing debt instruments such as notes and bonds; these are fixed obligations.

Financing corporations.

Corporations require money both for current operations and for expanding their activities. Funds for current operating needs are called *working* capital; funds for investment purposes are called *permanent* capital or simply *capital funds.*

Working capital is generated from current sales. It may also be borrowed from banks or raised by selling notes, known as *commercial paper.* Such loans are temporary and are expected to be repaid from the proceeds of sales within a few months.

Permanent or long-term capital is raised from the sale of *securities:* chiefly notes, bonds, and stock. These evidences of corporate indebtedness or ownership are traded in security markets, giving them liquidity from the standpoint of an individual investor.

Bonds are debts of a corporation, signified by a promise to pay a fixed sum at a certain date with interest at a specified rate. These bonds may be secured by a mortgage on the specified properties, such as a railroad right of way. In this they resemble a mortgage on a house, except that, as bonds, they are split into a number of convenient denominations. Each bond is, in effect, a piece of the mortgage. If the corporation fails to pay the principal or interest, the holder of the mortgage, usually a trustee such as a bank, has the right to seize the property and to sell it for the debt.

More commonly today bonds are *debentures,* obligations secured by the general credit of the corporation rather than by the pledge of certain specific assets. A corporation with a good credit rating will not normally have to mortgage its assets.

A corporation desiring to raise capital by means of a bond issue, say in the amount of $10 million, will normally handle the sale through *underwriters,* a syndicate of investment banking houses that guarantees to the corporation the sale of its bonds within a certain time at a certain price. The underwriters do the actual selling of the bonds to the investing public, and are obligated to take up themselves any balance remaining unsold at the time specified.

Before offering the bonds, the borrowing company must file with the Securities and Exchange Commission a registration statement setting forth full details about the company's finances and the purpose for which proceeds from the sale of the bonds will be used. An abstract of this registration statement, known as a *prospectus,* must be furnished each potential buyer of the bonds so he will be fully informed about the nature of the asset he is buying.

A company may have more than one bond issue outstanding, in which case the later issues will be secondary or tertiary claims on the earnings and assets. Railroads, for example, often have multiple bond issues outstanding. These are known as senior or junior securities, depending on whether they are a first or second, or a fifth or sixth, claim on earnings and assets.

A bond issue which is junior to an earlier issue is said to be subordinated to it.

Stock differs from bonds in being permanent rather than temporary capital and in signifying ownership in the company rather than a creditor relationship. Stock is known as *equity capital* as distinct from debt. If a company has one million shares of stock outstanding, each share signifies ownership of one-millionth part of the company and of all its assets and liabilities. If the corporation's balance sheet shows it to have a net worth of $20 million, each share is said to have a book value of $20. Its price on the stock market may be higher or lower than this, depending on earnings and other factors.

A company may have more than one class of stock outstanding. Sometimes it will have voting and nonvoting stock. When the Ford Foundation was established following the death of Henry Ford, the Foundation received nonvoting stock in the Ford Motor Company. The voting stock was retained primarily within the Ford family.

Sometimes a company will have both *preferred* and *common* stock. The preferred, as the name implies, carried a preference as to dividends and assets in the event of dissolution. The preference is usually for a fixed amount. If it is for $1 in dividends, the issue will be known as $1 preferred stock. In contrast, the common stock represents the residual claim to earnings and assets.

Financing partly by bonds and by preferred stock is one method of obtaining what is known as "leverage on the common." If a company is earning 10 per cent on its investment but is 50 per cent financed by bonds on which only 5 per cent must be paid, the return to the common is 15 per cent. Leverage naturally has an amplified risk if earnings should decline. If they should decline to just what must be paid on the bonds, the return to the common would be zero.

Corporations sell stock in the same way that they sell bonds, namely by employing an underwriting syndicate, filing a registration statement with the Securities and Exchange Commission, SEC, and accepting the proceeds from the sale of the issue. If the company is well-established and well-known, and its stock is widely held by the investing public, it may float stock by issuing *warrants,* which are rights to buy the new stock at a certain price, usually below the current market price. For example, a company whose stock is selling for $50 may issue warrants to each holder of 100 shares to buy 10 additional shares at $40. The warrants at time of issue are therefore potentially worth $1 per share. Holders of the existing shares may either use the warrants to purchase additional shares at the preferred price or sell the warrants to others who wish to exercise them. The value of the warrants will fluctuate with the price of the shares. If the stock should rise in price from $50 to $60, the warrants theoretically should rise to $2 from $1. A 20 per cent rise in the stock means a 100 per cent rise in the warrants, which have more leverage.

It will be clear from the foregoing that corporations have numerous options in financing their operations. If earnings are relatively steady from year to year, as are those of public utilities such as electric power and gas companies, there will be little risk in having substantial bonded indebtedness and a relatively smaller stockholder's equity. Public utility companies do use bonds and also preferred stock extensively. On the other hand, if earnings are volatile from year to year, as are those of machine tool companies, for example, the capital structure is simple, perhaps consisting only of a single class of common stock.

New types of corporate securities are continually being invented, to appeal to the preferences of investors, and to enable companies better to raise the capital needed for expansion. For example, the convertible debenture is now somewhat in vogue. This is a hybrid security, in essence a bond which carries the option of conversion into stock on specified terms. For example, a $1000 bond might be convertible into 20 shares of stock at $50 per share. So long as the stock is below $50, the option is relatively worthless; should the stock rise above $50, it would be advantageous for the bondholders to convert. Convertible bonds usually carry some premium over straight debt because of the conversion privilege.

The decision of how to finance business expansion is one of the most crucial a business must make. A new stock or bond issue will be carefully considered by the board of directors of a corporation and entered into only if it appears advantageous. In 1970, for example, many coporate expansion plans were being deferred because of the high cost of capital.

Geographic locations of industry.

Have you ever wondered why the steel industry is clustered along the Great Lakes; why so many light manufacturing plants are to be found near New York City and in New Jersey; and why meat packing is so concentrated in the Middle West? In part, there is an historic basis for this, but there was and still is also an economic basis. Certain locations did and do offer combinations of advantages resulting in unusually low costs for certain industries and processes. Businessmen, seeking to maximize their profits by taking advantage of low costs, concentrated their facilities in these favorable locations.

Take steel production for example. This is basically a materials handling business in which very heavy tonnages of iron ore, limestone, and coal have to be brought together at the blast furnace. Originally the best and most easily extracted iron ore in the United States was to be found in the Mesabi range of Northern Minnesota. This could be shipped by rail a short distance to Duluth, then loaded on a lake freighter and shipped to any port on the Great Lakes at moderate cost. Transport by water was much cheaper than any other method, rail, for example. Similarly, coking coal could be mined in Pennsylvania near Pittsburgh, shipped a short distance by rail to a Great Lake port, and then carried cheaply by rail anywhere to meet the iron ore from Mesabi. Limestone could also be found at many points near the Great Lakes. From these geographic and transport cost facts it follows that steel could be manufactured most cheaply at any one of the several Great Lake cities or at Pittsburgh, Pennsylvania. In fact, steel-making has concentrated at such points as Gary, Indiana, Cleveland, Ohio, and Pittsburgh, Pennsylvania.

Steel is a basic industrial material which is sold largely to other manufacturing plants or to the construction and shipbuilding industries. After steel is made into ingots and then rolled, forged, or drawn into forms and shapes used by other industries, it must be shipped to these plants which are the primary markets of the steel mills. Nearness to the market is also a major factor in industrial location.

Automobile manufacturing, a big user of steel, is concentrated in Michigan near Detroit. Being a Great Lake city itself, Detroit is a good location for a steel mill, or steel could be shipped cheaply from a mill in Gary to the auto plants in Detroit.

Similarly, Chicago and vicinity has numerous manufacturing plants making farm machinery, railroad cars, and building materials. All of these operations use substantial quantities of steel. This is close at hand from the mills at Gary, which is also near the market for steel. In the steel industry, because of the heavy tonnages involved, transportation cost of the materials and the nearness to the market for the steel are the primary factors in industrial location. Cost factors dictate why the steel industry is situated geographically where it is, along the Great Lakes.

Suppose one is not manufacturing steel but something very different—toothpaste. This is a light product, so transport cost of materials is far less important than it is with steel. Nearness to the market is important, as is nearness to the materials used; chemicals, polishing agents, etc. Toothpaste is advertised heavily, so nearness to advertising agencies, marketing specialists, and centers of population is also important. To make toothpaste one needs only a small factory, but one equipped with highly specialized automatic machinery.

When these factors are all weighed, it will work out that a location in or near New York City or Chicago will be the most advantageous place for such a factory; this is where such factories are, in fact, found.

Migration of the textile industry is another example of how economic factors can affect industrial location. Originally the textile industry was concentrated in New England. It was one of the first manufacturing industries to be established in this country, at a time when New England was much closer to the center of population than it now is, and when New England had perhaps the largest pool of skilled labor to be found in the country. Machinery was largely imported so a seacoast location was advantageous.

Over time, New England lost most of its advantages as a textile mill site. Markets for finished products moved farther away, skilled labor was available elsewhere, and machinery was no longer imported. New England mills grew old and obsolete; the industry migrated to new plants in North Carolina, Georgia, and elsewhere. These were closer to raw materials, such as cotton, had lower prevailing wage rates, and cheaper power. As New England lost its competitive advantages, it eventually lost the bulk of its textile industry.

Thus, industrial location does have an economic basis and is not a mere geographical accident. Many states today make extraordinary efforts to attract industry to aid in the development of their state or region. Unless an area has some peculiar combination of advantages to offer, it is unlikely to be conspicuously successful in its efforts to attract industry.

Summary.

We have now looked briefly at business as an economist sees it. We have seen that business exists to make profits and, it is hoped, to maximize these profits. In this effort, a businessman tries continually to broaden his markets, to grow, and to serve that market at as low a unit cost as he can. To produce whatever it is that a business sells, he combines factors of production, land, labor, capital, and technology, as advantageously as possible. The right or optimum combination of factors will give the lowest unit costs relative to the scale of operations being carried on. In his effort to reach the optimum combination of factors, the businessman will proceed largely by trial and error, doing a little more or less of this or that, or making adjustments at the margin, *marginal adjustments,* in the terminology of economists. When incremental or marginal revenue and incremental cost are equalized, profit will be at a maximum. Business is also limited by competition, both actual and potential.

The forms of business organization are the proprietorship, the partnership, and the corporation. Corporations are necessary to mobilize very large pools of capital to engage in large-scale business ventures. A corporation is a legal person, and hence investors in it have limited liability. Corporations function through boards of directors elected by the stockholders and through officers appointed by the board. They finance their operations by issuing various kinds of securities, such as stock, bonds, notes, and warrants. Corporate management tends to be a special kind of trained business executives, often with little or no ownership interest in the corporation they manage.

Chapter 3

THE PAST IS PROLOGUE—Economics as an Historical Process

This title phrase, which appears on the National Archives Building in Washington, carries the thought that the past is merely a curtain raiser for the future, and that one should study the past to be prepared to live in the future. A companion thought is that those who fail to study history are condemned to relive it—to repeat the mistakes and the errors of the past that have been exposed by time.

It is doubtful that one should study any subject solely from fright, although much of the hurried study of nuclear energy shortly after Hiroshima and Nagasaki was prompted by just this motive. Rather, one should study the past to gain understanding of the fact that institutions and ideas are continuous processes, evolving over time and changing in response to emerging problems, rather than spontaneous inventions without precedents.

History and economics are closely intertwined, in the sense that many historical movements, often thought to be purely political or social in nature, have strong economic overtones. Marxists, for example, go so far as to claim that all history has an economic basis, that it is an unending class struggle between the haves and the have nots, in which the underdogs, the proletariat, are bound in the end to overthrow their masters by revolutionary means.

This Marxian dialectic, no longer intellectually respectable save in underground circles, reflects a narrow and provincial view, because it neglects other forces that have shaped history. Organized religion, for example, has been a vital factor in history—at least as important during some periods as economic developments or who sat on what throne. Sometimes disease is the determining economic factor. Some historians believe that malaria, introduced into the Roman Empire by slaves brought from Africa, was the essential factor in the fall of the Roman Empire.

The purpose of the present chapter is not to review general history or the Marxian interpretation thereof, but to describe briefly a few ways in which economics is, and can best be studied as, an historical process.

There are several strands to this history. One is the history of economic problems; the problem of unemployment, for example, keeps recurring in different ages and has been dealt with in many different ways.

Another strand is the history of economic ideas or economic theories; "cheap money" has been proposed over and over again as a quick and easy remedy for depression, despite the fact that this panacea has always failed to cure.

Still another strand is the history of economic institutions. Banks were invented in the Middle Ages and still operate on the basic principles discovered then, although they are much more complex today.

In a word, you cannot really understand economics unless you put it in historical context, unless you see how the ideas and problems we deal with today evolved over time as old fallacies were discarded and new ones embraced. If you looked at the Mississippi River only as it appears at St. Louis, you could not say that you knew the river—you would need to know how it appeared at St. Paul, at Vicksburg, and at New Orleans to have any real understanding of its scope and its many moods.

Similarly, if your only reading of economics was the Council of Economic Advisers Report for the year 1970, you would have only a snapshot of the United States economy at this particular point in time; moreover, it would be basically a macroeconomic snapshot.

If a movie tells a story better than a series of snapshots, even though the snapshots are chronologically arranged, then looking at economics historically is better than looking only at snapshots of the present, which most current economic writings are. The financial press is full of stories about what the bond market did last week or will do this week; popular journals will report how Peoria is attracting industry and rebuilding its blighted inner city, or how New England is adjusting its business structure as textile mills continue to move South. These are all contemporary snapshots—important and interesting in themselves, but not telling the continuing story.

The recurrence of economic problems.

Similar economic problems have recurred throughout recorded history because these problems have always had the same roots—gaining and using wealth, trying to maximize benefits for a particular class, or a whole society. Ever since the Vikings and Phoenicians first landed on foreign shores and bartered with the local populace, we have had problems of international trade and theories concerning this activity. In the 17th century, when England was the premier exporter of manufactured goods, economists (then known as mercantilists) theorized that England should export as much as possible and accumulate treasure, currency and bullion. In equating the nation with a merchant, they failed to see that trade needs to be a two-way affair. If a nation only exports and does not import, its foreign markets will eventually dry up, while the treasure accumulated from exports will eventually raise prices in the exporting country. Mercantilist theories were finally recognized as incomplete because both these things happened. A nation is not like an individual merchant and cannot behave like one except at its peril. All this was known before—Spain had already been through the same experience; but the British mercantilists had not read the lesson of historical experience.

In the American Civil War, it was widely recognized that the antagonists, although fairly equal in strength when the war opened, would become progressively unequal so long as the contest continued. The South had virtually no industrial capacity to manufacture weapons, ships, etc., while the North had virtually all the manufacturing facilities of the nation. The hope of the South lay in England. Southern leaders thought English mills needed cotton so desperately that they would furnish military supplies in return, plus shipping to transport them. They failed to realize that there were other sources

Ship loading at New York. International trade is a two-way street. Most trade takes place among well-developed countries. The emerging countries are chiefly exporters of raw materials and importers of manufactured products. The United States has been strong in the export of high-technology manufactured products such as complex machinery.

of cotton and that British shipping would not go to war zones when there were safer and equally profitable routes to travel. So, as the war continued, it became less a battlefield contest than a war of attrition and a war of production; in such a contest, the South steadily lost ground and was eventually overwhelmed. In a sense, they had placed too much faith in international trade and in the inexorability of established trade patterns. These could change and they did.

At the end of World War I, the victorious Allies, having defeated Germany, were concerned to collect reparations, to impose as large a portion of the cost of the war as possible on the defeated power. They reckoned up a large reparations bill which Germany was to pay in installments. What the statesmen of that day failed to see clearly was that Germany could only pay this bill by a consistently favorable balance of trade—an excess of exports over imports. In 1925, J. M. Keynes published a book, provocative for its time, in which he argued that Germany could not pay because the Allies could not afford to receive these unrequited imports from

Germany; they would be too damaging to Allied trade and too inflationary to the reparations-receiving countries. Subsequent events proved Keynes to be basically correct. Reparations were scaled down several times and finally cancelled altogether. In the end, what Germany paid was more than offset by new loans and credits to her, primarily from the U.S.

If other countries failed to learn this reparations lesson, the Russians did not. Following the defeat of Germany in World War II, the reparations question again arose. The Russians never argued for cash. Instead they took their reparations in kind, by dismantling German plants within their area of occupation and moving them piecemeal to Russia. The lesson of this experience, perhaps, is that seizure is more effective than a forced loan or a deferred tax. At any rate, the Russians did not have a reparations-transfer problem. Instead, the Allies, in rehabilitating Germany, in effect replaced what the Russians had seized.

These examples, interesting as they each are, serve mainly to make the points that (l) in economics things are not always in the long run what they appear at the moment to be, and (2) even in times of greatest strain, such as wars, economic principles will continue to operate. Their effects may be delayed, but in the end they will out—as Shakespeare remarked of murder.

Although times and circumstances change, the classic economic problems of poverty, inflation, trade, and finance continue to persist and to cry for solutions. If there are any lessons which economics teaches, they are the old proverbs about not having your cake and eating it, how there is no such thing as a free lunch, and how too much money will eventually show its effects. If these appear to be old bromides, economics is an old subject—one of the oldest, although its principles have changed greatly over time. We do learn something as our horizons broaden. The old economists could think only of their city or their small country. Today we must consider the world.

One of the most durable economic fallacies encountered in all ages is that new inventions, machines, will permanently displace workers. Doubtless this view was expressed when the wheel was invented; it was certainly said of the spinning jenny and the power loom, as in our own day it is said of the computer. Inventions do displace some workers—those who carry things on their backs, who spin by hand, and who keep books with a quill pen. At the same time, inventions open up new jobs—for electronic engineers, computer programmers, and the like—in far greater numbers than they displace workers whose skills are obsolete. Generally the new jobs opened up are not available to those workers who are displaced, unless they undergo a retraining process. The lesson again is the old one, stated by Heraclitus, that nothing is constant except change. Some skills do not last a lifetime but need to be exchanged for other needed skills. A skilled maker of buggy whips needs to be retrained in some other specialty, perhaps as a television repairman.

Another durable fallacy in economic literature is the idea that home industry is threatened by imports, because other countries have lower wage levels. The fallacy resides in the failure to distinguish between high wages and high labor costs. If an industry uses advanced technology, which permits labor to be highly productive, individual wages may be high but total

Transformers. Transformers at the Kariba Dam and hydroelectric plant in Southern Rhodesia. This plant, the largest in Africa, will produce 1.5 million kilowatts of electricity and will serve two countries. Projects such as this will bring the industrial revolution to Africa and will propel this continent from a tribal society into the modern world of specialization and mass production. Photo courtesy the World Bank.

labor costs extremely low. This is true in U.S. production of chemicals, for example. It is only when a foreign industry has up-to-date technology plus lower wage rates that its competition need be feared. Even then, it is not wage costs alone, but total costs, that determine ability to compete. A country with low labor costs may have high interest costs or high material costs that offset its wage advantage. The fallacy is in mistaking a part for the whole, and drawing wrong inferences from the part.

Not only do economic problems keep recurring, but countries also go through similar stages of economic development, although at different times. One watershed is the industrial revolution, or the beginning of rapid growth in manufacturing activity.

The Industrial Revolution.

The industrial revolution refers to a fairly rapid change in production methods in which factories replaced handicraft shops. Occurring first in England, the revolution quickly spread to other European countries and to the United States. Factory methods, based on interchangeable parts and on the use of machinery, proved far more productive than the old handicraft methods, and thus made these earlier methods obsolete. The textile industry was the first to be mechanized in England and in most other countries; but the principles of mass production soon spread to other industries. Early factories were concentrated in urban areas; consequently, spread of the industrial revolution was a strong force for urbanization.

Working conditions in the early factories were extremely bad, with a great deal of child labor working extremely long hours. Gradually, legislation and the efforts of reformers moderated these harsh conditions somewhat.

The factory system also modified conventional economic thinking considerably. Adam Smith, a dour Scotch lecturer in moral philosophy, who published his Wealth of Nations in 1776, was the philosopher of *laissez faire* or unrestricted operation of the price system. Before his time there was a great deal of regulation and direction of economic activity. Smith argued that by letting things alone the economy would operate to produce the greatest good for the greatest number. Although challenged in detail, Smith's views dominated economic thought in the English-speaking world until about the time of the American Civil War. He is still regarded as the intellectual father of capitalist economics.

Although the industrial revolution occurred in the 18th century in England, and not too much later in some other European countries, still other countries did not experience its effects until much later. In Japan the revolution did not occur until the 1870's, following Admiral Perry's voyage which opened Japan to western influences. In India the revolution has begun only recently and is still not completed. Although India now has many modern factories, a great deal of production is still carried on in small workshops with hand tools. Many countries in Africa and Asia have yet to experience the industrial revolution.

The industrial revolution was essentially a fairly rapid change in manufacturing methods, but modernization is also important in other sectors of the economy. The term agricultural revolution is sometimes applied to the many changes in farm methods that have occurred during the past 50 years. Use of machinery, fertilizers, hybrid seeds, and irrigation have greatly increased farm output per man. While these changes in agriculture are less visible than the growth of factories, they are perhaps even more important for growth of the whole economy and for development of backward nations.

Fashions in Economic Thought.

If one reads the history of economic doctrines, as anyone who aspires to become a professional economist must, he is struck over and over with the fact that there is nothing new in economic philosophy. All the ideas we consider novel today have been anticipated, in one way or another, by thinkers of earlier ages. They may not have cast their views in the same form, or used the same language, but the germ of the thought is there if we bother to seek it out.

When J.M. Keynes produced his general theory of employment in 1936, in which he argued that unemployment was structural but could be cured by massive doses of government spending, his views were considered radical and, by some, even subversive to orthodox finance. But the student of the history of economic doctrines knows that many of these views were anticipated by Sir James Steuart in 1767, 9 years before Adam Smith.

One reason economic theories are so seldom totally original is that economic problems are not novel but are merely new manifestations of the same old problems. One fact very clear from the history of economic doctrines is that theories are nearly always problem oriented; they seek either to explain the structure of problems or to point the way to their solution. If this be true, then there are seldom new theories—merely refinements, restatements, and rearrangements of old theories.

Since economics is an old subject or discipline, it is like mathematics, which is also an old subject, and unlike nuclear physics, which is a new subject. Nuclear physics is new because the whole basis of the science, the atom, was totally unknown until quite recently. Mathematics is an old subject because man has always needed to count and to reckon; similarly economics is old because the problems of food, shelter, and exchange have always been with us. Economics began, if indeed it had a discrete beginning, when the first caveman traded a club to his fellow caveman for a haunch of wild boar.

An old problem in economics, one which has been the source of much confusion and fallacy, is the tendency to reason from the small to the large without change in the logic. For example, people have always reasoned that what is good for a household must also be good for a group of them, or for a region, or for a nation. Experience has repeatedly shown this reasoning to be false, but it keeps recurring, even in our own time. For instance, we may read in a popular magazine like the *Readers Digest* that some small village has solved its unemployment problem by thrift and attracting a new industry; the article contains the clear implication that the nation can do the same thing, although this is clearly impractical. All regions cannot simultaneously attract new industries without robbing one another. Policies of this sort are what the British call "beggar your neighbor" policies—policies in which one area grows richer while its neighbors grow poorer in a kind of economic poker game. It is plain that a nation cannot for long practice such policies without inviting retaliation, so that in the end all parties lose.

Most reasoning that a large economic unit should behave like a small one turns out to involve "beggar your neighbor" reasoning. It is a good thing for a family to save as much of its income as possible, provided that in so doing necessary consumption is not denied and sheer miserliness practiced. But for a nation to follow the same policy may well mean that inadequate consumption results in unemployment, and that the efforts to save heavily are self-defeating because incomes fall so that actual saving runs far short of planned or intended saving. Reasoning from a part to the whole in economics is always dangerous and often downright misleading.

Although economics is an historical process, it is easy to misread economic history and to draw from it the wrong inference concerning future developments. For example, late in World War II there was a great deal of conjecturing by economists as to what the shape of the postwar world would be, and what problems would be most urgent. Euphemistically, this was called postwar planning. Most American economists who engaged in this exercise saw a big depression as the chief possibility. They reasoned war expenditures would be greatly reduced and that unemployment would result. Perhaps they were too much influenced by the 1930's, when unemployment was the main problem. Whatever the source of error, they could hardly have been more wrong. As we all know, the postwar problem was inflation, not unemployment. This should hardly have been surprising had we read the lesson of history properly—inflations have nearly always followed wars, although frequently it has been the defeated powers that have suffered the inflations while the victorious powers have reaped their reward in the form of depressions. There is no implication here that in winning World War II we really lost.

A soup kitchen for the unemployed in 1933. The Great Depression, beginning in 1929, brought widespread unemployment and profoundly influenced American ideas about economics and politics. Franklin D. Roosevelt, who became President in 1933, embarked on an experimental program to achieve economic recovery. His program included devaluation, public works, the NRA, and deficit spending. Still recovery was slow in coming. The entire decade of the 1930s was one of underemployment and unused capacity.

If you read current comment about the stock market in the financial press, you are bound to be struck with how often the commentators try to use past experience to predict the future. If the market traditionally rises in December, as some believe it does, this will be the basis for a forecast in November. If, as some others believe, what the market does in January presages what it will do for the rest of the year, then bull or bear forecasts will issue toward the end of January. When these forecasts are later reviewed and found to have been erroneous, the explanation is usually that some other factor, not foreseen at the time, dominated the situation. Often this unforeseen factor is a political one, or a development stemming from some other country. The honest forecaster would say that he failed to take account of all the data and to give the right weight to all the unfolding trends.

Making cheese in New Zealand. This country offers a good example of an economy in transition between predominantly agricultural and primarily manufacturing. Most of its manufacturing industries are based on materials such as milk, wool, etc. which are produced in New Zealand but converted into a higher value form prior to export. Note the cleanliness of the plant and the finished wheels of cheese on the tables. We have many similar plants in such states as Wisconsin.

One of the classic arguments of economic policy has been over the issue of free trade vs. protection. Historically, the case for protection has been for developing home manufacturing industries, by keeping out cheap foreign-made products. The free traders, on the other hand, have been those who looked to the export of agricultural materials and who were quite content to import manufactured goods. In the U.S. before the Civil War, for example, the South was strongly free trade while the North harbored a good deal of protectionist sentiment. Other countries have also seen protective tariffs as a proper shield behind which to realize some of their aspirations concerning economic development.

Although the tariff question has been discussed and decided primarily on political grounds, economists have always looked on it primarily as a subsidy matter. That a protective tariff is, in effect, a subsidy is quite plain; it takes from the consumer and gives to the manufacturer. The real question in individual cases is whether or not it is an efficient subsidy. An efficient subsidy is one which produces a large amount of the activity it is intended to promote for a modest cost. An inefficient subsidy, on the other hand, costs a great deal and produces little or no results. If a country has at hand all the preconditions for a manufacturing economy—access to materials, good transportation, skilled labor, and sufficient capital, then a temporary tariff may cause a quick and substantial spurt in manufacturing activity. We could properly say in this case that the subsidy had been efficient. If, on the contrary, none of these preconditions exist in a state of readiness, little manufacturing activity will be generated even by a high tariff. A comparison of benefits and costs would force us to the conclusion that the subsidy had been inefficient.

Intellectual Schools.

The long history of economic doctrines has brought forth many "schools of economists," i.e., groups having broadly similar views which usually emphasize one theme while neglecting others. In our own time, for example, we have the University of Chicago school which wants nearly everything to be regulated by market processes and which distrusts all government intervention with these market processes.

In the period before 1776 economic thought was dominated by a school known as the *physiocrats,* who believed that only agriculture was productive in some fundamental sense and that other activities were parasitic, as it were, on the body economic. From this preconception sprang all sorts of strange notions that were partially eradicated by Adam Smith in his *Wealth of Nations.*

In recent years much has been heard in this country about the so-called *new economics.* Although its policy prescriptions differ somewhat from those previously in vogue, the *new economics* is in no sense new intellectually. Its advocates hold that the economy, if stimulated to full employment, thereafter could be regulated to remain there through fiscal and monetary policy.

The flaw in the new economics is that full employment and absence of inflation appear to be basically incompatible. We can have one or the other but not both at the same time, and so are faced with a hard choice between inflation and unemployment, which is most likely to be resolved politically in favor of inflation. The new economists still flourish and still believe that they can somehow reconcile the irreconcilibles; but their case remains, as the Scotch jury would say, "unproven."

Fashions in economic theory do change, largely in response to changing problems. The 19th century British economists, sometimes described as the *classical school,* were primarily interested in microeconomics. They made much more elegant than their predecessors the explanation of how individual prices are determined, how forces move toward an equilibrium, and how the product of economic activity is divided. They did little to increase our knowledge of business cycles, our understanding of the monetary process, or the effects of invention and innovation. Their focus was on parts of the economy rather than on the whole. Like pathologists they dissected the economy and studied the structure of its separate organs. They did not so carefully study it as a functioning organic process.

In the 19th century there was also a German school of economists known as the *historical school.* They studied the separate economies of different countries in great detail as historical processes. The difficulty with this school was that, in detailing the uniqueness of different historical trends, they neglected commonalities—they failed generally to set up theories or simplified explanations of economic trends. Those unfriendly to this school would say that they failed to see the forest for the trees, that they lost the main thread in a mass of historical detail.

The purpose of this commentary is not, however, to criticize this or that school of economic thought; this in itself is a separate and specialized branch of economics which depends on extensive reading of the original texts. It is basic training for professional economists but does not belong in an introductory survey of the subject. The point to be made is that economics, because it deals with great public issues of the moment, is a kind of current events subject. We cannot, however, expect current policies to spring ready-made from historical experience. This experience must be appropriately modified and updated. On the other hand, to neglect history and to deal with current events as something totally new is to lack perspective.

The Policy Objective.

Perhaps the basic purpose of economic study is the formulation of wise economic policy. While not all economists can participate in this process they can, by their studies and researches, develop data and insights that can be influential in the policy formulation process. Some of the greatest economists have participated hardly at all in public affairs; Adam Smith did not, for example. Instead these nonparticipants devoted themselves to developing systematic explanations of economic processes that lead indirectly to policy implications. Smith, for example, was the philosopher of *laissez-faire,* of let alone, or loosen the restrictions on business if progress is the objective. His notions in their day were contrary to the accepted or conventional wisdom; but they suited perfectly the emerging tide of industrialization that followed their appearance.

One of the central ideas of economics is that of interdependence. With industrial progress, production has become more and more specialized and more dependent on the exchange process. Robinson Crusoe has often been cited as an elementary example of economic processes because he had to produce for himself whatever he wanted to consume. He had the choice of devoting his energies to activities aimed at immediate gratification, e.g., hunting or fishing, or to more long-range projects, such as improving his house. Self-sufficient farmers in the early West of our own country were very like Robinson Crusoe. Save for a little salt and perhaps a few nails, they produced whatever they consumed.

Today's economy is a far cry from that of Robinson Crusoe. Business firms often produce only one product, although in far greater quantities than would be possible using simpler methods. Workers often perform only one task rather than completing a product by their own efforts. They merely assemble a component, or attach a part on an assembly line, or perform some small operation. Everywhere the trend is toward specialization because experience has shown that specialized production units can turn out more, and at lower cost, than can general-purpose units. We see this on the farm, in the factory, in the service trades, nearly everywhere we look.

With specialization goes exchange. One can only specialize if it is possible to exchange the specialized product of one's efforts for all the other things one needs and wants. Markets depend on organization and upon a monetary system that functions effectively and smoothly. Whenever a monetary system breaks down, as during a severe inflation, for example, we see a return to bartering, in which people trade goods directly for other goods rather than for money. Lacking confidence in the monetary system, they seek commodities that may be eaten, or worn, or are sufficiently scarce to maintain their value.

Modern economies are tremendously more complex and interdependent than those of earlier days. This may be seen in a number of manifestations. Today, copper prices are determined on a world-wide basis on the London metal exchange. A rise in the price on this exchange will quickly be followed by price adjustments wherever copper is bought or sold. Similarly, prices of corporate securities are determined daily on the New York Stock Exchange. Transactions all over the country are completed at these quoted prices which change from hour to hour.

We call these highly organized markets, as indeed they are. They have evolved into their present form as the volume of transactions has increased and as improvements in transport and communication have made the handling of larger volume possible. For a highly organized market demands quick communication and concentration of buyers and sellers in a definite geographic or intelligence area.

It also demands established formalities in terms of standardized contracts, agreed settlement times, and the like. A market economy, in a word, is a far more complex economy than a self-sufficient one. But it functions more swiftly, with greater uniformity, and at far lower cost to both buyers and sellers. Markets are among the more intricate and more creative aspects of modern interdependent economic society.

Intricately organized markets are but one aspect of an interdependent economy. Another aspect is standardization of weights, measures, screw threads, and other building blocks of mass production. Eli Whitney, who is remembered for his invention of the cotton gin, contributed a much more important principle to mass production, namely the idea of interchangeable parts, built to definite specifications and capable of being used in any finished product of a given type. Originally developed in a government arsenal in connection with the manufacture of military weapons, interchangeable parts became the basis for practically all of mass production manufacturing. But for Whitney's principle, the assembly line would not exist.

One of the trends in modern manufacturing that is most notable is the mechanization of entire processes, as opposed to individual tasks. We have long had machines that could perform particular operations. Increasingly, these are being strung together in series with computer-activated controls managing a whole series of different tasks. In machining metals, for example, tools are numerically controlled by computer tapes so that people are necessary, not for actual processing, but only for general oversight and for repair work on the complex equipment.

Chemical plants run in much the same way with automatic valves and gauges controlling the flow and processing of the material, and with people merely overseeing the process. Far from diminishing employment opportunities, this mechanization of industry has opened up many more job opportunities than it has extinguished. It has also made people far more productive, so that their wages can be higher, and at the same time, the goods they produce can be cheaper.

Much of economics is about efficiency—not mere technical efficiency in the sense of enabling machinery to run faster and spew out products faster, but functional efficiency in the sense of making better use of resources, whether these be materials, or energy, or people. An atomic power plant is efficient because the fuel to drive it is fairly abundant and cheap whereas reserves of both coal and oil are limited. Over time, both coal and oil are likely to become more expensive, whereas nuclear energy is likely to become cheaper. The direction in which we are heading is clear, although the rate of change cannot perhaps be accurately predicted.

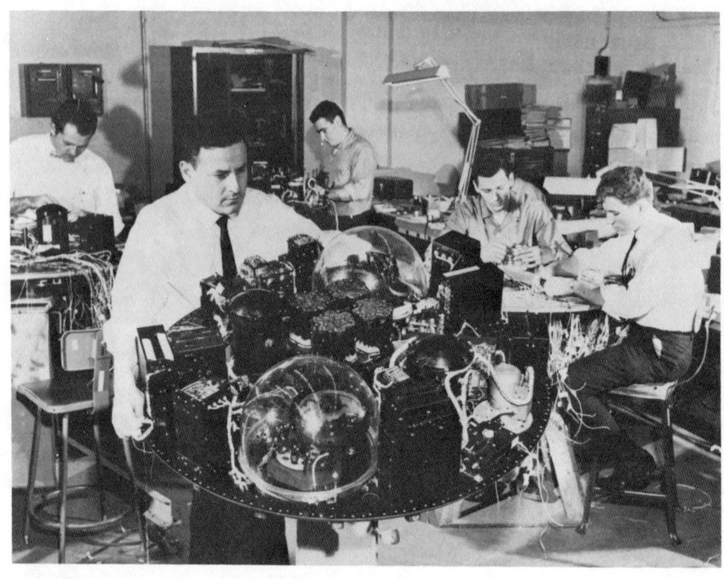

Assembling an early communications satellite. Today a number of these are in orbit, greatly simplifying telephonic and television communications. Satellites are an interesting example of government-business cooperation because government facilities are required to place them in orbit, after which they are operated by private business. In the not distant future the bulk of intercontinental communication is likely to be by satellite.

Economics deals with constant changes. The magnitudes we study are called *variables,* as in algebra. There are virtually no constants. The changes that are occurring are interrelated in the sense that movements of one variable produce corresponding changes in others. With everything in flux, you may well ask, what is the point in searching for principles? Are there any such principles, or do we merely have a system of constantly shifting relations, as in quicksand?

But even quicksand can be at rest or in equilibrium. When the equilibrium is disturbed, as when a horse stumbles in, the medium will react in a definite and predictable manner. There are laws of motion, just as there are laws of bodies at rest. A falling body accelerates in accordance with a well-known formula. There is a definite relation between the temperature and pressure of a volume of gas in a given space.

While economic principles are by no means so specific and precise as physical principles or laws, they are no less definite, nor do they lack predictive value. They are more qualitative than quantitative, loosely rather than rigidly related, and complexly rather than simply interwoven.

If the aim of economic study is policy formulation, we may ask how policy may be formulated in a meaningful way. This clearly depends on one's position in the economic structure. A wage worker is not in a position to decide issues of national policy, although he may influence these decisions by his vote, by writing his congressman, and in other ways. In his own sphere, his chief concerns should be to raise his own productivity, to make sure his training is up to date and in tune with technological trends, and that he makes rational decisions as a consumer. For example, it may be unwise for him to buy a house or a new car when interest rates are at a peak; by waiting awhile, he may reduce his financing costs considerably.

An independent businessman deals with economic policy in a broader context and has more wide-ranging economic decisions to make. He must decide when to expand and by how much; whether or not to change his location; whether to expand his work force and, if so, whom to hire; whether to raise additional capital by borrowing or by putting in more equity money; whether to enter the export business or confine his sales activity to the United States.

Public officials have the largest scope for economic policy determination and frequently the least training for the decisions they must make. The governor of a state must decide whether to ask for a tax increase or to try to reduce state expenditures, perhaps by cutting certain services that some of his constituents regard as essential. He must act in labor disputes to maintain law and order, must become involved in questions of education, and indeed in all manner of economic problems.

The President of the United States is the economic policymaker *par excellence* under our system. Most of the problems that come to him have both political and economic implications. He must deal with military spending, with health and welfare, with taxes and budgets, with crime, with education, with the environment, and other problems too numerous to mention.

Frequently, political and economic considerations will conflict. He may wish to close certain military bases for reasons of economy and because they are no longer needed; but he also realizes each closed base will be in some congressman's district and its closing will affect that district adversely, and perhaps modify the congressman's cooperation on some future occasion.

To help him with the task of formulating economic policy, the President has a formidable array of advisory services at his disposal. He has the Council of Economic Advisers, the Cabinet Departments, the independent agencies and the business and scientific community to call upon when he needs them. Although we have never had a president who was a professional economist, most presidents of necessity become quite skilled in economic affairs and in economic reasoning through constant exposure to economic problems. We have also had some rare examples of economic inanity from our presidents. Coolidge's notorious comment on the war debts—"They hired the money didn't they?"—is an obvious example.

Wise economic policy formulation consists mainly in keeping all elements of the problem in view, realizing the interrelationships among different factors, and anticipating what results are most likely to follow from what actions. It may be easier to settle a nationwide strike by allowing a generous wage increase, but an experienced President knows about setting a pattern, about how inflationary pressures can mount, and about how our competitive position in international trade is likely to be affected. In a word, he must balance many considerations which neither labor nor capital in the affected industry can be expected to take into account. His obligation is to the whole people and to the entire national interest.

One learns to formulate economic policy wisely through a combination of training and experience. Both are essential and they need to be combined in the right proportions. Increasingly, training is made available to the policymakers by consultation and advisory services; experience can also be supplied on a consulting basis; but the real experience necessary to the decision at hand is generally the policymaker's own. We can only hope that it will be full and suitable to the decision at hand.

In the second century A.D., Plutarch remarked that economy, which in things inanimate is but money making, when exercised over men becomes policy.

In a sense he was right. Policies always involve and affect people.

Chapter **4**

NOT TO BUY TOO DEAR—Prices and the Price System

In *Tom Jones,* Fielding tells us that "wisdom, whose lessons have been represented as so hard to learn by those who never were at her school, only teaches us to extend a simple maxim universally known. And this is, not to buy at too dear a price." Fielding's maxim was doubtless intended to be philosophic rather than economic; but it does illustrate an economic point, namely, that unfortunate buying, either by consumers or by business firms, can be unwise and can have consequences, at the least embarrassing and at the most disastrous. A merchant knows that an unwise purchase may leave him with unsold inventory that may have to be unloaded later at a distress sale. A consumer knows that a too costly purchase may become a white elephant and a future source of trouble.

This is by way of leading into the question: how are prices determined? What is the nature of the process in which they are set, changed, and finally settled? Everyone has some idea that prices are determined in markets, and that markets vary. Some are local, some regional, and some national or international.

Many prices are set initially by sellers; but sellers operate subject to constraints. They have to consider other sellers with whom they are in competition. They must consider costs, the alternatives open to potential buyers, and their own options of selling now or holding goods for future sale.

We also know that markets change. They may be strong this week, with prices rising, and weak next week, with prices falling. Some markets are seasonal. It is difficult to sell fur coats, for example, in the summertime, although extraordinary efforts are made by merchants to do precisely that.

In this ebb and flow of markets and prices, there must be some underlying system that determines how and why prices fluctuate. It is the task of this chapter to indicate in brief outline what this system is, how it operates, and why the pricing system is a general regulator of economic activity. In brief, one aspect of the system is this: prices create incentives and disincentives to producers and consumers alike. When a particular price is rising, producers will try to offer more; consumers generally will want to take less. Thus, a price rise may be self-reversing, although the reversing process may take either a short or a long time.

Much of microeconomics is the study of pricing processes—how they do and do not work, what consequences they have, and what ramifications flow from price changes. You will find these ramifications to be very extensive, and very pervasive throughout the economic process; you will also find that the many prices for goods and services do actually constitute a system; not perhaps a neat system, nor a wholly orderly system, but one that works in its fashion and is basic to our entire economic process.

Supply and Demand.

If you have heard about economics at all, you have probably heard that it is about supply and demand, or the law of supply and demand. In a general way, supply and demand do determine prices, and prices are important in propelling the economic machine in particular directions; but the so-called law of supply and demand is less a law than a tautology, meaning a statement of the same thing in two different ways.

If you have ever attended an auction, of household goods or the surplus stock of a bankrupt merchant, you have seen supply and demand at work. The supply in this case is fixed, namely the list of items up for auction. The demand is expressed by the bids which the auctioneer elicits from the crowd. When a particular item is desired by several individuals, the bidding is spirited and the selling price may be high; when an item is unwanted because it is out of style, not very useful, or in poor condition, or even if in good condition but no one wants it, the bidding will be limited and the selling price low.

An auction illustrates one function which a selling price serves; it clears the market or insures that all items are sold for whatever they will bring. An auction is therefore an efficient market in this one respect; it does clear the stock and leaves no residual inventory left over. This is why auctions are popular for sales where quick liquidation is desired.

You might be surprised to learn how popular auctions actually are as a marketing method. The stock market is an auction market, as are the commodity exchanges such as the Chicago Board of Trade. Livestock is often sold at auction in stockyards to meat packers, as are fruit and vegetables in city markets to produce dealers. The United States Treasury sells 91-day bills, public debt instruments, at auction each week. The buyers are dealers, banks, and others with funds to invest for short periods. The auction is considered the best and cheapest method of selling in all the above mentioned cases.

In many foreign countries, particularly less developed ones, prices are determined by haggling in the market. There are no fixed prices, and every transaction is the result of a bargaining process. The seller will start by asking more than he expects to get, and the buyer by offering less than he expects to pay. There will be a long discussion over the quality of the goods, with many offers and counteroffers, at the end of which a bargain will be struck. If you have ever shopped in an Arab souk, or market, you know how time consuming and exhausting this bargaining process can be. If it must be repeated for every purchase, much time and energy can be wasted.

Most goods and services, however, are not sold at auction or by haggling but at prices fixed by the seller which the potential buyer is free to accept or reject. Normally a retail merchant will fix his selling prices by taking his cost and adding a percentage markup to cover overhead and profit. Stores of a given type, say jewelry stores, will usually have a fairly uniform percentage markup, although discounters may shave this percentage as a method of attracting customers. To do this successfully they need to have a lower overhead than other merchants or to try for a larger volume at a lower rate of profit in preference to a smaller volume at a higher rate. Few are able in the long run to emulate the merchant who sold every item at a loss but made it up on volume.

Having initially set his selling prices, our merchant does some advertising and waits for the public to respond. If he has made an unusually advantageous purchase, so that his prices fixed by the markup method are low, he may find that sales are brisk. An old aphorism says that a merchant makes profit when he buys, not when he sells. Nevertheless, sales are necessary to realize that profit.

If the merchant finds that sales are not brisk and his customers are saying they can get the same thing cheaper elsewhere, he may experiment by cutting the price and observing the effect of this cut on sales. Pricing, therefore, is really a process of trial and error, in which the seller tries to find the best combination from the standpoint of his aggregate profit. In the formal language of economics, this combination is reached when he equates marginal revenue and marginal cost.

When economists speak of supply and demand they mean something quite precise, namely arrays of potential quantities that would be offered or taken at different prices. Such arrays may be represented geometrically by curves. Taking quantity along the horizontal axis and price along the vertical, a demand curve will slope downward to the right, indicating that larger quantities will be taken from the market at lower prices; a supply curve will slope upward to the right, indicating that larger quantities will be offered at higher prices. At some point the two curves will intersect, indicating that at this price quantity demanded and quantity supplied will be equal, or that this particular price, at the intersection of the curves, will clear the market. If all buyers and sellers had perfect knowledge of what others would do, this is the price that would actually prevail in this market.

Demand and supply curves are not fixed but are continually changing. When our merchant, disappointed with his trade, decides to mark down

DEMAND AND SUPPLY ARE SCHEDULAR CONCEPTS

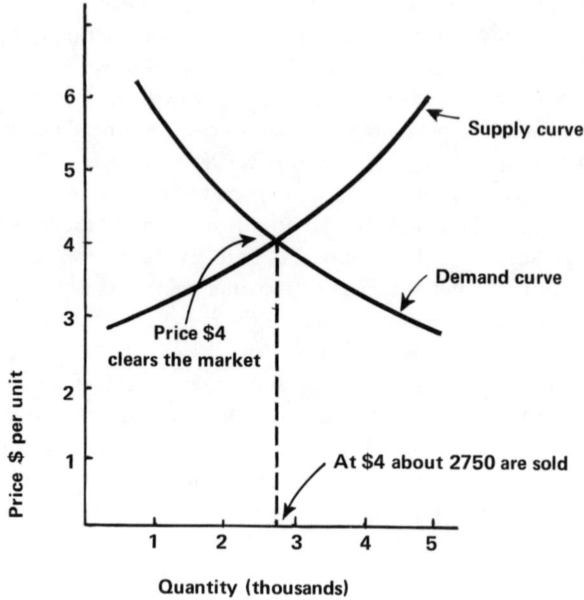

Demand and supply schedules for a hypothetical commodity. Notice the price per unit (vertical scale) and the quantities offered or taken (horizontal scale). The intersection of the curves marks a point where quantities demanded and supplied will be equal, or the market will be cleared. For curves such as this to define a market in which there are a number of both buyers and sellers, obviously good information must be available as to what both buyers and sellers are doing.

his selling prices he is in effect shifting his supply curve to the right, offering the same thing for less. If he sells more at the lower price he is intersecting the demand curve at a different point.

Merchants do not actually sit down with graph paper and attempt to construct demand curves for their products; they do, however, observe closely the effect of changing prices on quantities sold; this is very important to them. Any merchant knows that inventory turnover is very significant to his profits. Unsold merchandise ties up capital, runs the risk of becoming shopworn, and may become outmoded by style or seasonal changes. It is difficult to sell ice skates in the summer and bathing suits in the winter, although both efforts are made. It is better to have the right stock at the right time, move it rapidly, and replenish it often. This means a high rate of inventory turnover. Proper pricing is necessary to achieve this result.

Demand and supply schedules always exist within a certain time frame. At any particular time the demand situation, which might be illustrated by a curve, is based on given preferences and given incomes. Over time these change and demand shifts accordingly. A demand schedule for shoes in 1970 might be quite different from one for shoes at 2 P.M. on August 16. For very short periods supply schedules may be virtually fixed; over longer periods they have more variability. The merchant can reorder and the manufacturer can augment or diminish his output.

The important point to remember about demand and supply is that to an economist these concepts mean a range of possibilities rather than a single-valued given quantity. Price setting makes a single quantity of demand effective, namely the quantity that will actually be bought and sold at this price. Ineffective demand may be termed potential demand.

A little girl who was assigned the task of reading a book about penguins reported she had dutifully read the book which had taught her more about penguins than she wanted to know. If you were to read a little more widely in economic literature, particularly the textbook literature, you would hear more about demand and supply then you probably cared to. Let us note merely that these are rudimentary concepts of price theory, which is the economist's simplified explanation of how the price system works.

Elasticity of Demand.

We have seen how demand for any product may be represented by a schedule or a curve, sloping downward to the right, and indicating that larger quantities will be purchased at lower prices. For some purposes it is necessary to press beyond this point and ask how much larger for how much less?

This question leads to what economists call the elasticity of demand, or the relative steepness or flatness of the demand curve. If the curve is quite flat so that a small price reduction will result in a relatively large increase in quantity taken, demand is said to be elastic. More precisely, total revenue, which is the product of quantity times price, will be larger at the lower than at the higher price.

If the demand curve is steep, so that lowering the price results in only a very slight increase in sales, demand is said to be inelastic. Price times quantity will be smaller at the lower than at the higher price.

If price times quantity is exactly the same at the lower as at the higher price, the demand is said to have unit elasticity between these points.

If you have been exposed at all to the calculus, you will see immediately that elasticity is merely the slope of the curve or the first differential of the

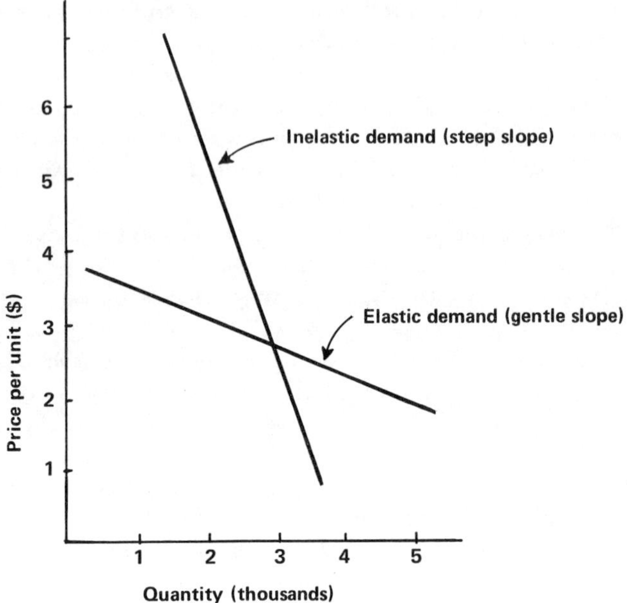

An elastic demand schedule is a relatively flat curve with little slope. An inelastic demand schedule has a relatively steep slope. Some demand schedules may be elastic in one part of their range, inelastic in another. A demand schedule of unit elasticity throughout its range would be known mathematically as a rectangular hyperbole. Suppliers will generally try to expand output in the face of elastic demand and to limit it in the face of inelastic demand.

equation which specifies the curve mathematically. Even without the mathematics, however, it is clear you can appreciate the difference between a steep curve and a flat one.

Now let us put the idea of elasticity of demand to work in a few elementary ways. Cigarettes are an object of excise taxation in most countries. One reason they are a good object for this type of tax is that raising such a tax, and consequently increasing the price of cigarettes to the consumer, does not significantly diminish their consumption. People smoke more or less because their habit weakens or intensifies, or because they are more or less concerned about their health, but not because the price is a little higher or lower.

Experience has shown that a government can raise the tax on cigarettes and be virtually certain this will yield more revenue. In other words, the demand for cigarettes is inelastic. In contrast, if a product or service the demand for which is highly elastic were to be taxed by an additional excise, it is not clear that any additional revenue would result.

Let us take another illustration—the pricing policy of a monopolist. A monopolist, by definition, controls the entire supply of something that is wanted—say the supply of "Coke" at a football game. If the demand for this product is elastic, he will maximize revenue by selling a large quantity at a relatively low price; if it is inelastic he would do better to sell less at a relatively high price. If demand has unit elasticity he will take in about the same amount regardless of where he sets the price. From this it is clear that one of the things a businessman wants to know when establishing a pricing policy is something about the elasticity of demand for his product.

Costs.

Just as demand is one blade in the scissors of price determination, the other blade is cost. The cost we are primarily concerned with is unit cost, or cost per unit of product. Cost has a number of elements.

A merchant selling dresses, for example, buys these from a wholesaler at a wholesale price. Let us say this is $20 per dress. To this cost for stock, he must add the cost of operating his store, paying his rent, his salesgirls, his heat and light, etc. These costs are sometimes called *overhead* or necessary operating costs to offer his stock for sale.

These overhead costs will vary somewhat, but not in proportion to his sales. For example, he might be able to handle 10 or 20 percent more sales with no significant increase in overhead. This would mean his overhead per sale would be that much lower.

In figuring his *percentage markup*, which is the basis for determining selling prices, the merchant will take overhead into account. Let us say that he figures normally to sell 200 dresses per month. If his overhead per month is $1000, this means he needs a markup of $5 per dress just to cover overhead. If he sells less than 200 with a $5 markup, he will not be recovering his overhead and will be operating at a loss. If he sells more than 200 he will more than have recovered his overhead and will have made a profit.

Suppose our merchant, knowing that his inventory costs $20 per dress, and calculating that his overhead is about $5, decides to price his dresses at $29.95. At this price he has some sales, but he also hears some potential customers say they can get the same thing down the street for $27.95. He reads his competitor's ads and looks at his show window; sure enough he is being undersold $2 per dress.

Now our merchant has a decision to make. Should he cut his selling price to or below the level of his competitors, or should he maintain his price and be content with a smaller volume? Knowing that his overhead will continue whether he sells dresses or not, our merchant decides to reduce his price not to $27.95 but to $26.95. At this new price sales again become brisk; but he must still anticipate what the next move of his competitor will be.

A self service grocery store. This one is located in Athens, Greece. Merchandising methods have changed substantially in recent years. The self service store economizes on labor and also allows the customer a close look at the merchandise. The self service concept is especially suitable when the typical customer buys many items at a time (groceries) rather than when the usual purchase is only a single item (clothing or television sets.)

It is clear from the above that price setting involves strategy. You make a move; your competition reacts to it; you must then counter their reaction, and so on. This process goes on continually in the business world. Its result is to move prices generally in the direction of costs.

The more competitive the market, the stronger will be the pressure for prices to move toward costs. The less competitive the market, the less pressure on prices toward cost.

For example, if our merchant has the only dress shop in town, and the alternative is to drive 25 miles to a larger city, he will be able to maintain a higher margin or markup. He will still have to keep in mind the possibility that, if his prices are too high and his profits too large, someone else may be motivated to set up a competing shop, perhaps across the street.

Economists are fond of dissecting costs into various elements. For example, they speak of variable costs, those which vary with units of product sold, and fixed costs, those which do not change with units sold. In the case of our merchant, the cost of the dresses is variable, the rent for his

Loading a container ship at Newark, N.J. The ship is built to handle these large containers which are shipped to the port by rail or truck. Handling freight in this way saves cost since the container is not unpacked until it reaches its destination. An important part of the cost of many products is transportation, of the materials to the factory and then of the finished products to the point of sale. Transport costs are an important factor in determining industrial location.

store is fixed. In a manufacturing, rather than a retailing, operation, the costs of labor and materials to manufacture the dresses would be variable, while the costs of advertising, warehousing, and selling would be essentially fixed.

If you want to be precise about the difference between fixed and variable cost, *fixed cost* is the total cost associated with zero output, that is the cost of being in business and ready to do business. *Variable cost* is the increase in total cost as output expands.

Overhead cost, which has been mentioned, is essentially an accounting conception meaning cost that cannot be assigned to units of production in any logical way except arbitrarily. If you are manufacturing dresses, you know each one takes a certain amount of material, thread, sewing and cutting time, trimming, etc. If you have a decent cost accounting system you can figure quite accurately what these direct costs per dress are. But there is also the cost of your showroom, of entertaining buyers, of advertising, paying designers, etc. These are overhead costs which can only be prorated to individual dresses in an arbitrary manner.

To make the matter just a little more confusing, while most overhead costs are essentially fixed, some may be variable. You can entertain buyers lavishly or frugally, for example. Likewise some direct or assignable costs may be fixed. An example would be depreciation on a sewing machine that is used only to sew dresses. The cost is assignable, but will be the same whether 10 or 100 dresses are sewn.

Although the various kinds of costs are of considerable importance in formal economic analysis, we need not pursue them further here. The essential point is that prices are closely related to costs. We might then ask whether prices are determined by demand or by cost.

The answer is, which blade of a scissors does the cutting? In reality they both do, although at different times the pressure may be greater on one blade than on the other. So it is with prices. When demand is very strong, as it is in wartime, for example, prices depend primarily on demand, with costs playing a secondary role. On the other hand, when demand is very weak, as in the midst of a depression, cost will be the primary price-determining factor.

The Price System.

We have seen how individual prices are determined by supply and demand, by buyers' choices and producers' costs. It is necessary also to gain some idea of how prices are interrelated, how they form a network of mutually interacting quotations and how this network directs the private sector of the economy.

A seller's prices are also someone else's buying prices; a basic price change, in steel for example, can spread in all directions like ripples in the water from a stone thrown in a pool.

Suppose steel prices are raised because the demand for steel is strong and costs are increasing. This price rise becomes an additional cost item to manufacturers of automobiles, office desks, refrigerators, and others who fabricate steel into end products.

These manufacturers in turn may consider raising their own prices to pass on all or part of the higher cost of steel. Whether they can do this successfully or not will depend on the demand and cost situations for their own products; it may be better strategy to absorb the higher steel cost and to make economies elsewhere; it may also be desirable to consider whether steel can be replaced in part by other products such as aluminum or plastics. This may mean redesigning some products. A businessman must be constantly considering how changes in the prices that affect him should alter his business decisions.

One function the price system serves is to allocate economic resources to their most profitable uses. If a man undertakes to build a factory and manufacture a new product, he must bid for resources that are now in alternative uses. He must offer attractive wage rates to draw labor to his operation and attractive interest rates and profit expectations to draw capital. His bids may cause other employers in the area to raise their wage rates in an effort to hold their workers. Ultimately, however, both labor and capital will flow toward those employments where rewards are greatest.

For the price system to work perfectly as a mechanism for allocating resources, we would need very quick responses to price and wage differentials. Actually we know that response is slow and incomplete. Resources may flow toward their most productive uses, but the flow is sometimes like molasses rather than water. Also there are many compartments in the container, some of which are barely connected with the others; the price system by no means works perfectly; but barring undue interference it does work.

There are many interferences with unfettered operation of the price system. Conservative economists regularly deplore these interferences. Labor unions in negotiations sometimes press for wages beyond the marginal productivity of the workers they represent. This zealousness can lead to strikes or to limiting the employer's profit unreasonably, to the ultimate detriment of the workers themselves; some workers may get high wages at the expense of others who remain unemployed.

Government may interfere in pricing in many ways. The most familiar is price controls in wartime. These may be necessary because of the inflationary potentials involved in shifting resources to wartime use; but many distortions also arise; these have to be worked out later when the controls are abandoned.

In New York City many apartments are still under rent control. This fact inhibits new building and leads to uneconomic use of the buildings where rents remain controlled. The longer controls last, the less appropriate to the existing situation they become.

In recent years some Presidents of the U.S. have tried to prevent price increases by "jawboning," by inveighing against these increases and throwing the light of publicity on them, often along with implied threats of retribution.

It takes a tough businessman to stand up to this kind of pressure, even though there is no legal sanction for the pressure. Most businessmen cave in under it, with the result that necessary price changes are sometimes delayed. This may, in some instances, be desirable. But, often, it is an extremely bad thing from a long-range standpoint.

In general, the price system works because changes in prices cause shifts in resources; these shifts are generally in the direction of more profitable, and hence more desired, uses. If price changes are sluggish, and resource shifts in response to these changes are also sluggish, then an optimum allocation of resources will not be secured.

It is interesting that in a socialist economy, where resources are centrally controlled and directed, a price system is still necessary. In fact it can be demonstrated that in a socialist economy pricing should be virtually the same as it is in a capitalist economy. The price system is an essential piece of economic mechanism rather than a reflection of a particular kind of economic organization.

Let us recapitulate what we have learned about prices so far. First, prices are determined in markets, which may be local, regional, national, or international. A market is simply a more or less organized institutional structure in or through which something is ordinarily bought and sold. The New York Stock Exchange is a highly organized auction market of national scope in which corporate securities are traded. The buyers and sellers are member brokers of the exchange; but they are acting as agents for investors of all kinds throughout the country. The market is highly organized because it has an integrated, high-speed information network for distributing price information and for transmitting orders. You can give a broker an order to buy a stock of XYZ Co. and within a few minutes the order will be executed on the floor of the Exchange.

The market for men's clothing in a particular town, on the other hand, is basically a local market. There are two stores in the town handling this merchandise. There are also stores in other cities 25 to 50 miles distant. Finally there are mail order houses such as Sears and Wards. These are the chief options open to a prospective buyer. We might describe this as a local market with slight regional overtones. It is not highly organized and price differentials can persist for quite a long time because the information network is incomplete. Newspaper and other advertising is about the only method of transmitting data on prices and availabilities.

The market for United States government securities is a highly organized, national, over-the-counter market in which public debt instruments, treasury bills, government bonds, etc. are traded. It is over the counter in

Exterior of the New York Stock Exchange. Stocks of about 1400 of the nation's largest and best known corporations are traded here daily. Member firms of the stock exchange are brokers who receive orders from customers all over the country to be executed in New York. The stock exchange is partially self regulating but is also closely supervised by the Securities and Exchange Commission.

that there is no regular meeting place such as the floor of the stock exchange. Instead we have about 20 dealers, banks and non-banks, that make the market by standing ready to buy and sell over the telephone. They are dealers and not brokers because they buy and sell for their own account, rather than for customers. They deal largely with banks and other financial institutions that use U.S. government securities as a near cash asset or a secondary reserve, easily convertible into cash on short notice. Thus, a bank wishing either to buy or sell treasury bills, simply calls a dealer to whom it is known, and makes a transaction over the telephone. Dealers also trade with one another, to balance their inventories, or to obtain securities wanted by customers.

The market for steel is basically a regional market with national overtones. If you are a manufacturer who uses steel, say a maker of office furniture, you may place your order direct with a steel mill, either for immediate or future delivery. You will be quoted what is known as a basing point price, say freight on board Loraine, Ohio, plus transportation to your plant in Youngstown. All other steel users in your area would get the same basing point price, although shipping cost would vary.

If you are a small user of steel you would probably order not from the mill but from a warehouse in your area. The warehouse operator is basically a wholesaler who buys from the mill but keeps an inventory with which to fill orders. From the warehouse you get quicker service at a somewhat higher price than you would get from the mill. Prices are basically fixed by the seller, but there may be some negotiation over quantity, discounts, etc.

These few illustrations are sufficient to make the point that markets differ in their geographic scope, in how highly they are organized as to information and mechanism for executing orders, and how as a matter of established business practice they function. Market organizations have evolved, over the years, into the form most suitable to the business being done, and the established practice of customers. Forty years ago grocery stores used to offer personal service and delivery. Today they are primarily self-service and cash and carry. The change has been largely a result of economic forces. Retailing in the old way has become much too expensive for the ordinary citizen. Only the wealthy can afford to patronize the old type grocery store.

Likewise, 40 years ago the Stock Exchange was almost totally unregulated, except for such self-regulation as the members imposed upon themselves; and this was not very onerous. Now this market is very closely regulated by federal law and by a regulatory commission, the Securities and Exchange Commission, which specifies in great detail the terms under which short sales may be made, brokers' capital requirements, and many other matters. At the time this is written there is pending before the Congress a bill to create an insurance system, similar to the insurance of bank deposits, that would cover customers' accounts with brokers.

The most important thing to remember about prices is how they are interrelated. Compare them to a spider web if you will or, better still, remember Alfred Marshall's dish full of marbles. When one price changes, a number of others change in consequence. These secondary changes in turn produce tertiary changes and so on until a new position of equilibrium or rest is reached. In practice, equilibrium within the price system is never reached, but adjustments are always in process, just as particles in a pile of uranium are constantly rearranging themselves.

Second, prices depend both on demand and on costs. Whenever prices are above costs, forces tending to increase supply will be set in motion. When these forces have had time to work and supply is actually expanded, prices will be brought lower, nearer to cost. Contrariwise, when prices are below cost, forces will work to reduce supply and to raise price. The only exceptions to these general principles are cases where supplies are fixed, as in paintings by old masters, or where supply is under the control of a monopolist, who does not increase supply merely because prices are above costs. Similarly, sharecroppers do not reduce their crops merely because prices are unprofitable. They continue to produce because they lack alternative possibilities of employment.

Third, prices exhibit all different degrees of flexibility. Some change hourly; others remain unchanged for very long periods. Some are virtually uncontrolled, as in an auction; others are subject to a high degree of administration, as in the case of basic steel prices. Some prices respond quickly to changes in demand and cost; others sluggishly. We must be prepared, in studying the price system, for great variations in the behavior of different prices.

Fourth and finally, prices always involve a buyer and a seller. Your selling price is my buying price. A retail merchant buys from wholesalers and sells to retail customers or final consumers. A manufacturer of office furniture buys steel, hardware, and paint and sells desks and chairs. A wholesale distributor of manufactured food products buys from manufacturers and sells to grocery stores. Businesses are based on buying products and services, adding value to them by processing, distributing, and reselling to other businesses or to consumers. Thus prices are intertwined in a network.

Changes at one point will spread outward to other prices. Some prices change quickly; others move sluggishly. The more highly organized the market, the quicker prices will change and the more nearly uniform they will be throughout the market. Comparison shopping and competition are the forces making for price uniformity. Prices are determined by demand and by cost, working together, as the two blades of a scissor.

Chapter 5

IT'S SYSTEMATIC—The Price System, continued

In 1769, nine years before Adam Smith's *Wealth of Nations,* Sir James Steuart, a Scots expatriate who lived mostly in Europe, wrote that real value was determined by three factors: (1) the amount which a workman could on an average produce in a given period of time, (2) the value of the workman's subsistence and necessary expense, both for supplying his personal wants, and providing the instruments belonging to his profession, and (3) the value of the materials employed by the workman.

Today we do not hold so closely to a cost of production theory of value; but we still consider cost a most important factor in price determination, especially in setting prices relative to one another.

The point has been made in the previous chapter that individual prices are knit together in a price system. Let us examine in a little more detail how this system operates. For prices to be knit together we need competition, flexibility of prices themselves, and movement of the factors of production—land, labor, and capital—in response to price differentials.

Land, of course, does not actually move, but its use may change, for example, from a pasture to a parking lot and eventually to a building site. Labor actually does move from job to job in response to wage differentials and in search of better work opportunities. Capital moves to alternative uses when an investor sells his stock in General Motors and reinvests in Sears Roebuck. It also moves when a bank makes a loan to firm A and not to firm B.

Suppose a firm has invented a new and better product—say an improved computer or the proverbial better mouse trap. It puts this new product on the market; soon sales are brisk. The product is priced high enough to cover all costs and to leave a substantial margin of profit. What happens next?

Before long other firms, seeing the excellent business the first firm is doing, are in the market with imitations. If the original product is protected by patents, marketing the imitations may run the risk of patent infringement. Let us assume, however, that no patent rights are involved and that the imitators are free to offer their imitation products without fear of reprisals.

Because of competition, sales of the original firm making the new product will stop increasing as the imitators draw off some portion of the original firm's market share. What has happened as the imitators entered the field is that factors of production have been drawn to this new opportunity because of its superior profit prospects. Technology has created an economic innovation which has drawn resources from alternative uses or from unemployment to producing this new product. This is how the free enterprise system responds to a new profit opportunity.

In general, business firms respond to rising prices by producing more and to falling prices by producing less. To produce more they must use more resources—more labor and capital and, perhaps, more fixed facilities. If copper prices fall, less will be mined; if bread prices rise, bakeries will turn out more bread to capitalize on the expanded opportunity for profit.

UNIT COST FUNCTION OF ABC MFG. CO.

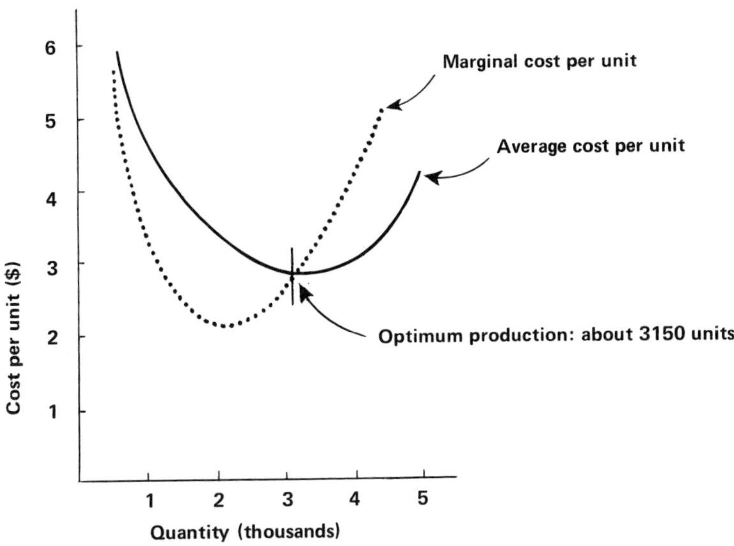

Diagram showing the relation of average and marginal unit cost. Notice that when average cost is falling, marginal cost will be below average; when average cost is rising, marginal cost will be above average. Therefore the two curves will intersect when average cost is at a minimum. This minimum average cost point is also the optimum scale of production for a particular plant; but the plant will not necessarily operate at this point unless demand has been perfectly forecast.

A firm's facilities will be scaled to a most efficient level of output. Below that level the plant will have idle capacity—machines not being used, too large an office staff, etc. Above that optimum level of output, capacity will be strained, overtime will have to be paid, and facilities will be generally inadequate to handle the work load. As a result, unit costs will rise.

It follows that deciding on the scale of facilities to be maintained is a crucial business decision, and one which should be based on a long range forecast of demand, including an allowance for normal growth. If a firm misjudges the facilities it needs, its plant will be either too large or too small, and this error will take a long time to correct. Meanwhile, costs will not be minimized but will be somewhat higher than they would be if the plant were the right size. It is seldom possible to make a strictly marginal adjustment in the size of facilities. Investment in plant and equipment often has to be made in large, discrete amounts rather than in tiny increments. It is apparent also that a firm whose U-shaped unit cost curve has a broad base is in a better position than one where the base of the U is narrow.

A modern machine for making newsprint. This one located at a paper factory in New Zealand. Capital must often be invested in large discrete amounts rather than in small increments. This is what makes deciding on the optimum size plant a difficult managerial decision.

Looking at unit costs from a broader perspective, we speak of increasing and diminishing returns to scale, which describes the behavior of costs when more than one plant size is considered. For a certain size plant we have one U shaped cost curve, but if we consider a plant twice as large, the second U shaped cost curve may be generally lower than the first. In this case, returns to scale are increasing, or costs are lower as volume is bigger. The chemical industry, for example, is in this position. It finds that by building continually larger plants, unit costs can be continually reduced. The problem, of course, is to sell the increased output of the larger plants. In part this is accomplished by reducing prices.

An example of diminishing returns to scale might be underground mining of metals. As the scale of production increases, it is necessary to dig deeper shafts and tunnels, to spend more for shoring and supports, and to have larger pumping and ventilating systems. Thus costs per ton of ore mined tend to increase rather than diminish.

Industries with increasing returns to scale tend to have large plants and concentration of production among relatively few companies. Industries with diminishing returns to scale have smaller plants and a larger number of firms able to compete. All industries show increasing returns up to a point and diminishing returns past that point. The point obviously varies greatly from one industry to another. At one time economists believed that, in the long run, prices tend to approximate cost of production, including normal profit. By this is meant principally that any differential between price and cost of production causes resources to flow toward or away from the point where this differential exists. The long run, in this sense, is not an actual slice of chronological time but an analytical construct, a situation where all forces operating for change have time to work themselves out.

But persuasive though this construct is, we know the real world is in fact never like this. Changes are always taking place, as they do along a seacoast when the breakers are rolling. Before adjustments to change 1 have been completed, change 2 has occurred and modified the adjustments being made to change 1. Similarly, change 3 will overtake and modify the adjustments flowing from changes 1 and 2; and so on *ad infinitum.*

This does not mean that the economic construct of the "long run" is without utility; on the contrary it is a useful law of motion of economic forces. It is useful just as it is useful to know the laws of motion of molecular particles, even though these particles are in constant motion. If you will remember Alfred Marshall's bowl of marbles, these were always moving in the direction of equilibrium, even though perhaps they never reached it. The equilibrium, in Marshall's sense, was essentially the state reached in the long run, after all outside shocks had been absorbed.

Our theme, however, is the interrelationships among prices and the fact that, taken together, they constitute a system, an imperfect one perhaps, but still a system. One category of cement that holds the system together is the possibility of substitution.

If copper prices rise, the producers begin to mine and smelt more copper.

The users, the wire mills, brass mills, and frying pan makers, faced with higher costs for their material, endeavor both to raise their own selling prices and to economize on the use of copper by employing aluminum, plastics, etc. The copper price rise is both a profit opportunity to the copper producers and a cost increase to the copper consumers.

Substitution possibilities work rather slowly and should hardly be regarded as mechanisms that operate to mitigate temporary price fluctuations. We come back again to the propensity of economists to divide the adjustment process into short range and long range, with this division again not being based on a definite interval of chronological time. The short run is not one month and the long run is not five years. Rather, the long run is the period when certain processes, such as substitution, begin to work in a perceptible way and to have some effect on the pricing process.

The purpose here is not to compound confusion by raising the question of what is "short" and what is "long" in economics. The difference, after all, is one of degree, not of kind. When copper prices rise, some substitution of other materials for copper will begin almost immediately. However, since this substitution involves redesign of products and processes, it is not likely to be significant if the higher copper prices are expected to prevail for one week only and then revert to the previous level. Only if copper is expected to continue to be dear for an extended period, or perhaps permanently, will substitution become significant.

The interrelationships among prices are often more subtle and more pervasive than we would probably believe if we did not look at the matter in some depth. Again let us take an example. If constructions costs are rising rapidly, propelled both by rising wage rates and a strong demand for buildings of many types, both housing and commercial structures, how do these rising construction costs affect other prices?

First and most obviously, the strong demand for buildings puts upward pressure on prices of construction material—cement, lumber, hardware, etc. Second, since construction is a component of many business plans for expansion, the rising costs raise investment requirements and place limits on the actual expansion of business facilities. Some firms postpone plant expansion, or build a smaller addition than they had planned, simply because costs have risen beyond their expectations. Rising costs will also influence some consumers who perhaps had planned to buy new houses but who decide now to defer their purchases in the hope that housing prices in the future may be lower.

Construction costs will influence rents on existing structures, tending to raise them because costs now are higher. Through rents they may influence the overhead costs of merchants and consequently their selling prices at retail. Thus, higher construction costs may have a pervasive influence over much of the economy, transmitting this influence through price movements. We live in an exchange economy, where one man's selling price is another's buying price, and where resources flow toward rising prices and away from falling prices.

Consider, if you will, another example. During World War II, when the financial problems of the Federal government were acute, some thought was given to the possibility of taxing coffee and tea, which are almost entirely imported; since both products are widely consumed and relatively low in price, the demand for them is probably quite inelastic. A modest tax, say of 5 or 10 cents a pound, would undoubtedly have been passed along to consumers in the form of higher prices, with little effect on the quantity consumed. A few people might have discontinued use of these beverages, but probably not many. Such a tax would have been a good revenue source from the standpoint of the government.

If coffee and tea were more expensive, some adjustments would have been made in family expenditure patterns. They would have been slight, perhaps, but still perceptible. Perhaps more soft drinks would have been consumed. Perhaps outlays on clothing would have declined slightly. The tax was never imposed, so we cannot know exactly what its effects might have been. Maybe we would have had another Boston tea party!

The point to be made is a simple one—the effects of price changes have a way of ramifying throughout the economy—causing shifts of resources, adjustments in expenditure patterns, and producing profits and losses at many points. Prices really do form a system, knit together in more ways than we may at first realize.

Prices are interrelated in another way, namely as determinants of income. The merchant's income depends on the prices he charges. A rise in the price of copper means not only additional profits for copper producers but also more wages for copper miners and more sales for the makers of mining machinery. A fall in the price of scrap iron means not only cheaper input for steelmakers; it also results in less income for those who collect and process scrap for recycling and for the railroads and trucklines that transport it. Although we could trace the effects well beyond this point, they would tend to be smaller and less significant. Nevertheless, all the marbles in the bowl can be affected to some degree by the removal of just one of them.

Demand and supply—a second look.

Having seen something of how prices are interrelated, let us take a more in-depth look at the old cliche that prices are determined by demand and supply. Demand, we have seen, refers to a schedule of quantities buyers are willing to take at various prices; supply, to a schedule of quantities sellers are willing to offer. As prices rise, buyers are normally willing to take less and buyers to offer more. Prices serve to clear markets by matching quantities bought and quantities sold.

Demand, however, does not materialize from thin air; it is the outcome of a more fundamental process. Consumers have incomes and they have tastes; both change over time, which makes the pattern of demand shift and twist. Fads like the hula hoop, for example, result in a sudden surge of demand for some commodity or service and then as quickly fade away. We have efforts to develop demand, as when the fashion arbiters decree midi-skirts will be worn, only to discover that women's tastes are not so easily swayed as they hoped. We have also sustained advertising to the effect that a particular brand of toothpaste will make us healthier, or more irresistible, or at least less repulsive. Often this advertising is an insult to the intelligence—a variant of the old theme of Adolf Hitler—that the big lie, repeated often enough, comes to be believed.

If consumer demand depends on tastes and incomes, the demand for all consumers' goods is simultaneously determined. With a given income we consume more of A at the expense of less of B, C, and D. As incomes rise, we may demand more of all products simultaneously. As incomes fall, demand for all products may shrink simultaneously.

If the demand for consumers' goods is determined by tastes and incomes, how do we explain the demand for *intermediate products* such as caustic soda or steel ingots or double-knit fabrics? Obviously, the demand for this type of product is derived from the demands for final products. Business firms operate by anticipating demand and translating these anticipations into orders for intermediate products and inventories from which these orders may be filled. In these anticipations businesses are guided heavily by past experience; but they must also take growth and shifting expenditure patterns into account. Makers of successful new products often find that demand has outstripped their capacity to satisfy it—there are no more hula hoops in stock, although they will quickly arrange to have more produced.

Demand anticipation can be a most difficult and demanding aspect to business decision making. Suppose you are a manufacturer of ladies shoes. Your fall line has 50 different styles, each of which must be furnished in a dozen different sizes. The size distribution you can probably anticipate fairly well from past experience; 5 percent of orders will be for size 5, 12 percent for size 6, and so on. Demand for the different styles, however, is much less easily predictable.

At the same time you are trying to forecast demand, you know that the minimum economical production run is 5,000 pairs, and that if you do

10,000 pairs your cost per pair will be 7 percent lower. Your problem is, how many pairs of what sizes and styles should you produce for inventory in advance of any orders? If you produce too many, you will be stuck with unsold inventory which will eventually have to be unloaded at distress prices. If you produce too few, you will find yourself unable to fill orders; your wholesalers may then turn to your competitors. But unsold inventory ties up capital; the firm must pay for materials and labor as well as for storage, with no return coming in. Thus it is apparent that deciding what to

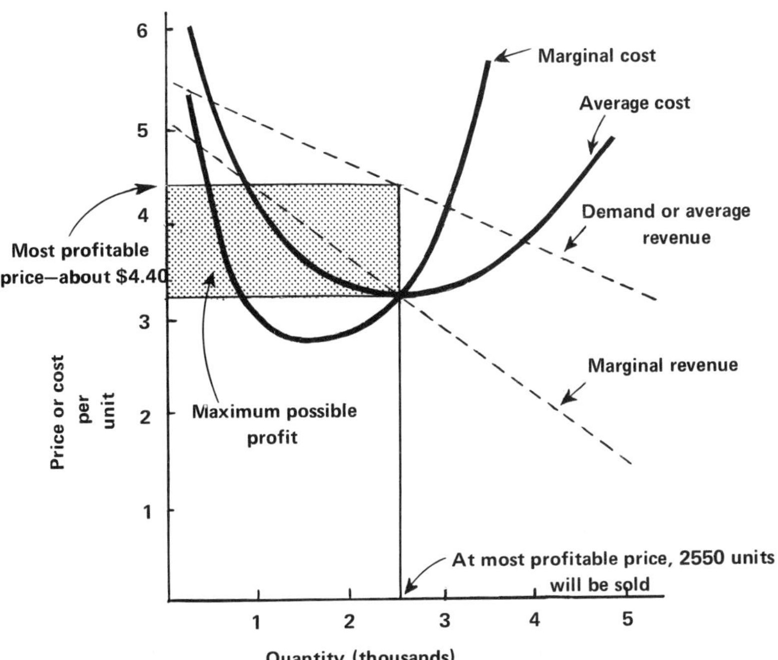

Diagram illustrating the process of profit maximization. The principle is equating marginal revenue with marginal cost. This defines the level of output at which profit will be maximized. Given the above demand and cost curves, the most profitable price will be about $4.40 per unit, at which price about 2550 units will be sold. The shaded area represents total profit, while the rectangle below it represents total cost. Any other price would yield a smaller total profit.

produce and in what quantities is indeed a crucial business decision, one that can affect profits very decidedly.

The point already made is that supply is related to cost, not merely in the long run but at all times, albeit in a complex way. Although supply may at times be only loosely related to cost—as when a merchant must sacrifice his stock to meet overdue bills—in most instances it will be closely related to cost, because supply is based on costs as well as on anticipations of demand which may be correct or incorrect. One cannot disregard costs and hope to remain in business; nor can one be highly successful in business without making quite accurate long-range forecasts of demand.

Demand is based on two things—tastes and incomes. Tastes determine what consumers want, either because these things are necessary, or because they satisfy special desires or contribute to image-building, or whatever. But wants unbacked by purchasing power remain ineffective. A man may want a Cadillac in the worst way, but without the necessary $8,000 his demand for Cadillacs is zero or ineffective. Only when he goes to the dealer with cash or credit in hand does his demand become effective in the market.

Cadillacs are priced at $8,000 because General Motors has determined this is the price at which they can make and sell this automobile, covering their costs and leaving a reasonable margin of profit. They also know that the potential demand for the Cadillac at this price is sufficient to insure their profit. In arriving at the $8,000 price, General Motors has not overlooked the Cadillac's competition; they are well aware of what Lincoln Continentals and Chrysler Imperials sell for and what they offer in performance and features.

So the private enterprise sector of the economy operates by responding to prices and to price movements. Although the private enterprise sector is the largest in the American economy, there are other sectors where prices do not govern in quite the same way. Let us notice briefly how decisions are made in these sectors.

Imagine yourself a member of the House of Representatives Appropriations Committee attending a budget markup session. The National Institutes of Health have petitioned for a $10 million program for cancer research. In their hearing they have explained how they propose to spend the money and what results they expect from the outlay. Your problem is to decide whether benefits from the proposed program will outweigh the costs and whether or not you should vote for the appropriation. You know that cancer research is important and that lives may be saved; you also know that other government programs are important and also yield public benefits. Should they or the cancer research program have priority?

In this case there are no selling prices to guide you; there are merely costs. The benefits may be substantial but they are largely intangible—lives saved, costs of prolonged illness avoided, etc. The alternate or competing program may be for unemployment benefits; these again have intangible benefits but they may be extremely important, at least to those who receive them.

You have a third difficulty. Neither cancer nor employment strikes all the people, only some of them. Are you entitled to spend large sums to benefit only certain classes, as against all the people? Should the money be spent instead on an anti-pollution program that would benefit everybody, rather than only those who have cancer or are unemployed? These are not easy decisions, and they have many ramifications. Their role in determining future tax rates is but one example.

If you find decision making as a potential Congressman too difficult, imagine yourself a trustee of the Ford Foundation, attending a meeting where future grants are being decided. One proposal you must consider would strengthen a university in a particular underdeveloped country; another proposal is for research in urban problems in the United States; a third is to support a center for the fine arts—music, painting, drama, etc. Which project is the more worthwhile, and how do you compare them?

Trustees of the Ford Foundation in session. Foundations such as this disburse large sums of money in grants for educational, social, or humanitarian projects. They try to apply benefit cost calculations to see which project will produce the greatest social benefits per dollar expended. Their job is difficult because results of projects are often indefinite, intangible, and delayed. Who is to say, for example, how or when the benefits from improved education can be measured?

Clearly, decisions in the absence of a price system are difficult decisions that must be made largely on subjective grounds. The price system may not make the right decisions, but at least its decisions are objective, reflecting the preferences of many people rather than just a few. Some years ago, people bought automobiles with ugly tail fins, which were both vulgar and unfunctional. Nevertheless, they were the style and they sold. Happily, good taste reasserted itself and the tail fins quickly disappeared. This is part of the genius of the market economy. If consumers do not want tail fins or midiskirts they "vote" against them in the market place and the offending items quickly disappear, having suffered the fate of commercial failure. Unfortunately, we lack a similar mechanism to correct a wrong decision by the Appropriations Committee or the trustees of the Ford Foundation.

Function of the price system.

The importance of the price system in a free enterprise, market economy is that it serves to allocate resources to the production of those commodities and services that are in demand, for which people are able and willing to pay. These products may be worthless patent medicines, or miniskirts, or steel ingots; they have in common the fact that people are willing to buy them at profitable prices. We have seen that, when the price of a product rises, more resources flow toward its production; when the price falls, resources seek alternative uses where profit prospects are better. In a modern market economy these resource shifts in response to price changes are constantly going on; they are the essence of the economic adjustment process.

Although some resources are allocated in accordance with criteria other than market prices—in government and in the nonprofit sector, such as by philanthropic foundations—prices are the main allocative mechanism to give the economy vitality and direction, to make the decisions no other mechanism could make as well and as objectively. It follows, then, that interferences with the pricing mechanism, except for well-established public purposes, such as the regulation of public utilities, are to be avoided whenever possible. During a war we have mandatory price controls because with the excess demand of wartime we should otherwise have profiteering and price gouging; but when the war is over, we find we have many distortions resulting from the controlled prices.

We have also seen that a centrally planned economy needs a price system quite as much as a free enterprise economy does. When the Soviets undertook to organize the Russian economy after the Bolshevik revolution, they soon discovered that they needed prices to make their system of planning work. The prices they use to this day are arbitrary ones that produce many distortions in the allocative process; but they are unable to do without some prices, even arbitrary ones. Lack of a freely functioning price system is, indeed, one major inefficiency in the Soviet system.

The price system is not only an allocative mechanism; it is our principal method of determining incomes from the productive process. Skills that are valuable and much in demand are highly compensated; those that are less valuable and more abundant draw smaller incomes. We may regard this process as unfair in that it does not take into account the drudgery and disagreeableness of some work; it pays large incomes to movie stars and other entertainers whose contributions are not necessarily culturally uplifting; and it pays only minimal incomes to those who lack special skills and aptitudes. Nonetheless it is an objective system determined by the play of prices rather than by anyone's judgment as to what is fair and proper. We may not like the system, but it works. Indeed, it is difficult to imagine a system that would work better.

One who has control of the supply of some product or service is called a monopolist. One attribute of this control is that he is able to manipulate prices to his own advantage; to set them high if he wishes, or lower as he feels he will maximize his profits by a more reasonable price policy. One reason we have antitrust legislation is that monopolists potentially interfere with the free functioning of the price system and thus retard its operation as the allocator of economic resources. It is not that competition in itself is so desirable; indeed it probably does not operate to promote technical progress as well as monopoly; it is merely that the price system as a whole cannot operate as effectively if some prices are controlled while others are free. Controlled prices always run the risk of being either too high or too low; either sort of error disturbs the optimum allocation of economic resources.

If one looks at the myriad of prices that prevail on a given day, it is possible to gain some idea of how complex the economy really is. For each of the thousands of individual products we use there are manufacturers' prices, wholesale prices, retail prices, used or second-hand prices, regional prices, national prices, international prices. In addition, there are thousands of prices for service items: haircuts, surgeon's fees, repair charges, restaurant charges and all the rest. It is hard to believe that all these prices are interconnected; yet to some degree they all are. If repair charges were too high, consumers would demand more durability in their durable goods; manufacturers would be compelled to supply it. If haircuts were priced too low, barbers would be overwhelmed with customers.

Prices and price movements are constantly giving signals to the economy—signals that say produce more of this and less of that, signals that say sell here instead of there. These signals guide the flow of economic resources without a central plan to produce what people want; it is really quite a wonderful mechanism when you ponder it; it is also an impersonal mechanism for harmonizing our economic interests, without one person telling another where to work and what to do. Any alternative economic mechanism has much more of compulsion in it.

When Adam Smith wrote that, "it is not from the benevolence of the butcher, the brewer, or the baker that we expect our dinner, but from their regard to their own interest," he was merely expressing the function of prices and of responses to them in a simple form. Prices direct economic activity and control the flow of economic resources.

Chapter 6

CHARGED WITH A PUBLIC INTEREST—Public Utilities

In the 18th century, as trade among nations grew, the influence of regulated monopoly companies, such as the Merchant Adventurers or the East India Company, steadily declined. State intervention was replaced by competition. The merchant created the industrialist.

Reversing this historical process, if competition declines and monopoly increases, we can expect regulation to grow and to become more detailed and complex. Within a limited area of economic activity this has, in fact, happened.

A nuclear energy electric power generating plant in California, about 200 miles north of San Francisco. This plant has a capacity of more than 68,000 kilowatts. Wholesale electric power rates are regulated by the Federal Power Commission. Photo courtesy Pacific Gas and Electric Co.

A certain group of businesses in this country are exceptions to the general rules of the free enterprise system. Their selling prices are controlled or regulated by a public body, usually a regulatory commission consisting of appointed officials. These businesses are often known as public utilities. They include telephone, electric power, gas and water companies, railroads, interstate trucking concerns, and some others. Banks and insurance companies are also closely regulated, but this regulation relates primarily to matters concerning their financial soundness and does not normally extend to the prices they charge.

The group of public utilities or price-regulated companies are, in the main, "natural monopolies." That is, they provide a service which is usually better and more cheaply done if one company serves an area than if there is competition among a number of different companies. Imagine what it would be like to have six telephone companies serving an area instead of only one. They would have to duplicate networks of poles and wires; to reach everyone you might have to have six telephones in your home instead of one, and so on. The same principle applies to electric power and gas distribution. A single company with a single set of facilities is obviously the best system. A natural monopoly in this sense means simply that a single company can provide the best and cheapest service. In recognition of this situation a utility usually receives from a local government a franchise or an exclusive right to operate. In return for this franchise it agrees to submit to regulation, including rate setting.

The cardinal rule of rate setting.

Public utility rate regulation, in turn, is normally based on the principle of approving such rates as will yield a fair return on invested capital. While this may sound simple, rate setting is actually a complex and difficult task, with its own ground rules and procedures that have become fairly standardized over the years.

Once initial rates have been established, changes come about as the result of petitions made by the company to the commission for, say, a rate increase. These petitions are accompanied by extensive calculations showing what the proposed rates will do to operating revenues, what expenses will be, and therefore what net income will remain. In rate hearings testimony will also be heard from utility users and the public concerning the effects the proposed rate increases will have on their constituents.

In the end, the commission will render a decision granting all, part, or none of the proposed rate increase. The object of these proceedings is always to keep rates as low as possible and still allow the utility to earn a fair rate of return on its invested capital. This capital has been contributed by shareholders as in any other business. Unless they get a proper return on their investment, the utility will not be able to raise new capital as required. Their service will consequently deteriorate, and they will be unable to meet all the demands on them.

Heavy fixed investment.

Most utilities have in common the fact that they are capital-intensive businesses; i.e., the investment in fixed assets is very large in proportion to sales. This means these utilities are constantly borrowing funds in the capital market through the sale of bonds, etc. With a large bonded indebtedness, they are sensitive to changes in interest rates. During an inflationary period they are "squeezed" (because of the formal procedure necessary to obtain rate changes) between higher interest charges and rates that lag behind other prices. Offsetting these disadvantages is the fact that income is quite stable. People continue to use electricity even though their incomes drop.

Who regulates utility rates depends on whether or not a utility operates in more than one state. The Federal government has the power only to regulate commerce and hence power rates among the states. Within a particular state, regulation is by a state-appointed commission.

The oldest Federal regulation is of railroad rates and is exercised by the Interstate Commerce Commission (ICC). This body dates from the 1880's; it has a complex job because of the nature of railroad rates. These rates are not based on the cost-of-service principle, but rather on what is known as the value-of-service principle, or charging what the traffic will bear. Coal, for example, is hauled for a low rate per ton because it is a bulk, relatively low value commodity. Automobiles, on the other hand, pay a much higher rate per ton mile because they are a more valuable cargo.

Rate structures.

Railroads have the characteristic that fixed costs per ton-mile are relatively low. If a railroad is operating published schedules, as it must, the additional costs per ton of freight are quite low. It pays the railroad to accept coal or other bulk cargoes at low rates so long as these cargoes cover the variable costs and yield something to apply against fixed costs. This is better than not having the traffic at all. So railroads have quite complex rate schedules, with rates generally being graduated in accordance with the value of the commodities hauled. Trucks, which now compete extensively for haulage with the railroads, also have these complex rate schedules.

There are other characteristics of railroad rates that are interesting. On transcontinental traffic, for example, there is competition among several rail systems and also competition from coastwise shipping through the Panama Canal. Because of this competition, cross-country rail rates are kept relatively low, whereas rates between a coastal point and an inland point are subject to less competition and hence tend to be higher on a ton-mileage basis.

However, the ICC has a rule that the rate for a short haul cannot be higher than for a long haul when the short haul is included in the long. Thus, the rate from New York to Omaha cannot be higher than from

Home of the Interstate Commerce Commission in Washington, D.C. The ICC exercises regulatory authority, including rate setting, over railroads and interstate trucking operations. Oldest of the regulatory commissions, it has been charged with helping to keep the railroads technologically backward, and with allowing them to be saddled with financial problems including heavy fixed debt and inability to raise new equity capital. In most foreign countries railways are operated as government enterprises. We may well come to that in this country also.

Trucks at a warehouse in Detroit. The tractor trailer trucks shown here are especially popular because the trailer can be left for unloading and picked up later. Interstate freight rates charged by trucks are regulated by the Interstate Commerce Commission.

New York to San Francisco, because Omaha is a way-stop on the longer haul. The purpose of this rule is to minimize discrimination in freight rates against those locations where there is no competition, but which are served only by a single rail line having in effect a monopoly position. The reasons for the rule are fairly obvious. In the absence of regulation, certain locations would be charged extremely high freight rates.

Thus rate regulation is a matter not only of the level of rates, but also of the rate structure. A structure is wanted that will be fair to all classes of consumers and will not require some classes to subsidize others. This can be extremely difficult and is largely what makes rate regulation so complex.

Railroads and interstate trucking are the province of the ICC but interstate electric power and gas rates are regulated by the Federal Power Commission. Electric power rates are not so complex as freight rates, because there are fewer classes of consumers and only one commodity—power—is furnished. One complicating factor, however, is that there are "peak-load" rates and lower "off-peak" rates. The peak-load problem is common to many utilities but is especially important in the case of an electric power company, which has to have sufficient capacity to meet the peak demand for its services. With power, there will be a daily peak plus a weekly one and perhaps also a monthly peak. Utilities can calculate fairly accurately from records of past service what the peak demand on them will be, and they all attempt to smooth out the load curve as much as possible by offering reduced rates for service in certain hours. For example, electric water heaters, if run only during off-peak hours, may qualify for this reduced rate.

Virtually all power rates are composed of two elements—a demand charge and a quantity or use charge. The demand charge is essentially a fixed charge for being hooked up to the service and being able to use it. In an electric power company, the quantity charge is per kilowatt-hour used and is often graduated, so that beyond a certain quantity one gets to a lower rate bracket. This is like a quantity discount for buying any kind of merchandise. Gas and water rates are usually structured in the same way, with a demand charge and a quantity or use charge.

Telephone rates are also generally like electric power rates, with a demand charge for being hooked to the system, and use rates, which may or may not be metered for local service. Long-distance rates, of course, are charged separately on a distance and time basis. These rates have been kept quite low, and, in fact, long-distance telephone service is one of the very few items in household budgets that is cheaper now than 20 years ago. Installation of dial equipment and automatic switching are the technological advances that have made these savings possible.

Telephone operators at work. Such operators are rapidly being replaced by automatic switching equipment. Their replacement is being accelerated by the policy of offering lower rates for direct dialing than for operator assisted calls. Interstate telephone rates are regulated by the Federal Communications Commission.

The Technology factor.

Utilities do not have to compete for customers, but they do need to compete with other businesses in the area of technical progress. One reason for our good telephone service is that the telephone company has always sponsored research and development work and has made every effort to modernize its facilities. This has been done along with expansion, so that service to the consumer has constantly improved.

By contrast, the railroads are now in difficulties partly because they failed to keep pace with technology and to improve their service. Consequently, they have continually lost freight customers to the truck lines and passengers to the airlines, and, as a result, are in severe financial difficulty, as witness the problems of Penn Central, formerly two of the richest of all railroads.

The railroads have a long history in this country. From about 1830 to the end of the last century was the great period of railroad building. During most of this period the railroads were unregulated and they competed fiercely with one another. They received heavy construction subsidies from both the Federal and state governments, mostly in the form of land grants along their rights of way. If these lands were held for a time, their value increased greatly as improved transportation developed the economies of areas along the rail lines.

In the Midwest, for example, towns that had become well established withered and died if the rail lines went elsewhere. On the other hand, mere villages on the rail lines grew to prosperous cities because of available transportation. With the growth of trucking, location on a rail line has become less necessary for prosperity.

Although the railroads were a powerful force for economic development during the last century, they have largely ceased to play this role. Although there have been some technical improvements in rail transportation, notably piggyback freight, where truck trailers are carried on freight cars and then unloaded to finish their journey, the railroads have generally failed to keep pace technologically with the rest of American industry. This technical backwardness is basic to their present difficult economic position.

How much of this backwardness is attributable to regulation is an open question. Certainly it may be said that the ICC has not actively encouraged technical progress but has been rather content for the railroads to continue operating in their traditional manner. This is clearly one of the perils of regulation—that it may not actively encourage innovation because the utility is allowed to keep few if any of the gains that result from innovation. An unregulated company, in contrast, can appropriate the gains from innovation, at least until their competitors follow suit and adopt the same innovation.

One obligation that public utilities accept is to serve all customers in the area of their franchise on standard terms. This obligation helps to determine the capacity they must have, and hence what their overhead costs will be. An unregulated business does not have this problem. It can turn customers away if it lacks the capacity or the products to serve them. If a utility is in a growing area it will be faced with regularly enlarging its capacity and hence with raising capital for this purpose. Its success in the capital market will be an important indicator of whether its regulated prices permit an adequate return on investment.

One consequence of long-term rate-regulation is that its scope seems constantly to broaden. In part, this is because regulatory agencies assert jurisdiction over a larger and larger field as practices develop that are designed by the utilities to circumvent regulation. In part, it is also attributable to a natural tendency on the part of governmental bodies to extend their jurisdiction—a sort of Parkinson's law of expanding functions. Extending the scope of regulation is a tendency that needs to be resisted, lest the scope of regulation be extended to areas where operation of the price system is itself sufficient to protect the interests of consumers.

The rate base.

One problem regulatory commissions have had historically to contend with is inflation of the rate base. In the 1920's, for example, there were numerous combinations of operating utilities and numerous holding companies that owned the controlling interests in several operating companies. Frequently these operating companies were acquired at inflated prices,

prices based on the expectation that earnings would continue to grow indefinitely. When the depression that began in 1929 had run a few years, these overvaluations became strikingly apparent.

The problem for the regulatory commission is simply that, if the rate base, or amount of fixed investment in the company, is inflated, rates to give a fair return on this investment will be too high, since the stated investment is itself too high. Thus regulatory commissions must, in effect, audit a utility's plant accounts to see that this plant is actually worth what its book value claims to be. If the plant accounts carry obsolete or outmoded facilities at more than their true worth, "write-downs" are needed to bring the accounts in line with current values.

This is a difficult and time-consuming aspect to regulation, since valuation of a going concern is not a precise art. Reasonable men can differ on what a plant is actually worth. If the utility were selling its services in a free market, its earning power could be attributed to its plant and facilities. In the case of a utility, however, this would involve circular reasoning, since earning power with controlled rates depends on what a fair value for the plant is. Thus, the usual method of valuation, capitalization of earnings, cannot be applied in this case. We must go from fixed assets to earnings at controlled rates. Regulatory commissions have to be constantly on guard against efforts to inflate the rate base or investment accounts; inflation of this type leads to unjustified earnings for the utility.

Operating trends.

Some technical developments in public utilities that have occured over the past several decades are worthy of notice. In the electric power industry interconnections among various power systems have developed rapidly. To the extent that different regions have peak loads occurring at different times, this enables some saving to be made on capacity. You will recall that the dominant factor in capacity needed is the ability to meet peak demand. If this can be met partly by importing power from some other region, less generating capacity will be needed.

Also, power systems have become better balanced between hydro- and thermal power. A hydroplant, which uses falling water to generate electricity, is normally the cheapest plant to operate, although construction costs may be high. But hydropower is variable, depending on stream flow, the weather, and other factors. Thus, companies dependent on hydropower often have standby capacity in the form of a thermal plant, operated by coal or oil. This standby plant can be operated whenever the output of the hydro-facilities is less than normal, or it can be used to meet peak loads, with the hydro-facilities carrying the base or normal load. These economies in generating facilities have been known for a long time, but have only recently come into more general practice.

In the gas industry the trend has been toward increased use of natural gas delivered by pipeline, and decreased use of locally manufactured gas. Where a pipeline exists, the natural product is usually better and cheaper; it can be stored to meet peak demand just as locally manufactured gas was stored for this same purpose. Distribution is the same with either product. Increased use of gas for home heating has rapidly expanded the demand for this product.

In the railroad industry technological change has been slow to come. Passenger business has been lost to the airlines and freight business to the trucking companies. Railroads are still the cheapest method, except for water, for transporting bulk commodities such as coal, iron ore, sand and gravel. Railroads were the first industry to have rates regulated; regulation has perhaps been closer and less forward looking than in some other industries, such as telephone service.

Then, too, the enormous investment railways have in right of way, stations, etc. may have limited their freedom to adapt to changing circumstances. At any rate, no developments seem to be at hand that promise to reverse the decline in railway revenues and earnings.

The accumulation of deferred maintenance of railways is such that modernization would require the injection of a very large amount of fresh capital, which possibly only the government is in a position to provide. Whether this will eventually result in government ownership and operation, or merely in a series of financial rescue operations, is difficult to predict.

Valuation.

Although not a burning issue today, valuation of utility property was quite an issue in the early days of public utility rate-regulation. The question then turned largely on whether property should be valued at original cost, less depreciation plus additions, or at replacement cost. The latter is the more significant measure of cost in economic terms, but the former is essentially what is recorded in company accounts and is conventionally used as the measure of capital invested. In the choice between these two methods of valuation, much depended on whether prices had been rising or falling. In a period of rising prices, original cost will lag progressively behind replacement cost; when prices are falling, original cost will be progressively higher than replacement cost. Most often regulatory commissions have inclined toward use of original cost. This has meant that, when prices are rising, utility rates have generally lagged and utility profits have been squeezed, sometimes making it difficult to raise new capital.

One problem with replacement cost is that it is difficult to measure it with precision; like daily quotations in the stock market, it changes constantly. Original cost, in contrast, has an aura of definiteness. The actual cost of a piece of equipment bought five years ago is certain, even though its present value may be uncertain.

Depreciation is a large element in public utility valuation, because the facilities are normally capital-intensive, with depreciation being a major

DEPRECIATION OF AN ASSET
COSTING $100 OVER A 10 YEAR LIFE

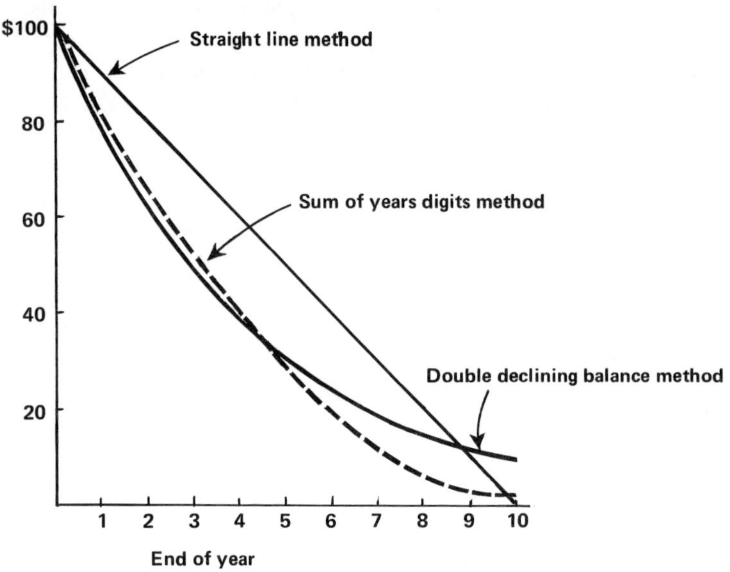

Chart showing depreciation of an asset over 10 years by three different methods. Plotted are the undepreciated values at the end of each year. The straight line method derives its name from its plotting, which forms a straight line. The other methods provide some acceleration over the straight line during the early years. Since depreciation is a tax deduction, accelerating it by use of declining balance or SYD methods has the effect of postponing tax liability. This is of less importance to a utility than to an industrial company.

element of cost. Depreciation, however, is always an estimate. Suppose a new machine, say an electric generator, is bought at a cost of $1 million. The expectation is that it will last for 20 years and then be worthless;

i.e., have no salvage value. Depreciation is simply an accounting technique for spreading the cost of the machine ($1 million) over its service life (20 years).

The simplest technique for doing this is writing an equal amount, 5 percent, off each year for 20 years. This technique is called "straight line" because if the value of the machine were plotted on a graph for 20 years it would follow a straight line from 100 percent to zero.

Other methods of depreciation involve some acceleration compared to straight line, i.e., these methods write off relatively more in the early years and relatively less in the later years. Instead of a straight line this would plot the value of the machine as a curve, concave toward the x-axis. Engineers and valuation experts maintain that this type of curve more accurately represents how a fixed asset declines in value than does the straight line.

Federal tax law gives a considerable latitude to which method of depreciation may be used. Since 1954, taxpayers have been entitled to use *declining balance depreciation* at *double* the straight-line rate. If an asset has an expected 10 year line, so that the straight line rate is 10 percent, the declining balance rate in the first year may be 20 percent. The second year it will be 20 percent of 80 percent (the undepreciated balance) or 16 percent. The third year, it will be 20 percent of 64 percent (the undepreciated balance) or 12.8 percent, and so on throughout the succeeding years.

In double-declining balance depreciation two-thirds of the cost is written off in the first half of service life (5 years in our example above), leaving only one third to be written off off in the second half of service life. By taking more depreciation in the early years, a company increases its cash flow but also diminishes its profits since more expense (depreciation) is being taken.

Thus, the utility companies are impaled on the horns of a dilemma. If they take as much depreciation as they can, in order to maximize their cash flow, they reduce their current earnings and also their rate base. This may imperil their future rates. In view of this problem, most utilities have been content to stick with straight-line depreciation, even though there is an immediate tax advantage in using an accelerated method. Unlike industrial companies, utilities are interested less in immediate profits than in long-run stability of earnings. Regulation gives them this kind of perspective.

Municipal ownership.

In the 1920's and 1930's there was a considerable movement toward municipal ownership of some utilities in this country. This movement carried furthest in water and sewage systems but also extended to electricity and gas in some regions. When a utility is municipally owned, its prices can be set at a level in the public interest and less detailed ongoing regulation is necessary. However, in electricity and gas, economies of scale are usually more important than in water supply. There is more to gain from being part of a large interconnected power system than a water system. Normally a municipally-owned power plant cannot be so well interconnected as a private company. Thus the trend toward municipal ownership of power facilities seems to have been arrested. There are still, however, a large number of municipally owned power plants in operation.

Public vs. private ownership and the regulation thereof used to be a hotly debated topic in the field of public utilities. Today this is no longer so. In the 1930's, when the Tennessee Valley Authority (TVA) was started, one theory was that this government-owned and operated facility would help regulation by providing "yardstick" competition to the private utilities in the area. The reasoning was that, if TVA could produce and sell power for a certain cost, this cost would be a proper model for private utility rates.

The concept of yardstick competition was essentially a failure in practice because no agreement was ever reached as to whether costs of the public and private plants were really comparable. Without such comparability, the yardstick concept is impractical. Although TVA is still operating under public ownership, its rates are no longer considered a standard for the private companies, whose rates are still regulated by the old method—i.e., set at a level sufficient to yield a fair return on investment.

One result of the general method of regulation used is that regulatory commissions have felt it necessary to extend their oversight of utilities to matters other than making of rates. Controls have been extended over accounting, over financing through issuance of new securities, over depreciation practices, and other matters. Whether all these auxiliary controls are really necessary is a somewhat controversial matter. The regulatory commissions have generally insisted these controls are necessary or desirable or both. They cite efforts by the utilities to circumvent regulation and some abuses in financing, accounting, etc. On the other hand it is difficult not to see some efforts to extend regulation is merely power seeking and not absolutely essential to the public interest. The point here is merely to indicate that this controversy exists. Its analysis belongs in a specialized course on the techniques and history of public utility regulation.

Financial companies.

Mention was made of the fact that banks and insurance companies are closely regulated. However, this is not a public utility type of regulation over the prices charged the public. There is plenty of competition among banks and insurance companies, so neither group of institutions is able to charge the public monopoly prices.

Indeed, interest rates which banks can pay on savings accounts are limited because there is *too much potential competition* rather than too little. If banks were allowed to compete for savings accounts by offering higher interest rates, this could conceivably lead the banks into unsound or speculative investments because these have the highest yield—also the highest risk.

Likewise insurance companies are limited in the investments they can make because they have large but uncertain liabilities to policyholders, extending over many years. The principal purpose of regulation is to make certain the insurance companies will have reserves on hand to meet these liabilities when they come due, as they certainly will at some future time.

Neither banks nor insurance companies are natural monopolies. Therefore the prices they charge the public do not need regulation as do the prices charged by an electric power company, which is the only source of supply for a particular region.

The general rule.

We come back to the general principle of rule of public utility rate regulation which is that rates shall be such as to permit a fair return on a reasonable investment. If rates are set too low, property of the privately owned utilities is being confiscated without due process of law. The remedy of the utilities is to bring suit against the regulatory commission on these grounds, usually in a federal court. Many such suits have been filed, and a number carried on appeal to the United States Supreme Court.

One leading case, which has influenced all subsequent utility regulation, was Smyth vs. Ames, decided by the Supreme Court in 1898. In its decision on this case the Court said in part:

> We hold that the basis of all calculations as to the reasonableness of rates to be charged by a corporation must be the fair value of the property being used by it for the convenience of the public. And, in order to ascertain that value, the original cost of construction, the amount expended in permanent improvements, the amount and market value of its stocks and bonds, the present as compared to the original cost of construction, the probable earning capacity of the property under particular rates prescribed by statute, and the sum required to meet operating expenses are all matters for consideration, and are to be given such weight as may be just and reasonable in each case. What the company is entitled to ask is a fair return upon the value of that which it employs for the public convenience. On the other hand, what the public is entitled to demand is that no more be exacted from it than the services rendered are reasonably worth.

As is plain from this language, the Court did not favor a single method of valuation, but would give consideration to all the different methods that might be used. The standards for regulation are extremely broad ones—of fairness and reasonableness in which the law so often takes refuge.

Another leading Supreme Court case, which seemed at least partially to overturn the Smyth rule after more than 40 years, was the Hope Natural Gas Case, decided in 1944. In its opinion on this case, the Court said in part:

> Under the statutory standard of just and reasonable it is the result reached, not the method employed, which is controlling. It is not theory but the impact of the rate order which counts. If the total effect of the rate order cannot be said to be unjust and unreasonable judicial inquiry under the Act is at an end. The fact that the method employed to reach that result may contain infirmities is not then important.

The practical effect of this decision, concerning which the Court was quite fragmented in its opinions, was to strengthen the power of regulatory commissions by rendering them less liable to judicial review on questions of valuation.

In summary, then, about all that may be said for the present legal status of valuation in public utility rate regulation is that the matter is still unsettled and still developing. As one economist, a specialist on public utilities, put the matter:

> The reasonable valuation of public utility property is a tough old bone on which many have chewed without getting good and satisfying results. By this time it shows the marks of first, a hopeful and then a disillusioned Supreme Court. of acquisitive managerial interests who emploited the Smyth rule for all it was worth before 1930, of valuation engineers who like to make money out of valuation studies, of commissions that finally are enjoying administrative authority and can make the companies uncomfortable under the Hope decision. The meaning of reasonableness, which is always something less than perfectly clear and conclusive in a democratic society, is more confused than crystallized by so many different gnawings on the valuation bone—Emery Troxel, *Economics of Public Utilities,* New York, Rinehart, 1948, pp. 283-4.

Thus, we see that regulation of public utilities is still an evolving art, in which government strives to balance the interests of consumers with those of property owners. At times the balance may appear to favor one party; at other times, the other. The fact remains that these monopoly industries, on which we all depend, are definitely charged with a public interest, and it is this interest which regulation serves. Undoubtedly, it does so imperfectly and with occasional biases. But we have yet to evolve an alternative system that will do the job better. Regulation seems to be here to stay.

Epictetus, a philosopher who lived in the First Century A.D., wrote that, "since it is reason which shapes and regulated all other things, it ought not itself to be left in disorder." One can only hope that, as our society grows more complex, our structures for reasoning will not become less orderly.

Chapter 7

THE WHOLE IS GREATER THAN THE SUM—Macroeconomics

In 1679 Sir William Petty, a remarkably accomplished man in many fields, but best remembered as the father of economic statistics, which he called political arithmetic, wrote in his notebook that to inquire properly into the state of any country, one should examine some 70 different characteristics, including: the title and weight of the moneys; how much silver in a day's wages of a laborer; how many horses and men till 100 acres, and with how many days' work; what arts, sciences, and trades do most flourish; what is the nature and extent of the present revenue, and what are the frauds and diversions practiced upon the same.

Petty's admonitions remind us that much of economics is measurement and quantification. This is especially important today when statistical sources and estimates are highly developed.

You will recall that macroeconomics was defined as the study of the whole economy rather than merely a part thereof, such as an individual firm, or a particular industry, or a limited geographic region. What we propose now to look at is the United States economy as an entity, producing and distributing both goods and incomes. It is largely (but not entirely) a closed economy in the sense that much of what we produce we sell to ourselves and consume ourselves. It is open in the sense that we do export to other countries some 3 percent of our gross national product, and we do import both materials and finished goods for use here.

Since macroeconomics deals with national aggregates, we need some idea about what information is available on this basis and why it is significant. First in importance is undoubtedly the *national accounts,* a series of interlocked tables dealing with the *national product,* its origins and disposition, the incomes that flow from economic activity, and the uses to which these incomes are put. Prepared by the U.S. Department of Commerce, these accounts have come to be considered basic to macroeconomics. Let us first try to grasp plainly what the national product is.

The national product.

An aggregate measure much used in appraising current economic conditions is that of the total output of all goods and services or the national product. In the United States we call this the *gross national product,* or GNP for short. This figure is calculated quarterly and published widely in the financial and general press. It is perhaps the most well-known and well used measure of economic activity that we have currently available.

The GNP measures conceptually the total output of *finished goods and services* produced in the United States; to avoid duplication the measure does not count both automobiles produced and the steel that is contained in these automobiles. Rather, the steel sold to automobile manufacturers is counted as an *intermediate* product and not directly as a part of the national product. Similarly, cement production that enters into buildings or highways is not directly a part of the national product, although indirectly it is.

National product estimates may be broken down in various ways as the tables on the following pages indicate. One breakdown is by type of product, including a vast array of such consumer goods as food items, refrigerators, clothing, books and magazines, etc. Similarly, services to consumers range from hairdressing to medical care, to movies, to repair services on durable goods of all types.

Another distribution of the national product is by type of income arising from productive activity. This distribution segregates wages, taxes, interest and dividends, profits, etc.

A third distribution is by industry in which the product originates, e.g., agriculture, manufacturing, distribution, finance, banking, etc. This distribution is significant because all of the product produced belongs to somebody or to some institution, that is to say, ownership claims arise simultaneously with production and are necessarily equal to the value of this production.

The national product is a dollar measure because only in this way can apples, shoes, machinery, and haircuts be brought together in a single comprehensive measure. Likewise, goods and services in the national product are valued at their current prices, at what they actually fetch in the market if there is a market through which they pass. Goods produced by private industry and sold to consumers are valued at actual prices paid in stores, supermarkets, and to dealers.

Services of government employees, since they are not sold in markets, are valued at cost—at the actual wages paid plus other necessary costs. Similarly, services performed by nonprofit institutions, such as colleges, research institutes, and societies for the prevention of cruelty to children or animals, are also valued at cost, since these services are not provided on a strict price-for-service basis.

The national product, as measured in the United States, is described as *gross* because it does not allow for the consumption of capital used up in the production process. Machinery and equipment enter the national product at *gross,* or full value, rather than at *net* value after depreciation.

Mr. Foote, a shoe manufacturer, sells shoes worth $1 million per year.

This $1 million becomes a component of the national product and a part of aggregate consumer expenditure. Mr. Foote also buys shoe machinery this year for $100,000. This likewise becomes a component of national product since this is a final sale of the machinery manufacturer. In the process of computing his net income for the year, however, Mr. Foote must subtract from his gross income of $1 million not only the costs of his labor, materials, supplies, and overhead, but also depreciation on the machinery, both the old and that newly purchased this year for $100,000.

Perhaps a reasonable estimate of this depreciation is $50,000; this is the amount Mr. Foote can legitimately deduct in figuring his income tax return. In compiling the aggregate national product estimates, however, no deduction is made for depreciation. Thus what is measured is the *gross* rather than the *net* national product.

Perhaps the net would be more meaningful; the British, for example, think so and use this variant regularly; but because depreciation calculations are tenuous and not firmly based, we have grown accustomed to using gross national product instead. It is a slightly more inclusive measure which does involve some duplication—namely capital consumption, whatever this amount may be.

If the GNP should rise from one year to the next by $50 billion, a not unreasonable increase, this rise may reflect a larger physical output and/or somewhat higher prices. In order to calculate what proportion of the GNP rise is due to increased output and what to increased prices, comparisons are often made on a *deflated* or *constant dollar* basis, on the theory that such comparisons are more meaningful than those in current dollars. If components of the national product are deflated or divided by appropriate price indices, it may be found that, of the $50 billion increase, only $20 billion is represented by increased output, whereas $30 billion represents the same output as last year valued at this year's higher prices. Constant dollar estimates of this type are known as real comparisons or deflated series, or comparisons with the effect of changing prices removed. They are not precise comparisons, since deflation always introduces some possibility of error; but they may be useful for certain analytical purposes, and are often so used.

In a distribution of national product by industrial origin, the contribution of each industry is the value added by that industry. The soft drink industry, for example, may have $1 billion of final sales to consumers—a veritable ocean of Coke and uncola—but out of this $1 billion of gross income it pays $500,000 to suppliers, $100,000 for taxes. The remaining $400,000 is *value added* by the industry; it breaks down into wages, interest, dividends, profits, and depreciation. Value added for each industry, plus indirect taxes paid by each, is what will sum to the national product

Mining iron ore in Australia. Mining is a decreasing share of the GNP in the United States although not of some other countries. The ore in this operation will move through a long tunnel, here being excavated. Metal mining is a business of handling heavy tonnages, which must often be concentrated before they are shipped. Once the bulk of iron ore used in United States steel mills came from the Mesabi range in northern Minnesota. Increasingly, we are turning to imported ores from such far away places as Liberia, Labrador, and even Australia.

Nurse training for the management of incubators in a modern hospital nursery. Services are one of the fastest growing components of the national product and medical and health services one of the fastest growing of all services. In preventing infant mortality and improving life expectancy, health services yield a high return in lives saved and better efficiency of the working population, present and future. Life expectancy has increased considerably over the past several generations, and will continue to increase as new medical discoveries are made and new methods of treatment developed.

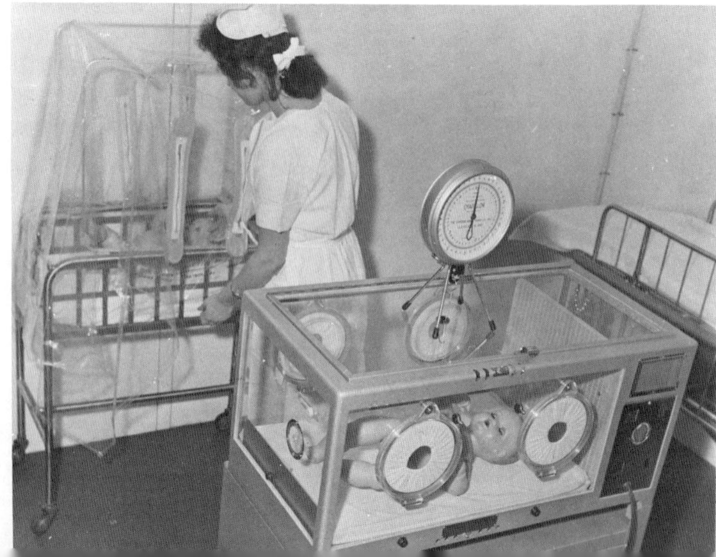

by industrial origin.

This distribution is interesting for what it shows about the changing character of production. In the United States, for example, value added by agriculture has been falling in relative terms (i.e., as a percentage of the total) while value added by the service industries has been steadily rising. This is characteristic of advanced industrial countries with a relatively high standard of living. For an undeveloped country, Cambodia, for example, agriculture will still account for a high proportion, 50 percent or more, of the total national product. This same high ratio would also have held for the United States in, say, 1850 when we were still primarily an agricultural, rather than a manufacturing and mercantile country.

With this background in hand, we are ready to look at some actual gross national product statistics. Let us take a comparison between a recent year, 1969, and 1929, 40 years earlier.

GROSS NATIONAL PRODUCT OR EXPENDITURE
(Billions of dollars)

	1929	1969
Personal consumption expenditure	77.2	576.0
Gross private domestic investment	16.1	139.6
Net exports of goods and services	1.1	2.1
Government purchases of goods and services	8.5	214.7
Total: gross national product	103.1	923.3

Source: U.S. Dept. of Commerce, Office of Business Economics

From this table it is clear that Gross National Product has grown ninefold in 40 years, although a substantial part of this increase has been in prices rather than in quantity of goods and services produced. If GNP is revalued in constant prices of 1958, the increase is from $203.6 billion in 1929 to $727.7 billion in 1969, or about 3 1/2 times instead of nine times. In other words, a 350 percent rise in physical volume of output, coupled with a rising price trend, adds to a ninefold expansion of GNP in current dollar terms, or prices actually prevailing in the years covered by the statistics.

In terms of composition, you will note that government purchases show the largest relative increase over this 40-year span, while consumption is next. Although net exports increased absolutely, they declined relatively between 1929 and 1969.

A different structural aspect of the GNP is given in the following table, where emphasis is on the type of product rather than the type of expenditure.

GROSS NATIONAL PRODUCT BY TYPE OF PRODUCT
(Billions of Dollars)

	1929	1969
Durable goods	16.1	192.3
Nondurable goods	38.5	267.5
Services	35.6	377.5
Structures	11.4	95.0
Total GNP	103.1	932.3

You will notice that the totals are the same as in the previous table, but that the structure is different. Durable goods in the above table are those that normally last 3 years or more; nondurable goods normally have a shorter life. You will also notice that the largest relative increase in the 40-year period is in durable goods; the next largest in services. This category includes not only personal services but also government.

Still another distribution is by sector, or type of institution producing the national output of goods and services. This distribution is as follows:

GROSS NATIONAL PRODUCT BY SECTOR
(Billions of dollars)

	1929	1969
Nonfarm business	85.4	768.4
Farm business	9.7	27.0
Households and institutions	2.9	28.6
Rest of the world	.8	4.2
Government	4.3	104.1
Total GNP	103.1	923.3

Again we have merely a different aspect of the same totals.

One final distribution at this time shows the composition of GNP by originating industry; that is, value added by each industry. This distribution is in constant prices rather than in current dollars.

GROSS NATIONAL PRODUCT BY INDUSTRY
(Billions of 1958 dollars)

	1947	1968
Agriculture, forestry, and fisheries	17.9	24.6
Contract construction	12.9	23.8
Durable goods manufacturing	52.3	133.3
Nondurable goods manufacturing	39.4	87.2
Transportation, communication, and utilities	29.6	70.4
Wholesale and retail trade	52.7	119.9
Finance, insurance, real estate	35.6	95.8
Services	30.6	65.9
Government and government enterprises	32.4	68.6
All other	6.7	17.6
Total GNP	309.9	707.6

You will note that the time span in the table above is not 40 years but only 21; also the figures are in constant rather than current prices. Growth is especially noteworthy in durable goods manufacturing, in transportation and communication, and in finance and insurance.

Let us turn now from the consideration of the production of goods and services to the flow of income. For this purpose, we need first to pass from GNP to what is known *as net national income.* The transition is illustrated in the following table:

RELATION OF GNP AND NATIONAL INCOME
(Billions of dollars)

GNP	102.1	932.3
Less: Capital consumption allowances	7.9	77.9
Plus: Subsidies less current surplus of government enterprises	0.1	1.1
Less: Indirect business taxes	7.0	86.6
Less: Business transfer payments	0.6	3.6
Less: Statistical discrepancy	0.7	-6.2
Equals: National income	86.8	772.5

You will notice that the two largest adjustments involved in passing between GNP and national income are capital consumption allowances or depreciation, the element of double counting previously mentioned as being contained in GNP, and indirect taxes, or taxes primarily on things rather than on people. The tax on liquor is a good example of an indirect tax.

National income, which is compiled on an industry-by-industry basis, is basically a measure of the value added by each industry. If liquor taxes were counted as part of the value added by the liquor industry, that industry would have a high value added, much higher than some other industry of equal importance whose product was not taxed. To facilitate comparisons among different industries, and to put them all on a comparable basis, all indirect taxes are arbitrarily excluded from the national income.

National income is basically a measure of the incomes earned by individuals from participation in the production process that yields GNP. This distribution by type of income is seen in the following table:

NATIONAL INCOME, BY TYPE OF INCOME
(Billions of dollars)

	1929	1969
Compensation of employees	51.1	564.2
Business and professional income	9.0	50.2
Income of farm proprietors	6.2	16.1
Rental income of persons	5.4	21.6
Corporate profits before taxes	10.5	88.7
Net interest	4.7	30.6
Total: National income	86.8	771.5

In the above table, business income includes the net before taxes of proprietors and partners engaged in business, and also the incomes from independent professional practice of people such as physicians, lawyers, accountants, etc.

From national income to aggregate personal income and its disposition is another two short steps illustrated in the following table:

NATIONAL AND PERSONAL INCOME
(Billions of dollars)

	1929	1969
National income	86.8	771.5
Less: Corporate profits and inventory revaluation	10.5	88.7
Contributions for social insurance	0.2	54.4
Wage accruals less disbursements	0.0	0.0
Plus: Government transfer payments to persons	.9	61.9
Interest paid by government and consumers	2.5	28.7
Dividends	5.8	24.6
Business transfer payments	.6	3.6
Equals: Personal income	85.9	747.1
Less: Personal tax and nontax payments	2.6	117.1
Equals: Disposable personal income	83.3	629.6
Less: Personal outlays		
Consumption expenditures	77.2	576.0
Interest paid by consumers	1.5	15.3
Personal transfers to foreigners	.3	.7
Equals: Personal saving	4.2	37.6

To interpret the above table properly, a few notes are needed. Inventory revaluation refers to the process of passing from book inventories, which are a blend of price and quantity change, to an estimate of quantity change alone, expressed in current prices. Government transfer payments are not payments for current contributions to production; for example, they are welfare payments, and social security payments, and unemployment relief checks. Disposable income is what individuals have left over after taxes to spend or to save. Personal transfers to foreigners are remittances to family members living abroad, such as an aged mother still in Poland, or a daughter going to college in Paris.

The table above is noteworthy not only for the large increases in all the magnitudes over the 40-year period, but also for the burgeoning of particular items. In 1929 we had no Social Security System, which now accounts for the bulk of government transfer payments. Taxes, as you can see, have

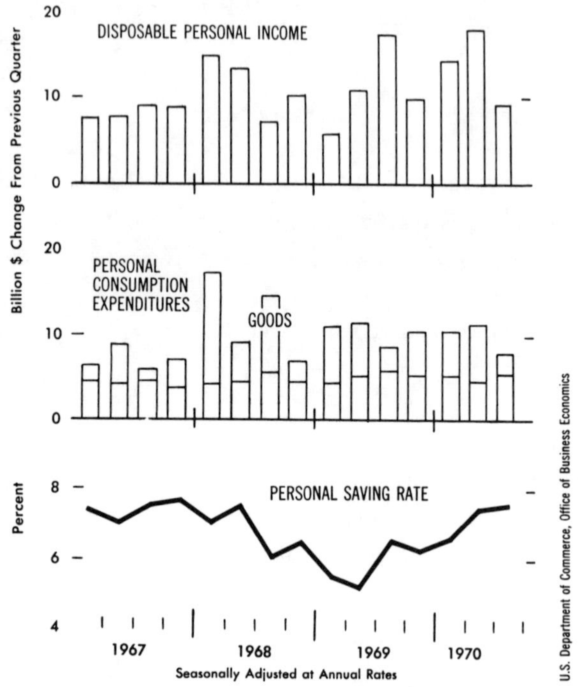

Disposable income, personal consumption expenditures, and saving, presented in terms of absolute changes from the previous quarter. Note that disposable income increased in each quarter but the increases varied from about $6 billion to about $18 billion. Personal consumption expenditures varied relatively less than did disposable income. Consequently the savings rate also varied considerably about an average of roughly 7 percent. In 1971 the savings rate remained high, contributing to more than normal unemployment.

grown some 40 fold; government is that much larger and more expensive, at both the local and national levels. Consumption expenditure has grown both in amount and in variety as we have approached more nearly the affluent society.

In brief, the national product and income tables tell us what the United States economy has produced, what incomes it has generated in this production process, and how these incomes have been used, the results of economic activity on a national basis. The tables tell us little or nothing about how and why these results were achieved, or how different they might have been under other circumstances, or the factors that were responsible, in a fundamental sense, for the achievement of these results.

For the answers to these and related questions, we need to look at other figures. One such constellation of figures pertains to the human resources used in production, the people who, by their work and efforts, have made this production possible. Consider, then, the following table:

POPULATION, LABOR FORCE, AND EMPLOYMENT
(Millions of persons)

	1929	1969
Population	121.8	203.2
Armed forces	.3	3.5
Civilian labor force	49.2	79.1
Employed	47.6	76.7
Unemployed	1.6	2.4

Source: U.S. Bureau of Labor Statistics

As you can see from this and the earlier table on GNP, over the 40-year period from 1929 to 1969, about 60 percent more people at work have managed to produce about 350 percent more goods and services, valued at constant prices. Evidently there have been factors at work to make people more productive.

There are, indeed, many such factors—including better education and skill in the work force, a movement from less to more productive occupations, more capital equipment per worker, higher technology, and a better organization of productive activity. Naturally this increase in output per head has also meant higher incomes and a better life for the average worker. For example, average gross weekly earnings in manufacturing rose from less than $25 in 1929 to more than $134 in 1969. Improved productivity made much of this increase possible.

Manufacturing capacity, as measured by Federal Reserve figures, has grown from an index of less than 77 (1957-59=100) in 1948, to nearly 208 in 1969, or nearly threefold. Business expenditures for new plant and equipment have increased from $19 billion in 1947 to $75 billion in 1949, a nearly fourfold increase. Not only has the labor force grown more productive, but it has more capital and technology to work with, a fact that also helps to explain the rise in output per head.

Another factor, less easy to measure, is the growth in markets. In 1929 many products were sold only locally or regionally which today are marketed nationally or internationally. Adam Smith wrote many years ago, in 1776, that division of labor is limited by the extent of the market. Revers-

Assembly line in an automobile body plant. The auto industry is a typical mass production industry where specialization and division of labor enable millions of cars to be produced and marketed each year. Broadly defined to include parts and components, the auto industry is the largest of our manufacturing industries. In recent years imports, chiefly of smaller cars, have been claiming a larger share of the U.S. market. The spots on the roofs of bodies in the foreground are reflections of overhead lights rather than the latest in polka dot styling.

ing his dictum, we arrive at the proposition that broadening markets make possible more extensive division of labor, or else require more mechanized and more productive mass production methods. Buggies were made by hand in small shops: automobiles are made in large mechanized factories by the millions.

One of the central concerns in economics today is growth in production, in incomes, in markets, in profits, and in other categories as well. Much of macroeconomics is concerned with reasons for growth or the lack thereof and with policies that will promote growth, along with full employment, higher living standards, and other generally accepted objectives. Thus macroeconomics is largely concerned with such questions as how best to insure that the economy will operate reasonably close to capacity, what to do if it does not, and similar matters.

These are macroeconomic policy questions; with others they occupy the forefront of most current economic discussion. Let us turn, therefore, to the subject of economic policy and see a little something of what it is all about.

Economic policy.

One of the strongest reasons for studying economics is to appraise public policies, and perhaps contribute to the development of some yourself. Policy can, of course, be appraised from a number of vantage points—from sheer prejudice, from false analogies about the whole from a part thereof, or simply from instinctive or visceral reaction. It can also be appraised analytically, against a background of knowledge, and with a feeling for the relevant interrelationships. Such an appraisal should reflect a sounder and more enlightened viewpoint.

Policies are nearly always directed to issues, and issues may be stated in various ways, some of which prejudice the resultant policies. The old lawyers' question in cross examination—have you stopped beating your wife?—shows how an issue may be set up as to lead to alternative solutions, all of them unsatisfactory. Just as there is no good answer to the lawyer's question, there may be no good answer to an economic policy question phrased in a certain way.

Suppose the issue is, what is the best method of cooling off the economy and slowing down inflation in early 1970? The alternatives are numerous—a tight monetary policy, some tax increases, wage and price controls, reduction in government expenditures, and so on. Often the recipe will not be for one course instead of others but for a little of this and a little of that, in what one hopes will be a harmonious blend—a chef's creation instead of a mulligan stew.

Very often policy makers in the Federal government do not actually make policies; they make choices. Issues arise and claim their attention. The alternatives and their options are laid out for them, largely by their staff members. They then make a decision which calls for action of a certain kind or perhaps no action at all, or perhaps only apparent but not real action.

Policy is the consequence of a series of such decisions. Given definite premises and a remembrance of past decisions and their consequences, policy can be either a steady, step-by-step march toward a definite goal, or a haphazard meandering in concentric circles.

Suppose you do not make policies, or choices, but merely, as a concerned citizen, have an interest in policies and in their consequences. Consider, for example, the problem of disinflation in 1970. You know that tight monetary policy bears with special severity on housing, so choosing that alternative will probably mean less housing than would otherwise be available. You also know that administering wage and price controls means a large bureaucracy, which takes a long time to set up and an even longer time to dismantle. You also know that tax increases take a long time to legislate and often come out of Congress looking very different than when they went in. It is largely considerations such as these which determine the choices that are made, which may or may not, over time, add to a consistent policy.

It is important not to confuse policies with objectives—a confusion too often encountered. If someone says his policy is to encourage economic growth, we may accept this as a statement of an objective; it is the actions he proposes to take or not take in pursuit of that objective that constitute his policy. Whether or not these actions and inactions will actually result in movement toward the announced objective is a matter for judgment and the verdict of history.

One reason the effect of economic policies is so difficult to judge is that these policies rest on a foundation of assumptions about things that will and will not happen. By the time the effects of a policy can be apparent, so many effects of other policies and other events are also working that we have a tangled skein that cannot be unravelled. Thus, policy appraisal involves partial analysis or systematic unknitting. Often by the time effects of a policy are fully apparent, the policy itself is no longer considered important, so radically have problems and approaches to them changed.

These are a few of the reasons why both policy formulation and policy appraisal or evaluation are extremely difficult. That they are difficult does not make them any less important. We are guided as to the future largely by our experience with the past. While this often involves such miscalculations as preparing for the last war and locking the barn when the horse is already missing, there is a countervailing danger of preparing for contingencies that never happen and for disasters that never occur.

Much depends on our view of whether the economy is a resilient entity, capable of healing its own wounds and correcting its own excesses, or a frail and delicate fabric, constantly being ripped and torn by the winds of change, and thus in need of continual patchwork. One's underlying economic philosophy depends, to a considerable extent on how one answers this question.

A careful reading of the history of economic doctrines reveals that economic theories and analyses have always been problem oriented. First came the problem—of poverty, or unemployment, or financial crises, or whatever. Next came the analyses of the problem by the construction of simplified models or theories, in which the main factors, or what were believed to be the main factors, were isolated and their effects traced. From this a solution emerged, if indeed there were any solution. Sometimes the verdict was gloomy, simply that progress was either impossible or unlikely.

Throughout history economists have always tried to solve problems or more accurately, to recommend solutions. Most economists have not had sufficient authority to solve problems personally, although some have been ministers of finance or held other posts of secondary authority. Generally they have *not* been kings, or presidents, or prime ministers. In recommending policies they have sometimes been partisan, but more frequently they have endeavored to be objective and to concentrate chiefly on the economic rather than the political face of problems.

Bomb damage, Berlin, World War II. Those who saw West Germany in 1945 thought it would take years to restore production and the amenities of normal life. Yet within a few years, thanks to Marshall Plan aid and the efforts of the Germans themselves, the economy was booming. War damage, horrible as it is, offers an opportunity to modernize cities and industrial plants that would not be present in a period of peace. The damage in this picture is minor compared to that suffered by other streets at other times. Atomic bombs would have levelled whole areas instead of merely wrecking structures as in this photo.

In the remainder of this book you will encounter many references to economic policies and to economic policy issues or problems. Remember that policies arise from problems and are efforts to solve problems. Remember also that problems change as our society develops and becomes more complex and interdependent. But many problems recur again and again. Inflation, for example, is a problem after every war, and during that war as well, although it may be partially suppressed. Some problems, such as poverty, are always with us.

History teaches us that, however new and unique a problem may seem, one rather like it has occurred in another time and another place. Economic training helps us to see problems in perspective and to understand their interrelations with other problems. It also helps us—we hope— to move toward more realistic and more fundamental solutions. At any rate, this is the stuff of economic policy formulation and appraisal.

In *War and Peace* Tolstoi wrote that, "if the will of every man were free, that is, if every man could act as he chose, the whole of history would be a tissue of disconnected accidents."

Fortunately we are not creatures of free will, and history is not accidental but systematic.

Chapter 8

THE ROOT OF ALL EVIL–Money and Banking

The book of Timothy advises us that the love of money, rather than money itself, is the root of all evil. Our concern at this time, however, is not with evil or its roots, but merely with money—what it is, what it does, and how it enables the economy to function. You may think you know what money is—coins or dollar bills in your pocket or purse. Actually it is a good deal more than that; the bulk of it is created by banks, written on paper.

Money is first of all the medium of exchange in which bills and wages are paid; it is something that is lent and borrowed; it is generalized purchasing power potentially exercising command over all goods and services that are offered for sale. The alternative to using money as a medium of exchange is barter, a most cumbersome system in which goods are traded directly for other goods.

The trouble with barter is that, if you wish to trade something, say a horse for a cow, you must find someone who both has a cow and wants a horse, in a word, someone whose wants are the opposite of your own. Moreover, there is always the denomination problem. One horse may not be equal in value to one cow but to 1 1/2 cows or 7/8ths of a cow. This makes a trade difficult.

If you have ever traded at a swap shop, you know how awkward barter can be. Thus only very primitive economies, such as those of the Australian aborigines or certain African tribes, still operate on a barter basis. All other economies use some medium of exchange, some kind of money.

The functions of money.

In an exchange economy like ours, money serves several purposes. It is first of all a unit of account, or common denominator in which prices, wages, loans, and taxes are expressed. Each country has its own unit of account; the relations among different national currencies are called foreign exchange rates. The United States dollar does not have the same value as the Hong Kong dollar, although the two currencies bear the same name.

Besides its unit-of-account function, money serves as a store of value; whether it is a good or bad store of value depends on the stability of its value over time. You might, for example, have had $100 in savings in 1950. This sum might have been deposited in a bank or savings and loan association to draw interest at a fixed rate, or it might have been hidden in a mattress or some other supposedly safe place. (Following the numerous bank failures in 1932 and 1933, many people were chary of banks and actually kept their savings in coffee cans, fruit jars, and holes in the wall.)

If you had put away $100 in cash in 1950 and were to bring it out to-day, you would find that its purchasing power had shrunk considerably, that it would buy a good deal less now than in 1950. Thus the dollar would have been a poor store of value over this period; you would have fared much better had you bought two or three shares of stock in some well-established corporation.

The decline in the value of money over time is called inflation. It is attributed to many causes, including increasing wages, excessive government expenditure, failure to tax vigorously enough, excessive expansion of bank credit, inadequate saving, and so on. The root cause of inflation is what a Greek director in the International Monetary Fund is fond of calling, in words derived from Greek roots, "numismatic plethora"—too much money, in relation to the goods and services to be exchanged.

One of the classic inflations, and one which has been the subject of much study, occurred in Germany in 1922 and 1923 following World War I. Germany, having lost this war, was faced with rebuilding productive capacity, with meeting heavy reparations payments levied against her by

Headquarters of the Federal Reserve System in Washington, D.C. This building houses the Board of Governors of the Federal Reserve System and their staff. Actual operations of the system are located in the twelve Federal Reserve banks in various cities throughout the country. The Open Market Committee meets in this building, normally once every three weeks.

Courtesy Federal Reserve System.

the victorious Allies, and with depression and unemployment at home. The German government, with inadequate taxable capacity and unwillingness to reduce government expenditures, resorted to the expedient of simply printing paper money, with no backing.

As this fresh money was put into circulation, prices rose, requiring the government to print even larger quantities of money the next month. The whole process was an ascending spiral in which everyone tried to get rid of money as rapidly as possible in exchange for goods—knowing that the money would be worth less and the goods worth more next week. A rather ironic joke, because too true, was that formerly a German went to market with money in his pocket and brought home his groceries in a basket; after the inflation had gathered momentum he carried his money to market in the basket and brought home the groceries in his pocket.

The German inflation was a ruinous process. It destroyed savings, undermined confidence in the financial system and in the German government, and contributed in no small measure to the rise of Adolf Hitler a decade later. Other countries have also experienced ruinous inflations, usually with drastic long-run consequences. Our own Southern states suffered a ruinous inflation following loss of the Civil War.

In this country during the great depression of the early 1930's there was considerable agitation for various inflationary schemes to promote employment or merely to make relief payments. In 1934 we actually devalued the dollar by raising the buying price of gold from $20.67 to $35 per troy ounce. This meant that the stock of gold held for monetary purposes immediately stood for nearly 40 percent more dollars, since each dollar was defined as containing less gold. At the same time, gold dollars were actually removed from hand-to-hand circulation and concentrated entirely in monetary reserves.

The history of different monetary systems is fascinating reading because it is intertwined with political and general financial history, with wars won and lost, with sovereigns overthrown, with governments changed, and with the rise and fall of both personal and national fortunes.

In older times, good currencies were based primarily on precious metals, gold or silver, equal in value to the nominal value of the monetary unit they represented. In a London museum, for example, you can see an old pound sterling—an actual coin containing a pound of silver, 92.5 percent pure. It is a handsome coin, nearly 3 inches across and perhaps 3/8ths of an inch thick. Incidentally, sterling silver today still means 92.5 percent silver and 7.5 percent alloy.

Likewise in the United States before 1934, you could go to a bank with $20 and buy a double eagle—a coin weighing nearly an ounce and made of gold .9 fine; that is, with a 10 percent alloy. Such coins still exist but may no longer legally be circulated. They are, as collectors items, also worth two or three times $20.

Over time, virtually all currencies have moved away from a metallic base or backing and have become paper, backed primarily by the faith and credit of the government that issues them. This has happened partly because the supply of gold and silver in the world has not increased as rapidly as has the volume of trade and payments that need to be financed by money. It also stems from the fact that sovereigns and governments have always, from time to time, debased or devalued their currencies when hard pressed for funds. Another reason for the changing nature of money has been the rise of banking, a subject in itself that will be discussed in the next few pages.

Perhaps the most important function of money is that, as a medium of exchange, it is generally acceptable in payments of debt, for purchases, etc. You are willing to take a piece of paper called a dollar because you know others will accept it from you on the same basis. You might, however, be less willing to take a Malayan dollar, both because it is only worth 33 cents in the United States and because the corner store or supermarket does not take Malayan money—to them it is not a proper medium of exchange, although it is in Kuala Lumpur.

Governments have always monopolized the manufacture and issuance of money because this is an essential attribute of sovereignty. Our Constitution says the Federal government shall have the exclusive right to coin money.

Forms of money.

Money has always been more than coins. About the only definition of money that makes sense is that money is whatever people generally accept as a medium of exchange. The American Indians used wampum for this purpose. In Africa, until recently, cattle were money. On the island of Yap, in the South Pacific, large stones, especially shaped and ornamented, and some of them even under water, served as money. The stones themselves were too large to move, but payments were made by simply transferring title to different stones.

Actually these stones were very like bank deposits today, except that they were fixed in quantity whereas bank deposits are highly variable. The Yap islanders had a kind of built-in protection against inflation in that their money supply could not easily be increased.

Today most payments are made not by handing over currency, but by writing a check, an order on a bank to pay so much money to such a person or institution. Likewise most checks received are not cashed for currency but are merely deposited in a bank. Bank deposits are clearly money because they are accepted as such. Let us examine what bank deposits actually are and how they come into being.

To do this properly, imagine, if you can, that you are back in the Middle Ages. You are a goldsmith, an artisan, with a shop located on a back street in Florence, or perhaps in Amsterdam. Your name might be Cellini, or it might be Goldsmith. But whatever your name, you spend your days hammering gold into vases, tableware, and other objects desired by the wealthy.

Handling gold at the Federal Reserve Bank of New York. All the gold shown here belongs to foreigners but is held in New York under earmark. When one country sells gold to another it is simply shifted to a different vault. Each bar in the photo weighs about 65 lbs. and is therefore worth somewhat more than $27,000. Photo courtesy Federal Reserve System.

You also buy and sell gold to and from other smiths and the general public. Because gold is valuable you have a strongbox in which to keep it secure from thieves and bandits.

I am a merchant up the street who does not deal in gold but in silk. However, I have accumulated some gold to pay for my next consignment of silk; since I have no strongbox and know of yours, I come to you and ask you to keep my gold until I need it. You agree to do so, put the gold away, and write me a receipt for two standard bars or 10 ounces, whatever the amount may be.

You are now a banker who has accepted a deposit and given a warehouse receipt saying you will pay me so much gold on demand. Other merchants learn of our arrangement and bring you their gold for safekeeping. Soon you have virtually all the gold on the street. A number of warehouse receipts, liabilities of yours, are outstanding against it.

I make a deal with another merchant on the street. The deal requires that I pay him 100 florins. I tell this merchant my money is with the goldsmith but I will go get it and pay him. He says there is no need because he keeps his money with the same goldsmith. Instead, he asks that I give him a paper saying that 100 florins, on deposit with you, now belong to him. I do this. I have written and he has accepted a check on you the banker.

Before long these papers are being generally exchanged along the street but all the gold remains stationary in your strongbox. Because you are a shrewd merchant and banker you get an idea. You say to yourself, why should all this gold remain locked up and unproductive? All the merchants are unlikely to want their deposits at the same time. I can keep part of the gold but can also lend part of it to other merchants who have no warehouse receipts with me. At this point, perhaps, you change your name to Moneylender.

In the coffee house you talk to a merchant who is hard pressed. He has bills to pay but not enough money to meet them. Because you know he is an honest and successful merchant, you offer to lend him some gold at ten percent interest. He gives you his note and you give him a warehouse receipt, exactly like those you gave the other merchants who left their gold with you.

Now observe what has happened. You have invented the *goldsmith* or *fractional reserve* principle which is the whole basis of commercial banking. You have more warehouse receipts outstanding than you have gold in your box, so you have only fractional reserves (the gold) against your liabilities (the warehouse receipts). You have also created some money. Your warehouse receipts are accepted as money by the merchants on the street. By making a loan you have added to the money supply.

If this story sounds fanciful, it is nevertheless exactly the way the business of banking began, and it illustrates most of the principles of commercial banking that are still applicable today. When the First National Bank makes a loan to a merchant today, it credits his account, increasing his ability to write checks to his creditors and suppliers, and it creates money, since checks on the First National Bank are accepted as money.

You may well ask why it is that, if banks can create money merely by making loans, we are not flooded with money and subject to ruinous inflation. For an answer, we must look at the nature and management of bank reserves.

Moneylender, our original Florentine goldsmith, knew he could not lend all the gold in his box, because any merchant who owned one of his warehouse receipts might come to him for gold at any time; he was obligated to pay on demand. Perhaps, over time, he discovered it was prudent to lend 50 percent of the gold in his box and keep the other 50 percent as a reserve against the demands of merchants having deposits with him. The 50 percent reserve ratio that he kept was dictated purely by his financial prudence and his knowledge of his customers.

If, with the arrival of a fleet of ships or at tax time, the merchants should want more gold than Moneylender had on hand, he would be insolvent and probably forced out of the banking business. So he made deals with other goldsmiths to borrow gold from them in time of emergency. In this way he expanded his reserves to include both the gold he had on hand and what he could borrow on demand. Consequently, he expanded his ability to make loans by reducing his reserve ratio, perhaps to 40 percent.

Today the First National Bank operates on the same principles and subject to the same constraints as old Moneylender. By making loans the First National Bank creates money, i.e., deposits, since these deposits, subject to check, are accepted as money. Its reserve is not gold in a box but its own deposits in the Federal Reserve Bank, a central or banker's bank. The amount of the First National's reserve is prescribed by regulation of the Federal Reserve Board rather than being dictated by the bank's own prudence.

The power of commercial banks to create money, a power no other financial institution has, has made banking subject to close and detailed government regulation, a regulation from which Moneylender was free; but the fundamental nature of the banking business has not changed in 500 years.

If banks can create money, as they can, we clearly have in banking an engine of enormous potential for the generation of inflation. Consequently, all governments attempt to exercise control over the amount of money that banks create. This control is called central banking or monetary policy. We shall examine what this is and how it operates in just a moment.

Liquidity.

Liquidity is money or, in the case of an asset that is not money, its nearness to money—the ease, quickness, and certainty with which it may be converted into money. An investment in common stock of a listed company is more liquid than an investment in land, because the former can always be converted into money in 5 days, whereas the latter may take considerably longer. A deposit in a savings and loan association is virtually as liquid as a bank deposit, since it may be drawn on at will; however, it is not money because orders on it are not accepted as money, whereas orders on a bank deposit are.

Liquidity for an individual is not the same as liquidity for the whole system. For example, 91-day Treasury bills, obligations of the United States Government to pay in 3 months, are considered highly liquid as a bank asset. Any bank holding them can convert them into cash very quickly by calling a Government securities dealer and selling to him.

However, all banks could not do this at once, because the capacity of dealers to absorb bills is limited. For an individual investor stocks are quite liquid because they can normally be sold and converted into cash in 5 days; but if all stockholders attempted to do this at once, the market would soon become disorganized and collapse.

Liquid assets command a premium over other assets which is expressed as an interest rate. If I buy a corporate bond paying 5 per cent interest, that 5 per cent may be regarded as a premium for the liquidity foregone in buying that bond. Because liquidity has a temporal dimension, long-term debt will normally require a higher interest rate than short-term debt. This may be observed in the interest rates on United States Government securities, for example.

A corporation is said to have liquidity problems when its cash on hand and cash flow are too small in relation to its current liabilities. In mid-1970 many corporations found themselves in this position because of rapid expansion in the past, rising costs—especially labor costs—and a slow-down in the rate of growth of sales. In some cases, the Penn Central Railroad, for example, liquidity problems forced *receivership.* A receivership is simply a court-supervised proceeding in which creditor claims are delayed until the company can be put back on a solvent basis.

We also hear from time to time of international liquidity problems, meaning a shortage of money that is internationally acceptable. Gold is the international money *par excellence,* but world gold production for many years has failed to keep up with the growth in world trade and payments.

For some years following World War II, the United States dollar was generally acceptable internationally as the equivalent of gold. It should be noted, however, that the United States could supply liquidity to the rest of the world only by running a continuous deficit in its balance of international payments, and thus supplying dollars to the rest of the world. In recent years there has been increasing concern about the status of the dollar as a reserve currency.

By creating special drawing rights, sometimes called "paper gold," the International Monetary Fund has added in recent years to the supply of international liquidity.

Money and prices.

We have already seen that too much money is associated with inflation. It remains to inquire whether this association can be expressed with a little more precision, whether there is some general principle, quantitative or qualitative, about the relation of money and prices. Economists have wrestled with this question for a long time and have come up with numerous formulations, some crude and some elegant.

Oldest is the quantity theory of money, which holds that prices depend on the quantity of money in circulation and will roughly double if the money supply doubles.

More refined versions are sometimes called equations of exchange; they take into account transactions or the amount of work to be done by money, and also the velocity of circulation, or the number of times money is reused during a given period.

One so-called "transactions" form of the equation of exchange may be written as:

$$MV = PT.$$

The equation is basically an identity since the left-hand member's M (the stock of money) times V (its velocity of circulation) expresses the total means of paying for transactions, while the right member's P (an average price for all transactions) times T (the total of transactions) equals all the transactions requiring to be financed by money.

Nevertheless, this formulation is a considerable improvement over the crude quantity theory, because it introduces other variables that have a bearing on the monetary equation. Velocity of circulation does vary, for example, with improvements in the check-clearing process. Likewise, the number and amount of transactions vary independently of variations in the monetary stock, for example, when the general level of business activity rises or falls.

A modern version of the old quantity theory, with implications for monetary policy, holds that the total money supply, defined as currency outside banks (therefore in the hands of the public) plus bank deposits should rise each year at a rate approximately equal to the rise in gross national product in constant dollar terms. Such a policy, it is contended, will keep prices roughly stable, whereas a larger or smaller increase will be inflationary or deflationary.

This formulation holds that velocity (in this case income velocity rather than transactions velocity) will, in fact, be approximately stable. This latter-day quantity theory is associated with Milton Friedman, an iconoclastic economist who teaches at the University of Chicago. It has never been accepted by the Federal Reserve Board. Were they to accept this view, most of the discretion would be removed from their function.

Central banking.

A central bank is a banker's bank; it serves generally the same functions for commercial banks that these banks do for their customers: it clears checks, holds deposits, and makes loans. Some central banks, such as the Bank of England, also deal with the general public; but this is because of their historical origins rather than their functions as a central bank. The central banks in the United States do not deal directly with the public, but only with banks.

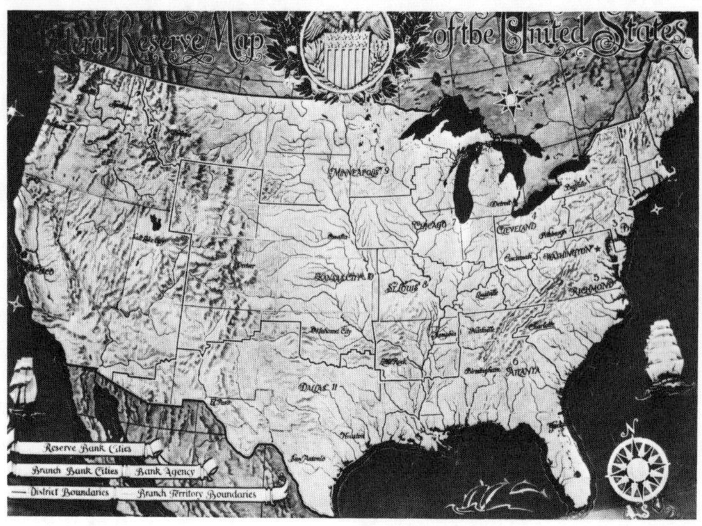

Map showing the division of the United States into Federal Reserve Districts. Notice that the solid lines which mark the district boundaries do not in all cases follow state lines. The cities in capital letters show the locations of Federal Reserve Banks; the cities in smaller type have branches. If you live in South Carolina, your checks will clear through the Bank at Richmond. If you send a check through the mail to Wisconsin, it will clear first through Chicago and then through Richmond. (Courtesy Federal Reserve System.)

A central bank is also the executor, and often the formulator, of monetary policy, which is policy concerning the volume of bank credit and when and by how much it should be increased or decreased. There are a number of instruments used to carry out monetary policy. Changing the discount rate is one.

The discount rate is the rate at which a central bank lends. When this rate is *increased,* it is a signal that credit will become tighter and that the central bank may become less willing to lend. A *reduction* in the discount rate, however, is interpreted as a signal that credit will be easier and the central bank more willing to lend. The discount rate is today more symbolic than actually effective, but it still has some significance as an instrument of monetary policy.

Central banks also hold the legal reserves of commercial banks and can affect these legal reserves by transactions or in other ways. Reserve requirements of commercial banks are fixed either by legislation, regulation, or custom; such reserves must be maintained at or above the required levels.

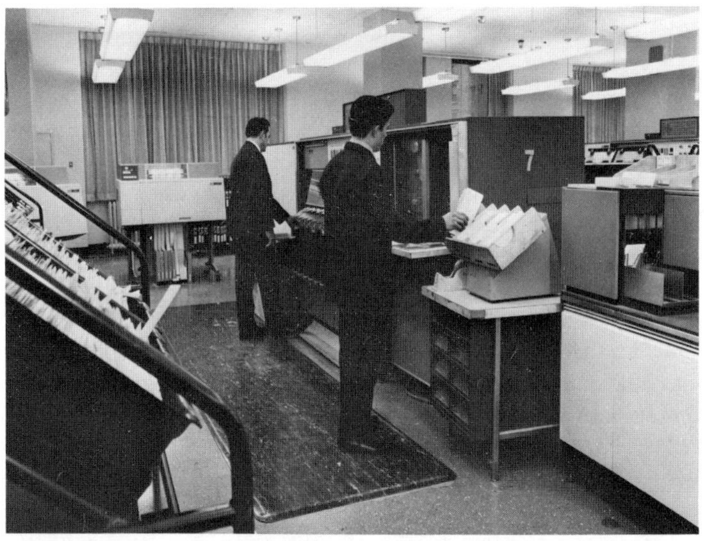

Clearing checks at a Federal Reserve Bank. This automated equipment can handle about 70,000 checks per hour. Because the Federal Reserve banks clear checks for all the commercial banks in the country, of which there are more than 15,000, special equipment such as this is needed because of the very large volume of checks in transit on any given day. (Photo courtesy Federal Reserve Bank of New York.)

Central banks also handle interbank settlement by bookkeeping entries, charges and credits to individual bank reserve accounts.

Suppose I, who bank in New York, send a check to you, who bank in Chicago. You deposit the check in your Chicago bank; this bank, being a member of the Federal Reserve System, deposits the check in the Federal Bank, which charges the check to the reserve account of the New York bank on which it was drawn. The net effect has been a reduction in bank reserves in New York and a corresponding increase in bank reserves in Chicago.

When one considers that not just one but millions of checks are drawn each month for business and personal purposes, it can be seen that the reserve accounts of individual commercial banks are in a constant state of flux; they must be closely watched if a bank is to maintain its proper legal reserve position.

Suppose the requirement is that an individual bank must keep a 20 percent reserve behind its deposits. This reserve is in the form of a deposit with the central bank; it is, in effect, the bank's checking account. Say, the bank has $5 million in deposits and must therefore keep $1 million in reserve. As the bank's deposits increase, it must supply more reserve; as they diminish, it can draw on its reserve which will then be more than 20 percent.

A bank's deposits increase in two ways: (1) by cash or checks drawn on other banks and lodged with the bank in question, or (2) by loans made to its own customers which are added to their deposit accounts. Similarly, a bank loses deposits when customers withdraw cash or when they write checks that are deposited in other banks. In this latter case, the bank also loses reserves to an equal extent as a result of the check-clearing process.

Consider now how an individual commercial bank can replenish its reserve account if this account is too small to meet the legal requirement. It can, of course, deposit currency for credit to its account. It can also sell some asset and deposit the proceeds in its account. The principal asset used for this purpose in this country would be United States Government securities, which the bank would probably sell to a dealer. Finally, the bank could borrow from the central bank, having the proceeds of the loan deposited in its reserve account.

Because it lends to commercial banks, the central bank is sometimes called the lender of last resort. This function may be extremely important during the period of acute credit stringency.

A central bank can also, on its own initiative, affect the reserves of the commercial banks under its control. By raising reserve requirements, from 20 to 25 percent, for example, the central bank could restrict the ability of the commercial banks to lend. Whereas before $1 of reserve would support $5 of commercial bank deposits, at the new requirement $1 of reserve will support only $4 of bank deposits. The commercial banks must either supply additional reserves or curtail their loans, the principal method of deposit creation.

Likewise, a central bank can, by selling assets, diminish the reserves of the commercial banks. Checks drawn on commercial banks to pay for these assets will, in the clearing process, reduce the deposits or reserves of these commercial banks in the central bank.

Thus when the central bank wishes to limit the growth in money supply, it can do so by selling assets—usually government securities. Similarly if it wishes to expand bank credit and augment the money supply, it can buy assets, usually securities, paying for them by checks which get credited to bank reserve accounts.

Like any bank, a central bank creates money (deposits) by making loans. The difference is that the central bank creates so-called "high powered" money, *i.e.*, bank reserves, each dollar of which can support several dollars of bank credit because of the goldsmith or fractional reserve principle.

Monetary policy in advanced countries is largely concerned with expanding and contracting the volume of bank reserves in accordance with the needs of trade and the economic situation. Central bankers sometimes describe their function as "leaning against the wind." When the wind of credit expansion is blowing too rapidly, leading to inflation, the central bank tries to brake the expansion by restricting the growth of bank reserves; when credit is contracting too rapidly, leading to unemployment and recession, the central bank will move to supply reserves more generously, in hopes that this will stimulate additional bank lending.

Normally, central banks do not order banks under their jurisdiction to make more or fewer loans; they merely encourage them indirectly to do so.

The Federal Reserve System.

Our central bank, the Federal Reserve System, is a curious blend of centralization and decentralization. Established in the administration of Woodrow Wilson, it consists basically of a governing board in Washington, and 12 regional reserve banks in various cities throughout the country. All nationally chartered banks are required to belong to the system; state-chartered banks may join if they wish and if they meet the requirements. Federal Reserve members have about 85 per cent of all bank deposits in the country. Member banks are required to maintain their legal reserves behind deposits in the form of a deposit account in their regional reserve bank. The governing board of the Federal Reserve System has the power to vary reserve requirements within specified limits.

Member banks may borrow from their reserve bank; if they do, they must pay the discount rate. Technically, this is fixed by each reserve bank with the approval of the governing board. Actually, all reserve banks charge the same discount rate, although a change may take a few weeks to spread to all. Each reserve bank has its own directors and officers and conducts its own operations in clearing checks, issuing currency, etc.; but a very close supervision on operations is maintained by the governing board.

Members of the governing board serve 14-year terms and are not eligible for reappointment after a full term. If appointed to someone else's unexpired term, they may serve this, plus a full term of their own. Certain board members have served as long as 27 years. One of the seven board members serves as chairman, being designated as such by the President for a 5-year term.

In theory, the board is politically independent, as a President of the United States will normally have only one appointment to make to the board each two years. Retirements and deaths will increase this figure somewhat.

In practice, the chairman, at least, must be quite responsive to the President's wishes, and the other board members will be in practice also. Just as the Supreme Court has been observed to follow the election returns, so the Governors of the Federal Reserve System are somewhat sensitive to the economic policies of the administration in power.

Nevertheless, independence of the central bank from political influence is a long tradition, developed by the Bank of England and honored to some degree by most other countries.

In addition to holding the reserves of member banks, the Federal Reserve Banks issue notes which serve as currency. Virtually all the paper money in circulation today is Federal Reserve notes, as you can see by reading the legend on a $5 bill. Formerly we had Treasury notes called United States Notes or "greenbacks" and also silver certificates; but both of these have virtually disappeared, save for a few buried in coffee cans or hidden in mattresses.

When a bank wants currency, it simply buys it from the Federal Reserve Bank for a charge against its reserve account. When it has too much currency, as is usually the case after the Christmas shopping season is over, it returns the excess to the Federal Reserve Bank and receives a credit or increase in its reserve account.

Reserve banks, like ordinary commercial banks, have reserve requirements of their own. In the case of the Federal Reserve Banks, this legal reserve is gold, kept in the form of gold certificates or warehouse receipts against gold held by the Treasury, largely in Fort Knox, Kentucky.

When $1 million in gold comes into this country and is bought by the Treasury for monetary purposes, it issues $1 million in gold certificates to the Federal Reserve. Likewise when gold leaves the United States, because the Bank of France wants to convert some claims against dollars, the Treasury calls in an equal value of gold certificates.

By law the Federal Reserve must keep 25 per cent of its note and deposit liabilities in gold. Reserves might be larger than this 25 per cent, and generally are. Should they drop below this figure, the governing board of the reserve system would have to suspend reserve requirements temporarily and take corrective action, including raising the discount rate, to restore this percentage. To date no suspension of reserve requirements has proved necessary.

In addition to gold and some loans to member banks, The Reserve Banks' other chief asset is United States Government securities, chiefly 91-day Treasury bills, but on occasion also some longer maturities.

The main policy-determining body in the Federal Reserve System is the Open Market Committee. This consists of the seven members of the governing board plus five of the 12 Reserve Bank Presidents. In practice, all 12 presidents attend meetings and participate in the discussion, but only five are voting members; voting membership rotates among reserve banks except that New York, which operates the system account, has a permanent voting membership.

The Federal Open Market Committee and staff members in session. The chief duty of this committee is to direct the purchase and sale of United States Government securities and in this way to influence the reserves of member banks. Purchases supply bank reserves while sales extinguish them. With a portfolio in excess of $40 billion, the Federal Reserve is a dominant influence in the Government securities market. (Photo courtesy Federal Reserve System.)

The Open Market Committee makes decisions for the whole reserve system on purchases and sales of United States Government securities; these decisions are taken primarily to influence member bank reserves in the direction thought desirable. When the Fed is purchasing securities, bank reserves expand; when it is selling, they contract.

All Fed banks participate in the open market account on a pro-rata basis; all transactions are handled by a trading department at the New York Fed bank, buying from and selling to specialist dealers, headquartered mainly in New York.

The Federal Reserve System is a delicate mechanism which has worked well, with few changes, since its founding nearly 50 years ago. The chief change from the original conception of the system has been the centralization of open market operations. The founders thought each regional bank would be more independent than it is; this soon proved impractical, given the integrated financial network we have in this country. Monetary policy does require a central point of direction, and this is found in the Open Market Committee.

Paul Warburg, an American banker who had much to do with the design of the Federal Reserve System and with passage of the Federal Reserve Act, wrote in his reminiscences in 1930 that, "the bank of issue should be able to act both as anvil and hammer." By this he meant it should at times be passive and at other times active in determining the funds available in the market.

The Open Market Committee acts in this way.

Chapter 9

THE PROMISES MEN LIVE BY—The Credit System

Some years ago a businessman, better known as the founder of the Book of the Month Club than as an economist or author, wrote a book with this title. His message was simply that the economy runs on credit and that credit is based on promises. So promises to pay are the promises by which men live, and the basis on which business operates.

The book, written in the 1930's, was a good one which illustrated very well the pervasive influence of credit in our modern economic structure. It is still worth reading, although its thesis is not at all novel and was not when it was written. At any rate, credit, the credit market, and the closely related market for equity or permanent capital is the subject of this chapter.

Ours is a money economy which functions because people and institutions buy from and sell to one another. They also lend to and borrow from one another. Many transactions involve the use of credit, which simply means deferred payment with or without an interest charge. This is the age of the credit card, with its slogan of buy now and pay later, and its concomitant problems of bad debts, computer errors, lost and stolen cards and all the rest.

Credit has always been a feature of a money economy, but the use of credit is growing with the end not yet in sight. Businessmen have always extended credit to one another, although often offering discounts for prompt cash payments. Credit to consumers and particularly installment sales are a more recent development, originating primarily from a desire to sell big ticket items such as automobiles, furniture, and other durable goods.

In 1900, families owned few durable goods except furniture; today nearly every household is equipped with refrigerators, washing machines, air conditioners, and other appliances our grandmothers never had. The American standard of living is founded on accumulation and replacement of durable goods. Only about three decades ago, the slogan was a car in every garage; today with approximately 85 million motor vehicles in service, many garages contain two or three cars.

As our economy has grown larger and more specialized, the volume of money payments has grown enormously. Likewise the kinds and volume of credit have proliferated. Business firms compete in credit terms as well as in price, quality, and service. Consumers shop for credit as they shop for merchandise, often buying these goods rather than those because the payments are less, rather than because the quality is superior.

If one sets out merely to list the different forms of credit, the list could easily become a long one. Merchants extend retail credit to their customers, and in return receive mercantile credit from their suppliers, wholesalers and manufacturers. These suppliers in turn receive credit from their suppliers, or from banks or other financial institutions. The types of credit vary from open book-credit (charge accounts or accounts receivable) to notes (often called commercial paper) to bonds (long-term evidences of indebtedness). New forms of credit, such as revolving charge accounts, are constantly being invented, and we may expect this evolution to continue. But all credit has the common characteristic of buy or borrow now and repay later. Credit may be likened to the oil that lubricates the wheels of business to keep them turning.

Credit is based on confidence that the buyer or borrower will pay. Thus we have investigations to determine whether one is credit-worthy; we have credit ratings to guide those who supply credit; these ratings are based largely on past experience in payment of debts. One's credit rating is a valuable

Branch office of an American commercial bank in Athens, Greece. In operating abroad, American banks not only finance international trade and deal in foreign exchange, but also make loans both to foreign companies and to American companies operating branches or subsidiaries abroad. Only the larger American banks operate foreign branches. Certain British and French banks have operated foreign branches for many years.

asset, to be kept intact for future use and not destroyed by over or ill-considered use.

Most forms of credit are based, directly or indirectly, on bank credit, because only commercial banks have the power to create money which they do largely by making loans. The retail store is willing to extend credit to you because it can borrow from a bank to carry inventory, or to pay rent and wages. The supplier is willing to extend credit to the store because it, in turn, can borrow from a bank or some other financial institution and thus meet its own expenses while waiting for its customers to pay. And so on throughout the economy.

When credit is described as *tight,* this is basically because banks are restricting the volume of their lending and this effect is spreading throughout the economy. We have seen that the Federal Reserve can cause credit to be tight by selling securities, thus reducing member bank reserves, and causing these banks to limit their lending. Similarly, credit is easy when the Federal Reserve is supplying bank reserves by buying securities on net balance.

Just as we have many different forms of credit, we have different interest rates applying to these different forms. The institution able to borrow most cheaply is the United States Treasury. The base or minimum rate in the whole interest rate structure is the rate the Treasury pays on 91-day bills. These are sold at auction each Monday for issue on Thursday.

The rate varies with Federal Reserve policy and is a good indication of that policy. When the rate on Treasury bills is declining from week to week, this means the Fed is supplying relatively more bank reserves. When the Treasury bill rate is rising, the Fed is tightening the monetary screw.

Next to the Treasury bill rate, and normally only fractionally above it, is the *discount* rate or rate at which Federal Reserve banks lend to member banks. This discount rate is adjusted from time to time and is a signal of monetary policy to come. When the Fed raises the discount rate, it is a warning to the banking system that credit is likely to become tighter. Lowering the discount rate means credit is likely to ease.

Next in importance, although somewhat higher, is the *prime* rate or rate at which commercial banks lend to their largest and best customers, normally large corporations. The prime rate is so called because other rates for bank loans are scaled upward from this base rate.

When banks lower the prime rate, it means they have abundant reserves and want to make more loans. Because banks compete, normally the prime rate charged by all of them will be either the same or very close to the same. Changes in the prime rate usually follow changes in the discount rate very closely, but sometimes change before the discount rate moves.

Two other rates that are quite sensitive to changes in credit conditions

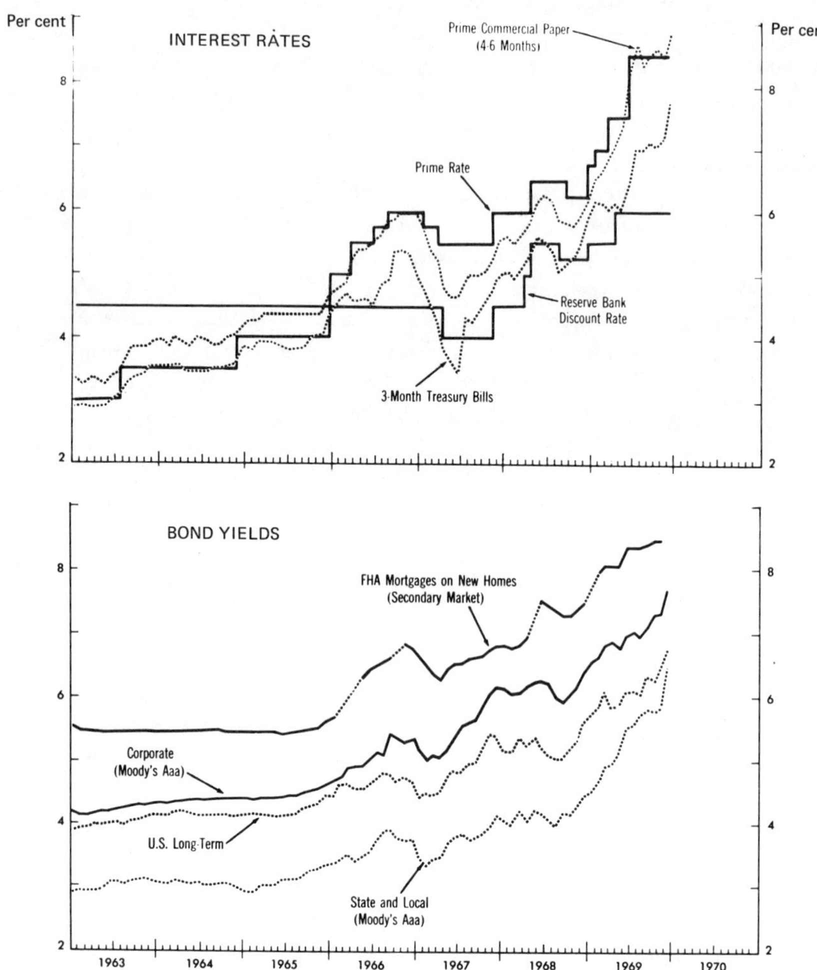

Chart showing the movement of various interest rates. The top panel shows short term rates, including the Treasury bill rate, the Fed discount rate and the prime rate charged by commercial banks. Notice how all these rates move together and how the Treasury bill rate and the Fed discount rate are usually very close to one another. The lower panel shows long term rates as measured by bond and mortgage yields. The state and local rate is lowest because these securities carry exemption from Federal income tax. Corporate rates run higher than United States Government rates, while mortgage rates run higher than those paid by corporations. Interest rate movements reflect changes in the demand for and supply of money and capital.

are the *bank acceptance* rate and the *commercial paper* rate. Bank acceptances are credit instruments normally originating in international trade. The exporter draws a draft which is accepted by a bank in the importing country, thus giving the importer short-term credit. Naturally the bank gears the rate at which it will lend to importers to the rate it charges other borrowers. There is an organized market for bank acceptances, so rates on these instruments reflect the rates on other credit instruments.

Commercial paper means notes issued by large, well-established corporations who borrow in this way simply by selling their own notes. Again, there is a well-organized market for this paper so corporations may resort to it directly rather than going through banks. Buyers of commercial papers may be banks, or other financial institutions such as insurance companies, or even nonfinancial corporations with a temporary surplus of funds to invest. Commercial paper is usually short-term debt of six months or less. The borrowers who use it are finance companies and other companies that borrow regularly and in large amounts. They are well-known national corporations.

Most open book credit, charge accounts and the like, is not charged for as such. However, the cost of granting this credit is calculated in the price of the goods or services being sold. If the credit price is the standard price, any consideration for prompt cash payment is usually given in the form of a cash discount. This is common in mercantile credit but not in retail credit.

When you buy for cash in a department store, you are paying part of the cost of the credit which the store extends to me, because I have a charge account and pay my bill 30 days later. Although retail merchants do not charge overtly for short-term credit, they do charge for extended credit, as in the case of installment purchases or revolving credit plans.

Hopefully, enough has been said to convey the idea that there are organized markets for credit, just as there are for goods and services. For example, there is a well-organized market for corporate bonds, or long-term credit extended to corporations. Many of these bonds are traded on the stock exchanges, just as corporate stocks which are not credit but equity instruments are so traded. The difference between equity and debt instruments is often a thin one, as in the case, for example, of convertible bonds. Let us, therefore, examine in some detail how stock markets operate, since they illustrate many of the features of highly developed credit markets.

The stock exchange.

Actually there is not one but numerous stock exchanges—the New York, the American, the Philadelphia-Baltimore-Washington, the San Francisco, and so on. Of these the New York *(the Big Board)* is by far the largest in volume of trading; it also handles stock of the largest and best-known American companies.

The stock exchange is an auction market in which brokers buy and sell for the account of customers. The exchange itself is a self-governing association, composed of members who each own one or more seats which admit them to membership and permit them to trade on the exchange floor. Only members are permitted to trade; nonmembers must place their orders through a member firm.

As a self-governing association, the exchange operates much like a corporation. It has a board of directors who make the rules and elect a president and other officers; generally today these officers are full-time paid employees of the association rather than members in their own right. The association rules cover listing requirements for stock to be traded; these include such rules as (1) the company must be adequately financed, (2) its stock must be widely owned, and (3) it must regularly report profits and other operating results to the public.

The members of the exchange are normally brokers. Each brokerage house will have one or more floor traders who do the actual buying and selling on the basis of orders from their home offices. A small brokerage house, for example, might have offices in 10 cities but only one floor trader in New York, assisted, of course, by helpers to take telephone messages, confirm orders, and so on.

If you have watched the exchange during trading hours, you know the action clusters around various posts where different stocks are traded. For example, rails (railroad stocks) will be at one post, chemicals at another, steels at a third.

The exchange operates during fixed hours each business day. It opens at 10:00 a.m. and closes at 3:30 p.m. At the opening, floor traders will have in hand certain orders, received from their offices that morning. These may call for buying or selling certain stocks at specified prices or "at market," meaning whatever the prevailing prices are. These orders are arranged in an order book which is continually being revised during the day as new orders are telephoned in. Normally purchases or sales are made in multiples of 100 shares. This is known as a *round lot.* Smaller transactions of 10 or 50 shares are known as *odd lots* and are handled with an odd lot dealer who specializes in handling these small orders.

When the bell sounds and the market opens, floor trader A, representing Bache and Co., has an order to buy 100 shares of Dow Chemical at the market. He goes to the appropriate post, cries out his offer to buy, and gets a nod from floor trader B, representing Burnham and Co., who has on his book an order to sell 100 Dow. The price is the same as the closing price of the day before, $75 per share. If there are serveral offers to buy, the seller will mark up the price—to 75 1/8. If there are several offers to sell and only 1 to buy, the buyer will mark down his offer—to 74 7/8. Prices on the New York exchange conventionally move in 1/8 increments, i.e., 12 1/2 cents per share. In the market for United States Government securities, where volume is larger and price movements normally smaller, quotations are in increments of 1/32 or about 3 cents per $100.

If traders A and B make a deal for 100 shares of Dow, they exchange slips of paper specifying the issue, the quantity, and the price. These slips go to their record clerks, with the information transmitted back to the home office that placed the orders; the offices will then bill customers who have bought and notify customers who have sold to deliver the certificates, if they are not already in the broker's custody.

Throughout the day a continuous stream of orders will flow to the floor traders who normally execute them very quickly, within a few minutes. The stock exchange is a highly organized and efficient market depending for its functioning on high speed communication. Orders to New York from Washington, D.C., for example, are transmitted by leased wire. You can place an order with a broker in Washington, D.C., and often get a confirmation back within 15 or 20 minutes. If the volume of trading is unusually heavy, it may take a little longer.

As trades are made on the floor they are put "on the tape," which is now a closed circuit television hookup, and reported back to brokers' offices all over the country. Thus, by reading the tape or watching the screen, brokers and customers know what issues are trading, what prices are rising and falling, and whether trading is brisk or dull.

At the end of the day a complete record is compiled of all shares traded with their high, low and closing prices. This is the record you will find on the financial pages of your morning newspaper covering trading the previous day.

Stocks rise and fall in value for a number of reasons, some real and some purely psychological. A good earnings report for the quarter just concluded will normally propel a stock upward, whereas a poor one will depress it. Some piece of business news, for example, a trade association report that demand for chemicals is unusually strong, will tend to boost chemical stock prices. A report that the Federal Reserve system is supplying more bank reserves is regarded as a good sign and will normally boost prices. Buyers and sellers of stock are always trying to anticipate developments and to act on the basis of what they think current news means for the future rather than its immediate significance.

The stock exchange is a national, even an international, market despite its physical location in New York City. Orders come from all over the United States and from foreign countries via high speed communication.

NEW YORK STOCK EXCHANGE TRANSACTIONS

New York Stock Exchange Transactions

Friday, September 10, 1971

Stock Prices on a particular day. These are stocks listed on the New York Exchange. Shown are sales, in lots of 100 shares, opening, high, low, and closing prices for the day. Notice also that the prices change in one eighths of a point. This is $12.50 per 100 shares. Notice also that to the left of the name appear the high and low prices for the year to date. Companies whose stock reaches new high or low prices on a particular day will usually be specially mentioned on the financial page. Courtesy the *Wall Street Journal.*

It is this communication that enables the market to handle efficiently 10 or even 20 million or more shares per day.

You have doubtless heard of "bulls" and "bears" in Wall Street. A bull is a person or broker who expects stock prices to rise; a bear expects them to fall. By extension, a market in which prices generally are rising is a bull market; a bear market is when they are falling.

Not all stock prices move together since each responds to its own influences and to the expectations of those who own it. Some stocks will be rising when shares generally are falling; some will be falling when the general trend is up. Such stocks are known as strong and weak performers, respectively.

Because the New York exchange handles some 1,300 different issues, shorthand or summary numbers, averages, are compiled to give the general trend. The Dow Jones Industrial Average, covering 30 widely held and traded stocks, is well known. It is compiled every hour the market is open and is generally available about 1/2 hour later; for example, the 11 a.m. average will be available at about 11:30. Other averages are the Standard and Poor's 500 stock average, and the New York Times average of all stocks traded on the New York exchange. Being broader, both these averages naturally take longer to compile and are not available at intervals throughout the day but merely each morning for the day before.

One important person in the stock market who should be mentioned is the specialist—a trader who specializes in a particular stock such as General Motors. His function is to insure an orderly and continuous market in the stock in which he specializes. Thus, if there are sellers but no buyers at the moment, the specialist will buy to prevent a precipitous decline in the price of the stock in which he specializes. Likewise, he will sell when buyers are numerous and sellers are few. He does this not from altruism but because in the long run he benefits from orderly trading in the stock, which tends to attract investors.

In addition to the organized auction market, there is another market, called the over-the-counter market, for stocks. In this market shares are offered by dealers at prices they themselves set. Most bank stocks are traded over the counter instead of being listed on one of the exchanges. Likewise, the stock of smaller and new corporations is normally sold over the counter.

Although over-the-counter dealers fix their own prices for the stock they handle, there is a good deal of uniformity in the prices quoted by different dealers, who often buy and sell from one another as well as serving their individual customers. Moreover, investors shop from one over-the-counter dealer to another so that competition results in fairly uniform prices.

United States Government securities are traded primarily in a specialized

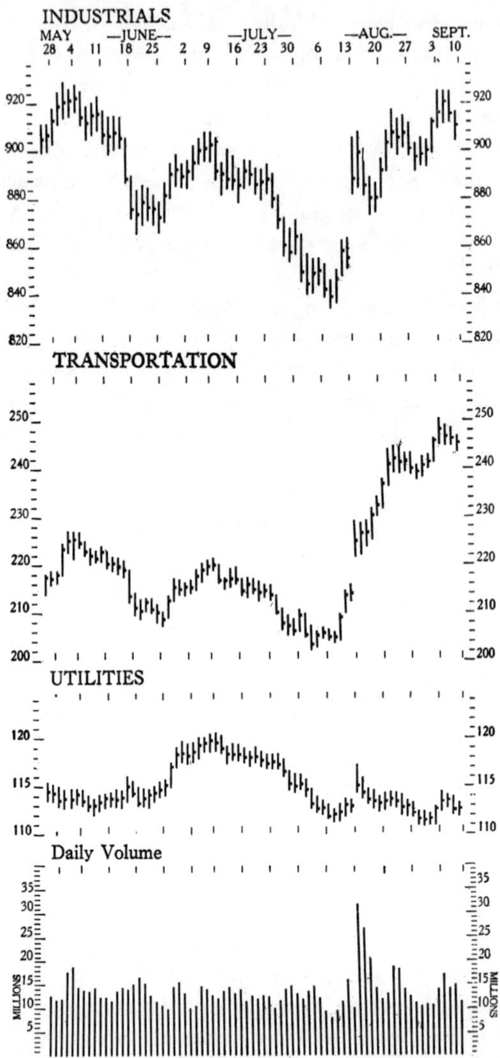

The Dow Jones Averages for about 4 months of 1971. These averages are widely published and followed as representative of price movements on the New York Stock exchange. The industrials cover 30 widely held stocks while the transportation and utilities indices cover 35 more. The vertical lines in the charts indicate high and low points for a given day. These averages are computed on an hourly basis and are often quoted on the radio within one half hour after compilation. Courtesy the Dow Jones Co.

over-the-counter market. Although these securities are listed on the New York exchange, banks and other financial institutions that trade large blocs of government securities do so primarily with a dozen or so dealers who are specialists in these securities. Some of these dealers are large banks that maintain special departments for this function; others are non-banks that specialize in the business. The market is national in scope, and business is transacted primarily by telephone orders to the dealers who are located chiefly in New York, but also in Chicago.

Verbal orders over the phone are binding and are later confirmed in writing. The business is highly specialized because prices of United States Government securities are sensitive to changes in interest rates and to modifications in Federal Reserve policy. Incidentally, a *dealer* is one who buys and sells for his own account; a *broker* deals for the account of others. A stockbroker in the New York market is usually buying or selling for and at the risk of a customer.

The government securities market.

Although this market handles a far larger volume of transactions than the stock market, it is less well known because the public participation is less. It is an over-the-counter market because it does not have a regular meeting place. Instead business is transacted over the telephone with a dozen or so firms that are dealers, i.e., who buy and sell for their own account rather than for customers. The customers in the market for treasury bills are primarily banks, but other financial institutions and non-financial companies also participate.

Suppose a bank has a temporary surplus of reserve funds it feels will not be needed for several weeks. If these funds are left on deposit with the Federal Reserve bank they will earn no interest. By investing them in treasury bills some earnings will be realized. The bank therefore calls a dealer in New York or Chicago; the dealer quotes a price, which the bank accepts. The sale is consummated over the telephone with written confirmation to follow later.

A few weeks later when the bank needs its reserve funds, it can call the dealer and sell its treasury bills, thereby replenishing its account at the reserve bank. Because of the well-organized and efficient market, treasury securities are a highly liquid investment, which banks and other companies can move in and out of for short periods with little risk of loss. Prices do fluctuate, but they move inversely to the trend of interest rates and do not have erratic short period price fluctuations.

The market for governments handles all treasury securities, not merely 91-day bills. The dealers trade a great deal with one another, which keeps prices uniform from dealer to dealer. Nevertheless a customer such as a bank may consult several dealers before making a purchase or a sale.

Dealers' inventories of different government securities naturally fluctuate considerably. When they are large, dealers borrow from banks to carry this inventory, just as any other merchant does. Dealers may go short by selling issues they do not own, borrowing to deliver and covering their short position by a purchase at a later date. As in the case of a short position in stocks, the dealer will gain if the price falls and lose if it rises.

The Federal Reserve conducts its open market operations with dealers just as any other bank would. The Federal Reserve deals with all the government dealers, rather than with a favored few or certain authorized ones. About half the dealers are large banks that have special departments for dealing in government securities; the remaining half are nonbanking companies.

Dealing in government securities is a technical and fast moving business; transactions are typically in millions of dollars, so that small price movements can be extremely significant. One thirty-second of a point, which is the conventional unit of price change, is $345 on $1 million of securities.

Other credit markets.

Other credit and capital markets are less highly organized than the stock exchanges and the government securities market, but some are national in scope and quite responsive to the ebb and flow of demand and supply. Both the commercial paper market and the market for bankers acceptances are national over-the-counter markets. In recent years the supply of bankers acceptances has greatly decreased, largely because foreign traders are better known to their suppliers and customers and hence have less need to use the bank instrument.

One charge that is often heard is that the credit and capital markets are organized largely for the benefit of big corporations and that small business has difficulty in obtaining access to these markets and obtaining credit from them. In part at least this allegation is true. A small company cannot borrow from banks at the prime rate; it cannot sell its paper in the commercial paper market; its stock is not listed on the New York Stock Exchange, but traded over the counter, perhaps only in its local area. This means the small business firm must pay more for credit and capital than its large competitor, and that it often cannot obtain credit when it is most needed.

There are certain institutional offsets to this alleged disadvantage. We have a government small loan program administered by the Small Business Administration; small business has some minor income tax advantages, and a preference in bidding for national defense procurement orders. All these, however, are minor advantages which undoubtedly do not offset the higher cost of capital and credit. To offset these disadvantages the small business must simply be more efficient than its large competitor.

In general, the credit markets have developed into the intricate institutions they are because they fill a real need. Business cash flow fluctuates considerably, creating a real necessity for business to borrow at some times and perhaps to lend at others. The market for credit has developed, just as the markets for lead or for shoes, because the demand was there and profits were to be made by meeting that demand. Banks make loans for the income they generate. Government bond dealers hope to buy at one price and sell at a higher one; investors buy stocks because they hope for income or capital gains or both.

The credit and capital markets are not basically different from other markets. Each has its own technical language and its own peculiar orientation, but each exists because there are potentially profitable business transactions to be made. Each has evolved in its own way, as determined by the characteristics and needs of its industry. Each is a dynamic institution, changing and modifying its customs and practices as conditions warrant. The computer, for example, has had a major impact on banking, stock brokerage, and the stock exchange itself. Other changes in technology, not yet apparent, will have their impact also.

Because the credit and capital markets deal in money, they are subject to close regulation. This is not the public utility type regulation designed to keep prices to consumers reasonable. It is regulation to prevent fraud, to make manipulation by insiders difficult, and to see that investors have full knowledge of the assets they are trading. Let us look briefly at the nature of this regulation.

Credit and capital market regulation.

Regulation in these markets is extensive but it is partly government regulation and partly self-regulation by the organizations themselves. For example the New York Stock Exchange is closely regulated, but mainly by the Exchange itself, which is a largely self-governing body. Regulation covers such topics as requirements for listing, capital requirements of member brokers, the commission structure on trading, and disclosure requirements. Regulations are implemented by fines, suspension of trading privileges, and in extreme cases outright expulsion. Similar self-regulation is practiced by the American exchange and the various regional stock exchanges.

Banking is a closely regulated industry but the regulation does not pertain so much to banks' participation in credit markets as to other aspects of the banking business. If the bank is a member of the Federal Reserve system its reserves are prescribed, as is the interest rate at which it can borrow. Not expected to be continuously in debt to the Federal Reserve, commercial banks traditionally use the discount window only for occasional accommodation, to be paid off as soon as practical. This is in line with the concept of the central bank as lender of last resort.

Other regulated aspects of the banking business are the rate which may be paid on savings accounts, the types of loans that meet examination standards, and the way reserves are computed. If a bank does not belong to the Federal Reserve system, and many state-chartered banks do not, the regulation is by the state department of banking. States differ considerably in the strictness of their bank regulatory activities. All banks that belong to the deposit insurance system are subject to some regulation from that system.

The stock exchange is not solely self-regulating but is also subject to Federal government oversight. The Securities and Exchange Act of 1934 laid down certain operating rules, such as those governing short sales, but is mainly concerned with the idea of full disclosure, so that investors will have the opportunity to know about the securities they are buying. Disclosure requirements apply mainly to new issues, but also cover such matters as public annual reports for established companies, prohibitions on dealings by insiders before information is published, and similar matters. The object of all this is to prevent rigging the market, a practice that was all too frequent before the securities acts became effective in the 1930's.

The government securities market is basically unregulated, but dealers go to great lengths to protect their business reputations and to honor their promises. In perhaps no other industry is one's verbal promise honored more scrupulously than it is among government bond dealers. They buy and sell millions over the telephone and always honor their verbal contracts, no matter how disadvantageous it may be. The whole industry depends on confidence and the scrupulous keeping of commitments. Any dealer who tried to back out of a verbal contract would quickly be out of business.

The aim of regulation in the credit and capital markets seems to be to insure that these markets operate fairly, without giving special advantages to any group, or without unreasonably limiting access to the market. The object is to make the market more effective and better able to serve the economy.

Although exception may be taken to the details of some regulations, there is little to quarrel with so far as the general objective is concerned.

Other credit instruments.

Most retail credit, evidenced by credit cards, and a good deal of mercantile credit, is the type known as open book. Payment terms are based on an understanding, such as 30 days. Accounts which are past due are known as delinquent accounts. Other types of credit are generally more formal than the open book type.

Some credit is evidenced by promissory notes. A note is like an expanded check. It promises to pay the holder at the end of a certain period a certain amount of money plus interest at a specified rate. If you have ever borrowed from a bank, you have had the experience of signing a promissory note. Sometimes a cosigner is required. This is a collateral promise that the cosigner will pay if the signer does not.

A note is known as a negotiable instrument. This means if the lender does not wish to hold it for its full term, he may sell it to another lender. When the note matures, the new holder will present it to the borrower for payment. At one time there was considerable traffic in negotiable instruments. There still is in commercial paper, which is the negotiable instrument of a large corporation that is borrowing. The borrowing company often will not know who holds its paper until it comes due and is presented for payment.

Bonds are likewise negotiable instruments and are like notes except the borrowing is for a longer period. Bonds are usually issued in standard denominations, such as $1,000 face value, and bear interest at a specified rate, the coupon rate. Suppose this is 6 percent. The bond may be listed and traded on the New York Stock Exchange and its price will fluctuate. If the bond is selling for 102, meaning $1,020 for a $1,000 bond, it is said to be at a premium, and its yield of $60 per year on $1,020 is less than 6 percent.

Long-term interest rates are often measured by the yield on bonds of a certain quality. Bond prices move inversely to interest rates, rising when interest rates are falling and falling when rates are rising. Bond prices also vary with quality, i.e., with the soundness of the borrowing agency and the likelihood it will repay. Thus, interest rates on corporate bonds are typically higher than those on government bonds. Municipal bonds, as we have noted, sell at low yields because of their tax-exemption privileges, which makes them especially attractive to high income investors.

Another credit instrument is the bill of exchange or acceptance. This is a negotiable instrument ordinarily drawn by the seller of goods or services. When accepted by the buyer or by a bank on his behalf, it becomes the same as a promissory note drawn by the buyer. Acceptances are used primarily in international trade. You can see they are more formal than open book credit.

Although credit originates in trade, it has an independent circulation from that of the underlying goods and services whose movement it finances. The manufacturer gives credit to the wholesaler, perhaps borrowing from a bank to finance himself until the wholesaler pays. The wholesaler in turn gives credit to the retailer, perhaps financing his own operations by issuing commercial paper. The retailer in turn gives credit to his charge customers, perhaps borrowing from a bank to finance these operations. The credit instruments, whether notes or bonds or accounts receivable, circulate independently of the goods they finance. Perhaps the retailer pays his debt first; perhaps it is the wholesaler or the manufacturer. At any rate, when the debts are paid, the credit is extinguished, to be replaced perhaps by credit originating in new transactions.

Drying coffee in Costa Rica. After picking, the coffee beans are soaked in water to remove the outer husk and then dryed in the sun as shown here. The beans must be turned frequently to make sure they dry properly. Coffee is a staple commodity in international trade which means it is traded in a well organized market and its movement to final consumers is financed by credit. Most coffee is shipped green and then blended and roasted in the consuming country. It loses flavor rapidly once it is ground.

Credit which finances the movement of goods is sometimes referred to as self-liquidating credit. It was formerly an axiom in the banking business that this type of credit was inherently sounder than finance paper, i.e., paper that originated in borrowing not directly related to the movement of goods. Today we are less certain of the value of this distinction and make less of it.

All credit is as good as the borrower. His probity and his concern for his business or personal reputation cause him to repay promptly, even though it is not always convenient to do so. Credit is a network of promises men live by. It depends on confidence that these promises will be kept. If they are not, the sources of credit dry up. When they do, business and commerce can be seriously affected.

Credit supplements cash. It magnifies and extends the money work that money can do. Only banks create money; but business firms of all types create credit by lending to their customers. Ours is an economy that runs largely on credit. Without it, our national product and employment would be smaller than they are.

In 1867 Disraeli said in a speech that "however gradual may be the growth of confidence, that of credit requires still more time to arrive at maturity." Credit is confidence amplified by money. Its growth may be slow but on this growth depends our hope of affluence.

Chapter **10**

A FOOL AND HIS MONEY–Personal Finance and Investments

Aristotle, sometimes credited with being the first analytical economist, outlined his ideas for an ideal commonwealth and found them at variance with those of Plato, his fellow philosopher. Whereas Plato's ideal republic was communistic, Aristotle opted for private property (including slaves) largely for incentive reasons. In his view, not the *abolition* of private property but a more *enlightened use* of it was required.

The enlightened use of private property is an old topic of economic study. Our concern in this chapter is to outline a bit of what this study involves.

In recent years retail trade has migrated to the suburbs of cities as have consumers. This shopping center, near Washington, D.C., is typical of hundreds to be found in the suburbs of large cities throughout the country. Migration of business to the suburbs has hastened the decay of inner cities, eroded urban tax bases, and greatly increased the demands on local government in expanding suburban areas. Suburban sprawl is the term sometimes applied to these growing areas.

The old adage about a fool and his money coming quickly to the point of separation illustrates one basic fact about economics. It is not enough to accumulate wealth by saving; it is necessary also to be prudent in the management of past saving or of wealth amassed in some other way, such as by inheritance. This chapter will deal with savings and with the manifold ways in which these savings may be invested. This is essentially personal or household finance. It is that ancient part of economics recognized by the Greeks and Romans and by all economists since their time.

Savings is of course that part of income not spent on consumption or taxes. It is a residual item that differs from individual to individual, depending on spending habits. Statistical studies of family budgets show that at very low income levels there is no saving, but dissaving or drawing on past accumulation. As income levels rise, saving first becomes positive and then increases more than in proportion to income. A moderate income family may save 5 percent of its disposable income or personal income after taxes; a higher income family may save 15 percent of its larger disposable income.

The distribution of saving by income size classes is more unequal than the distribution of income itself. The distribution of wealth, which is a result of past saving plus appreciation of property values, is more unequal than the distribution of current saving. It is a fact of life that the rich often grow richer while the poor grow poorer.

Let us assume you are newly established in a job and that you have current income from wages or a salary. As a new worker most of your income will go for consumption; with installment purchases you may even commit a good share of your income before you receive it. The car you buy and finance will cost you more than if you paid cash, for you must pay interest on the debt at a relatively high rate. The truth-in-lending law requires that finance charges be stated as an annual rate of simple interest. On the car you buy you will find this to be in the neighborhood of 18 to 24 percent, considerably more than you could earn on any safe investment.

Let us suppose, however, that you are actually willing and able to save some money from your weekly paycheck. What are the possible ways to invest those savings, and what are the relative advantages and disadvantages of each?

Bank deposits.

These are the most liquid form of savings and generally should be the first asset a saver holds. Bank accounts provide a liquid reserve for emergencies and a fund that can be kept in readiness for favorable investment opportunities should they suddenly arise. We have all had the opportunity to buy a bargain if only we had ready money. Experienced investment advisers nearly always suggest keeping a cash reserve on hand for just such unforeseen opportunities.

Bank accounts, of course, are of two kinds, checking and savings. A checking account, as the name implies, gives one the privilege of writing checks against his balance. It is a great convenience for paying bills, etc.; but the balance earns no interest. Indeed, banks levy a service charge on the checks drawn, to compensate themselves for processing, clearing, issuing statements and all the work that a checking account involves. A checking account is therefore liquidity pure and simple.

A savings account is not subject to check but is usually evidenced by a passbook. Balances left for certain periods, such as three months, earn interest at a stated rate, currently about 4 percent per annum. The maximum rate which banks can pay is regulated by the Federal Reserve Board and is kept relatively low to discourage competition among banks for savings deposits.

Savings and loan accounts are essentially like bank savings accounts except that savings and loan associations are not money-creating institutions, as banks are. Savings and loan deposits usually earn a slightly higher interest rate than bank savings accounts, and can normally be withdrawn on demand. The money lodged with savings and loan associations is primarily invested in home mortgages, that is, in loans to families to buy homes. The savings and loan association makes its operating expenses out of the difference between what it receives as mortgage interest and what it pays savers for their funds. Normally a spread of as little as 1 percent may be sufficient for this purpose; that is, it charges borrowers 6 percent and pays savers 5 per cent. Most savings and loan associations are mutual organizations; they have no stockholders but merely the capital that is contributed by individual savers. Any profits made are held as reserves against possible future losses. Occasionally a mortgage loan will not be paid and will go into default. In this case the lender will normally resell the property if no compromise with the debtor can be reached.

Life insurance.

Most workers who have dependents invest some of their savings in this form. Even if one has no dependents a small policy is often carried to pay funeral and burial expenses.

A life insurance policy is simply a contract between an individual and an insurance company in which, in return for periodic payments called *premiums*, the insurer agrees to pay a certain sum on the death of the insured to a named beneficiary. The premium, which may be paid monthly, quarterly, or annually, is based on age and the face value of the policy, which may be any agreed sum.

Suppose you buy a life insurance policy with a face value of $5,000. The premium is $20 per quarter or $75 per year. The insurance is what is known as *ordinary* or *whole life,* which means you agree to pay this premium as long as you live to keep the insurance in force. The $5,000 is payable to your beneficiary when you die. The beneficiary may be your wife, your children, whomever you name so long as they have an insurable interest in your life, meaning some dependency on your earnings, or some relationship to you such that you wish to make some provision for them in the event of your death.

There are other payment options for life insurance. For example, you may take what is known as an *endowment* policy. In this case you pay a higher premium but for a limited time, such as 20 years. In this case after 20 years the policy is paid up; no further premiums are due because there is sufficient reserve in the policy to carry the premiums from that point forward.

Every insurance premium is composed of two elements, the *current insurance cost*, and the *addition to reserve.* The current insurance cost will go up with age. In a level premium policy, where the premium remains the same, this means that when one is young the premium more than covers the current insurance cost, and when one is older the premium may be less than the current insurance cost.

Suppose in your policy for which you pay $75 per year the current insurance cost is only $50. This cost is based on statistical experience which indicates that out of 100,000 persons your age, 40 will die this year. This current cost also includes a charge made by the insurance company for handling your account.

If you pay $75 and the current insurance cost is only $50, the remaining $25 will accrue as reserve in the policy. This reserve means that, since the company's liability to you is still $5,000, they are in effect insuring you for $4,975 and agreeing to return $25 of your own money. Every increase in a policy reserve lessens the insurance liability to a corresponding extent.

If you examine an insurance policy carefully, you will find a table of reserve values or cash surrender values. This table indicates how reserve values in the policy change over the years. Should you decide to cancel your policy, you would receive the reserve or cash surrender value in consideration for releasing the company from its obligation to pay a death benefit.

So far we have been discussing an ordinary or whole life policy. There are other forms of life insurance contracts that may be suited to particular circumstances. For example, there is *term* insurance which is usually the cheapest policy form. Instead of lasting throughout life, such contracts extend for a definite term, such as 5 or 10 years. At the end of this term, the insurance lapses. There may or may not be options to renew at the end of this term, or before the term has expired.

Term insurance is particularly suitable for families with large responsibilities and limited incomes. The low premium means that a larger coverage can be carried than if the insurance were in a more expensive form. Term policies normally accumulate little or no reserve, with the premium barely covering the current insurance cost and the company expense. Since term policies are normally not very profitable to life insurance companies, they do not push them in their sales campaigns, but provide them if the customer wishes.

Annuities are the opposite of life insurance. Whereas one must die to collect insurance, one collects annuities as long as one lives. Both life insurance and annuities are based on life expectancy which is calculated statistically from mortality records for large numbers of people.

When one buys an annuity, the contract with the life insurance company specifies they will pay a certain amount, say $200 per month, commencing at a certain date and thereafter as long as one lives. The contract is based on accumulation before payments begin of the amount necessary to continue these payments throughout life. For example, at age 65 one may have a life expectancy of 17 years. Premium for the annuity plus earnings on the investment must be sufficient to pay the benefits for this period.

The insurance company does not know when any particular individual will die. It does know that among a group of people aged 65, 17 years is the average age until death. On these averages, it bases its rates.

Annuities are particularly attractive to people wishing to build a retirement income and not wishing to maintain capital intact. What one gets with annuity payments is partly a return of principal and partly earnings on the investment. If one lives longer than the average, the annuity will be a bargain. If one's lifespan is shorter than the average, then one is financing a part of someone else's annuity. When one buys an annuity one is in effect betting the insurance company he will live longer than the average. If this proves true, he will win; if not true, the insurance company will win.

If one works for wages, he will in all probability be covered by social security. This is a federal government system of old age and survivors insurance financed from payroll taxes. A certain percentage is deducted from the employee's pay and an equal amount is contributed by his employer. These contributions go into a trust fund from which benefits are paid to retired workers and to certain dependents of workers who die.

Generally children of a deceased worker are eligible for benefits until they reach age 18, or 22 if they are full-time students. The benefits are related to age and length of service of the employed worker, and to his average earnings during the period he was making contributions. The social security system also provides benefits to unemployed workers, but this is a separate system, not run on strict insurance principles.

For a young worker social security is a compulsory contribution system with benefits potentially a long way off. For an older worker, however, it is a promise of a retirement income not so far in the future.

United States Government securities.

These securities, which are considered an eminently safe form for investment of savings, are of two types, so-called *savings bonds* sold in relatively small denominations and redeemable according to a fixed schedule of values, and *marketable issues,* which are bought primarily by banks and other financial institutions, but are also available to individuals.

Savings bonds are issued on a discount basis, for example, one pays $18.75 for a bond worth $25 at maturity some years hence. The implicit rate of interest is approximately equal to that earned on a savings bank account, so there is little financial incentive to buy these bonds. They are actually sold primarily on payroll deductions, offering wage workers a convenient form of regular saving.

Marketable United States Government securities come in all types from 91-day Treasury bills to long-term bonds. For an indication of the variety of such securities available, read the price quotations on the financial pages of your local newspaper. As marketable securities, these fluctuate in price from day to day, falling in price when interest rates are rising, and rising when rates are falling. The quoted prices are in thirty-seconds of one point, one thirty second being about 34 cents on a $1,000 bond. Governments, like other bonds, are usually sold in $1,000 units or multiples thereof.

Government bonds are perhaps the most secure repository for long-term savings, although the yield is low compared to alternative methods of investing money. Most government bonds are held by banks and other financial institutions, who regard these securities as a secondary reserve, readily convertible should a need for cash arise.

State and local government securities, or "municipals" as they are called in the securities business, are another form of eminently safe investment. If one is subject to tax in the 50 per cent bracket, a 5 per cent municipal bond is as good as a 10 per cent corporate bond the interest on which is taxable. Because municipals are in such demand for their tax-exempt feature, they are not normally an advantageous investment for a person with only a modest income.

Government bonds are a conservative investment and as such belong in the portfolio of any investor who wants to minimize risks and still get some return on his investment. In a time of inflation, government securities may be a poor holding because the interest return may no more than compensate, or in some cases fail to compensate, for the rate of price advance. In such times one would be better advised to hold equities such as corporate stock or real estate.

Workers at the Bureau of Printing and Engraving, Washington, D.C. This bureau, a part of the Treasury Department, manufactures postage stamps, paper money, United States Government bonds, and similar matter. This old photo shows conditions as they were rather than as they are at present. The currency printing operation is one of Washington's prime tourist attractions. This picture dates from World War I. Note the flags and the blouses worn by the women workers. The moustaches give the men an almost up to date look.

Corporate securities.

The predominant forms are stock, which are shares in ownership, and bonds, which are evidences of indebtedness. As investments, stocks vary greatly in quality, in yield, and in price. Of particular importance is the *price-earnings ratio,* or *multiple.* If earnings per share on a particular stock are $4 and the market price is $40 the PE ratio is 10. Growth stocks with a good record of expanding earnings will command a fairly high multiple such as 20 or even 30, whereas stocks whose earnings record is poor or uncertain will command a lower multiple such as 7 or 8.

Stocks fluctuate in price with changes in earnings prospects and with changes in general economic conditions. In a "bull market," when stocks generally are rising, speculative activity and a general feeling of optimism will often persist for a considerable period. In a "bear market," when stocks generally are falling, pessimism will often carry declines past the point justified by economic conditions or prospects.

The stock market is always looking to the future and trying to anticipate economic trends and developments. Generally, stock prices today reflect what investors and speculators believe will be the case about six months hence. This is known as discounting future developments. If a particular company is having a good year and is expected to show a substantial gain in earnings, the price of the stock will rise in anticipation of this event. Similarly, if a company is believed to be in some trouble, the price of its stock will decline before the trouble actually develops.

The key to successful investment in corporation stock is careful research. You need to know what a company does, how well they do it, what their competitive position is in their industry, whether they are technologically up to date or backward, how capable the management is, whether their accounting accurately reflects their operating results, and many other facts of this nature. To buy stock on someone's "tip" that it is "about to go up" is to lead with one's chin, or to ask to be parted from your money. If one has neither the time nor the inclination to study carefully the stocks in which one considers investing, it is much better to invest in mutual funds and leave the decisions to others.

Corporation bonds are a good investment, offering both certainty of yield, and the return of principal at maturity. The yield is higher than government bonds, and good quality bonds are equally marketable so that they need not be held to maturity but may be sold whenever money is needed for some other purpose. Marketable bonds do fluctuate in price depending primarily on the trend in interest rates. When rates are rising, prices of outstanding bonds will be falling; when rates are falling, bond prices will be rising. This is because an outstanding bond, on which the contract or coupon rate is 5 percent, will be more or less attractive depending on what is happening to other interest rates.

Corporation securities are bought and sold through brokers who are members of organized stock exchanges. The largest and most substantial companies are traded on the New York Stock Exchange. Less well-established and smaller companies may trade on the American Stock Exchange. There are also regional exchanges in various cities throughout the country such as Baltimore-Washington, Chicago, Denver, and San Francisco. Generally these regional exchanges trade in securities of companies that are regionally rather than nationally known.

Many stocks are not traded on any organized exchange but merely "over the counter," as the term goes. This means the stock is bought and sold through security dealers who hold inventories of the stock in question and make a market for it on the basis of the bids and offers they receive. If you look up over-the-counter stock quotations in a newspaper, you will notice that they give both a bid and an asked price. The *bid* is the last offer to buy, while the *asked* is the last offer to sell. An actual transaction would be negotiated, probably, at a price between the bid and asked quotations.

Securities Exchange Commission, Washington, D.C. The SEC, set up in 1933 by President Roosevelt, was designed to overcome some of the bad stock market practices during the 1920's. It has regulatory power over new issues of securities, over trading on the stock exchanges, and other matters. The basis of SEC legislation is full disclosure of information to the prospective investor. The first head of the SEC was Joseph Kennedy, father of President John F. Kennedy, and a highly successful stock market speculator during the 1920's. He was picked to head the SEC because he knew all about market pools, rigging, and other insider practices.

Warrants are options to buy a stock at a stated price for a definite period of time. They are usually issued to existing stockholders in an effort to get them to buy more of the stock. Warrants, however, may be traded separately from the stock and often are. Their value will depend on the spread between the market price for the stock and the price at which one may exercise the warrant.

Suppose a warrant is issued to buy a stock any time in the next three years at $25 per share. The stock is currently selling at only $22. It would appear that the warrant is worthless. Actually it may be selling for $3. This means that buyers figure that there is a good chance the stock will be worth more than $28 at some time or times in the next three years. Warrants fluctuate relatively more in value than the stock to which they relate. Because they have leverage, they are a good vehicle for speculation. Investors who receive warrants on stock they own usually either exercise them fairly promptly or sell them.

Puts and *calls* are also options to buy or sell particular stocks at a fixed price for a definite period. A put is an option to put stock on the market or sell; a call is an option to call stock off the market or buy. Suppose you think that General Motors, currently selling for $50, is going up. Instead of buying the stock itself, you buy a call or option to buy it any time in the next 6 months at $50. For this you pay 3 points per share or $300 for a call on 100 shares.

If in the next 6 months the price goes to $55, you exercise the call, buy 100 shares and have a profit of $200 on an investment of $300. If on the other hand, the price drops to $45, your option is worthless; when it expires you have nothing except a $300 loss. Options are speculative devices with considerable leverage. They are not normally for small investors who are unable to take big risks.

Mutual funds are investments in pools of stock that are professionally managed. What one buys in a mutual is a proportionate share in all the investments of a fund. The advantages of a mutual fund are diversification and full-time management. Suppose you put $500 in a mutual fund. The fund management or investment advisors buy whatever stock they think best. If they make good judgments and their investments appreciate, your $500 may get to be worth more than that. If their investments are poor, your capital will depreciate.

Mutuals often have a sales charge of 7 or 8 percent of the amount invested. Those with no sales charge are known as "no-load" funds. They always have a management charge of about 1 per cent annually for picking and managing the investments. Some mutuals also have a redemption charge. Redemption is usually at net asset value at the redemption date. For example, if your $500 has appreciated to $520, this, less the redemption charge, is what you would get if you decided to redeem your investment.

Mutual funds are fine investments for people who want to own corporation stock but lack the knowledge or skill to select their own investments. They are a way of hiring someone else to make your investment decisions for you. For this, you naturally pay a price.

Mutuals vary greatly in performance. Some do well in bull markets but very badly in bear markets. Others do relatively well both in up and down markets. Some funds are conservatively managed while others speculate fairly recklessly. A small saver would do well to select a conservatively managed mutual if he wishes to put funds into this type of investment. Normally it will cost more to hire an independent investment advisor than to entrust funds to a well-managed mutual.

Real estate.

This can be an extremely good investment but it requires study and an ability to anticipate population and geographic trends. Also, real estate as an investment is not as readily divisible into increments suitable for a small saver as are corporate securities. More capital may be required to control a property than a small saver can conveniently get together.

Real estate may be bought primarily for the land value or primarily for the improvements on the property. A house or a store for rental purposes would be an example of property whose primary value was in the improvements. Land suitable for subdivision or for a shopping center would be an example where the improvements, if any, would be incidental.

Land values depend primarily on location or on fertility if used for farming purposes. A farm is a good investment but farming is now a highly capital intensive business, in which a large investment is tied up in equipment and in livestock if meat is a principal product. In certain areas of the country, farming is often done on a partnership basis with the tenant furnishing the labor and perhaps some of the equipment while the landowner furnishes the farm and perhaps some equipment also. Income is divided as agreed in the partnership contract. The majority of farms are operator owned, being essentially single proprietorships.

Land is often bought and held for relatively long periods by investors who feel economic growth will eventually make their land more valuable. To be right, they must have sensed the geographic direction of growth and bought their land in the growth path. It is also important that some intermediate use for the land be found while waiting for the growth that will appreciate its value. In rural areas land can sometimes be let for grazing or hay growing; in urban areas, it is often leased for parking lots or some other purpose while awaiting development.

If whole parcels of land are too expensive for the small saver, participation in real estate syndicates may be considered. These syndicates are basically partnerships formed for a particular purpose, such as buying a piece of land or a building. They are normally formed by a promoter who uses this device to stretch his own capital to buy a desirable property.

Syndicates may last a long time but are usually fairly short-run affairs. Often a few years after the property has been purchased it can be sold to advantage, whereupon the syndicate is dissolved, with a profit to each of the participants.

Syndicates can be a good investment if the property is carefully chosen and the purchase price is advantageous. Those which are most successful are organized by experienced real estate operators who know local property values and are in a position to sense growth trends.

In addition to actual real estate, one may participate in real estate loans by buying a mortgage or perhaps some second trust notes. These are junior mortgages which usually come into existence when a purchaser lacks a sufficient down payment to cover all settlement costs. These notes are often taken by a real estate firm in the first instance and then resold at a substantial discount to an investor.

Grand Coulee Dam, State of Washington. Multi-purpose hydro projects such as this have a very strong effect on land values in the area. The project provides water for irrigation, which increases the value of farm land in the region. It also provides cheap hydroelectric power which can be shipped considerable distances, making land attractive as factory sites. Aluminum plants and other plants needing large amounts of electric power have been attracted to the area. Finally, the dam provides recreation facilities for swimming, boating, etc., which enhance the value of the region as a tourist center.

If the buyer of the property is creditworthy, these notes can be a good investment. Often with the discount the yield will be 10 to 12 percent, much higher than can be obtained on conventional real estate investments.

Conclusion.

Many other ways in which to invest savings may be found. Indeed, the possible opportunities are limited only by the ingenuity of the investor. Many small business opportunities may be found for one who has some time as well as money to invest. Many of these opportunities are franchise operations in which advertising and supply problems are handled by the franchiser.

One should exercise considerable caution, however, before entering into a franchise contract. Often these are not at all advantageous to the franchisee, who often finds himself working for bare wages while most of the profits go to the franchiser. It may be much better, if one is going into business, to do so independently rather than through a franchise scheme. It all depends on the terms of the potential contract.

Engineers at work at an aircraft plant in California. The aero-space industry is quite volatile, with its stocks being alternatively good and poor performers. At present the industry is depressed with many engineers such as these laid off. Aircraft manufacture requires a large number of engineering drawings covering all details of airframe construction. Facilities for aircraft manufacture have been expanded to such a size in this country that the industry cannot operate profitably without a sizeable volume of military orders.

When one plans an investment program, a certain degree of diversification is desirable. One cannot be certain how an investment will turn out; it is usually not wise to put all of your savings in one basket. Often an investment that did not initially look so promising will turn out to be better than one with initial glittering promise. We can never forecast the future with total accuracy.

Although some diversification is desirable, many investors diversify too much. Each investment must be watched carefully, not merely from time to time but constantly. Too many stockholders do not read their annual or quarterly reports with the care they deserve. Often they miss significant details that would be signals to buy, sell or hold the stock they own. There is little need for a small investor to own a dozen different corporate stocks. Often he would do better by owning half that many and watching them more carefully.

Let me repeat that to be a successful investor requires constant reading and study. One must know not only what to buy but when as well; also when to sell and switch to something else. Investment prospects are constantly changing. Today's hot growth stock may be tomorrow's dull performer. You can buy bonds at precisely the wrong time. A choice piece of real estate along the proposed path of a major highway may be less choice if the highway is rerouted.

There is an old saying in the stock market that the small investor is always wrong. Some speculators carefully watch the odd lot market, where blocks of less than 100 shares are traded, primarily by small investors. If the odd lotters are selling General Motors, the speculator will buy it; if they are buying General Electric, he will sell it.

Like other investment rules of thumb, this one is by no means infallible. The small investors are occasionally right, although they seem to be wrong more often. Usually they are wrong in their timing more than they are in their choice of investment media.

In building an investment plan, it is usually wise to decide early how much risk you are willing to take, and how you want your returns to be balanced between income and appreciation. There is an important tax advantage in taking investment returns as capital gains rather than ordinary income. Usually the tax is only half as much.

Those with little wealth are normally in a poorer position to take substantial risks than those with more wealth. Young people normally take greater risks than older persons. Any investment program involves some risks but these can be minimized by judicious investments and by paying close attention to timing.

For most of us, savings are hard to accumulate. They require self-denial, thinking of the future more than the present, and biding our time. If saving is hard, surely taking the time and effort to study proposed investments carefully is in itself a good investment.

The fool and his money may soon be parted, but the wise man gains a little here and a little more there. Perhaps he never makes a real "killing"; but then he never suffers a calamitous loss either. Risk is unavoidable; but no one need hurry to embrace it more frequently nor more eagerly than necessary.

Chapter 11

IT'S IN THE BAG–Budgets

In old French the word budget, now used to describe a government's expenditure plan, means bag. With the fine feeling the British have for tradition, the Chancellor of the Exchequer, roughly equivalent to our Secretary of the Treasury, uses an historic old bag or brief case when he goes annually to Parliament to present the budget for the coming year. While officials of our government do not use an historic brief case, they also take an annual trip to Congress each January to present the budget of the United States Government.This is the President's plan for expenditures in the fiscal year to begin the following July 1.

If we think of the public purse as a bag or pocketbook, or as the Italians would say, a fisc, taxes are what fill the purse, while expenditures, which are first projected by budgets, drain the purse. If you wish to carry the analogy farther, borrowing also fills the purse, while repayment of borrowing helps to drain it. When the government operates at a deficit the balance in the purse is pulled down; when it realizes a surplus, because receipts exceed expenditure, the purse gets a little heavier.

This chapter seeks to set forth a few of the general principles of budget making and budget execution. These are important to an understanding of what is sometimes known as public finance, or how governments finance their operations and activities.

Government budgets are simply plans for revenue and expenditure covering a definite period, such as a fiscal year. They contain revenue projections based on existing tax rates and perhaps also proposals for new taxes for which enactment is sought. They also contain expenditure plans which have been provisionally approved and for which the sanction of appropriations legislation is sought. Most budgets are taken up annually; but for some state governments the budget period is two years; the budget is biennial. A budget is usually presented as the chief executive's financial plan; that is, as the program of the President of the United States or the governor of a state.

Budgets under our system are proposed by the executive arm of government but reviewed and finally enacted as appropriations legislation by the legislative arm. The appropriations legislation becomes the actual authority to spend money for specified purposes.

Budget making.

Let us examine how a budget-making process operates, taking for our example the budget of the United States Government which, by law, must be presented to Congress each January. In January 1972, the budget for fiscal 1973 will be presented. The Federal Government operates on a fiscal

President Truman delivering the state of the union address before a joint session of Congress in 1950. The state of the union message is closely followed by the budget message and the economic report each January. It has become the custom for the President to deliver the state of the union speech in person, whereas formerly it was merely sent to Congress to be read. Note the press gallery behind the clock and the public gallery to the left. Joint sessions are held in the House chamber.

year extending from July 1 to the next June 30. Fiscal 1973 begins July 1, 1972.

In theory the period from January through June is when the appropriations committees of Congress will act on budget proposals and enact the proper appropriations legislation. Actually the process regularly takes much longer than this. July 1 will come with half or less of the appropriations bills enacted, continuing resolutions enable government agencies to act on the same basis as last year until their appropriation acts are passed, often midway through the fiscal year.

Although the budget is presented to Congress in January, it has taken virtually all the prior year to make it up. The process begins with each individual government agency making its program plans and calculating the expenditures necessary to carry out these plans. Once the budget is made up within an agency it is presented to the Office of Management and Budget, which is part of the Executive Office of the President. This office examines each agency's request carefully, screens out duplication, advises whether the programs are in accord with the overall program of the President, and frequently makes cuts because a program has a low priority or because it appears overfinanced for the results likely to be accomplished.

When all agency requests have been examined individually, the whole is put together and examined by the President, usually in November and December. What he finally approves is what goes into the budget document and to Congress in January.

The appropriations process.

Once the budget has been received by Congress, following some general discussion of its philosophy and economic impact, it is handed over to the House Appropriations Committee, to be broken up among its subcommittees who examine the expenditure plans of each agency. The subcommittee on the State, Commerce, and Justice Departments, for example, then begins examining officials of these agencies, down to individual bureaus and offices, and writing an appropriations bill. In this process they may cut agency requests somewhat and may in some cases increase them beyond the President's request. For some years, for example, certain programs were regularly given more spending authority by the House than the President had requested. Sometimes this proved a true embarrassment of riches, in the sense that good programs did not exist to spend all the money that was appropriated.

More usually, however, the appropriations subcommittee will cut an agency's request by eliminating what it considers to be unnecessary frills. Unfortunately, agencies often inflate their budget requests in anticipation of these Congressional cuts. Although this inflation sometimes escapes the eagle eyes of examiners in the Office of Management and Budget, the examiners, with experience behind them, are not easy to fool.

Once an appropriations bill has been developed in the House and has passed that body, the whole process is repeated in the Senate. In practice, however, the Senate does not make as thorough a program review as the

House, but confines itself largely to acting as a court of appeal from House decisions. It may put back part or all of the cuts the House has made or, in rare cases, may increase an appropriation beyond the House approved figure.

These differences then all have to be ironed out in conference between committee members representing both bodies before an appropriation bill can finally be presented to the President for his signature. In rare cases the President may veto an appropriations bill. President Nixon did this in 1970 to the Health, Education, and Welfare appropriation bill, which he felt too far exceeded his recommendations for spending. Congress then had to develop a new bill which he finally signed.

Thus, spending bills become law exactly as other bills do, except the spending bills by custom and tax bills, as are required by our Constitution, originate in the House of Representatives, on the theory that the House is closer and more responsive to the will of the electorate than the Senate.

Promoting U.S. exports at a trade center in London. The U.S. has a number of these centers in foreign countries where U.S. products are shown, special exhibits put on, and contacts made between U.S. suppliers and potential foreign buyers. This particular exhibit dealt with high performance materials and was quite successful from the standpoint of new business developed.

Let us go back to the process of making up a budget to see what processes of reasoning it involves. An agency such as the Department of Commerce will have certain ongoing programs—the promotion of foreign trade, for example. Let us say that this year, for balance of payments reasons, a more aggressive program of promoting United States exports is desired. Programs are formulated for more trade shows, for wider distribution of marketing information, and for other activities aimed at promoting exports. When these programs' expenses are estimated, it may appear that the Bureau of International Commerce should have a 7 percent increase in its budget to finance these new and expanded activities. This 7 percent increase, when approved by the Secretary of Commerce, is then carried to the Office of Management and Budget for inclusion in the President's program. Let us say that this office approves it in toto following program examination; this 7 percent increase then appears in the budget submitted to Congress in January.

In due course it gets to the House Appropriations Committee where officials of the Bureau of International Commerce are examined in depth on the need for the new programs, on whether they are properly structured and will be appropriately staffed, and on whether the benefits anticipated will actually be realized. Let us say that the appropriations committee has some doubts about the program as contemplated and hence decides to give the bureau a 5 percent, rather than the requested 7 percent, increase in spending authority. This 5 percent increase is what is actually appropriated.

Appropriations committees often operate on the marginal principle, giving far more attention to requested increases than to justifications for continuing last year's level of spending. This often means that obsolete programs may get funded fairly easily, while new programs may have a difficult time securing appropriations; but this is the way the system works.

Budget philosophy.

It is all very well to say that a proposed new government program gets reviewed several times, both in the executive and in the legislative branch; but what kind of reasoning process does the review involve? Largely it is a process of trying to define, and wherever possible, to measure the public benefits expected to flow from the program, and the costs involved in reaping those benefits. If the program involves export trade promotion, the questions asked will be: How much can export trade be expected to increase? What benefits in the form of an easier balance of payments position, expanded employment in the export industries, etc., can be expected to flow from increased exports? What disadvantages (for example, restrictions by other countries against imports from the U.S.) might result?

As may be seen from the above, the benefits which should be given the most weight are social rather than private ones. Similarly the costs are social costs rather than merely private costs to the government or to business. Seen in this light, benefit-cost analysis as applied to budget making is merely a kind of applied economic analysis. Indeed, economists are coming increasingly to be recognized as having special qualifications as budget analysts.

Although budgets are commonly prepared and appraised on a year-to-year basis, most government programs extend over many years and cannot be properly evaluated on an annual basis. A program to promote safety on the highways, for example, needs to be looked at in a larger time frame. For this reason the U.S. Office of Management and Budget now requires all agencies, when presenting their budget requests, to provide not only

A committee of Congress in session. This committee is hearing testimony from a government witness. Committees get their information largely from hearing witnesses representing different organizations and varying points of view. When public hearings are concluded, the Committee goes into executive session and writes a bill, whether an appropriations bill or one on some other subject matter depending on the committee. When voted out of committee these bills go to the floor of the House or Senate to be debated and finally voted up or down, with or without amendments. The public is barred from executive sessions.

estimates for the year in question, but forecasts for the four following years, making a 5-year picture in all. It is felt that proposals can more accurately be evaluated if a 5-year span is considered. Although forecasts for 5 years ahead are hazardous, since the future cannot always be seen accurately, it is felt that the exercise of a 5-year-program review adds an element of depth to the whole budget review process.

The revenue side.

In addition to expenditure projections, budget documents usually also contain forecasts of tax revenues. These forecasts are sometimes made on two assumptions: (1) that existing tax laws and rates remain in effect, and (2) that new tax rates as requested become effective. In the British system, for example, the budget is required to be accompanied by tax proposals, if needed, to make the expenditure program effective. The United States system is a little different. Although tax proposals are sometimes made in the budget, the real business of requesting tax changes comes at a different time. This is because tax legislation is the province of the House Ways and Means Committee, whereas expenditure proposals are the business of the Appropriations Committee.

If new taxes are sought as part of the budgetary package, the Administration will prepare proposals which will be presented by the Treasury Department to the House Ways and Means Committee. This committee will hold extensive hearings with both official and private witnesses. It will then, in executive session, develop a bill carrying out the Administration proposals or alternatives of its own. When completed, this bill will be taken up on the House floor and, if passed, will be referred to the Senate. There, the Senate Finance Committee will duplicate the hearing and markup processes.

Tax bills are ordinarily amended on the Senate floor, whereas in the House they are debated under a closed rule which prohibits floor amendments. Thus tax bills nearly always go to conference.

The budget of the United States Government as presented in January is basically a cash budget, i.e., it shows payments to be made to the public and receipts to be collected from the public. Not all payments to the public require annual appropriations. For example, collections of payroll taxes for social security go into trust funds rather than into the general fund of the Treasury. Social security payments to retired persons and the unemployed may be made under standing legislative authority rather than annual appropriations legislation.

There is another budget used for economic analysis by the Council of Economic Advisers and other agencies concerned with economic policy. This is the national accounts budget of the United States Government

FEDERAL BUDGET (NIA Basis)

Defense purchases stabilized in 1969 but other expenditures continued to grow.

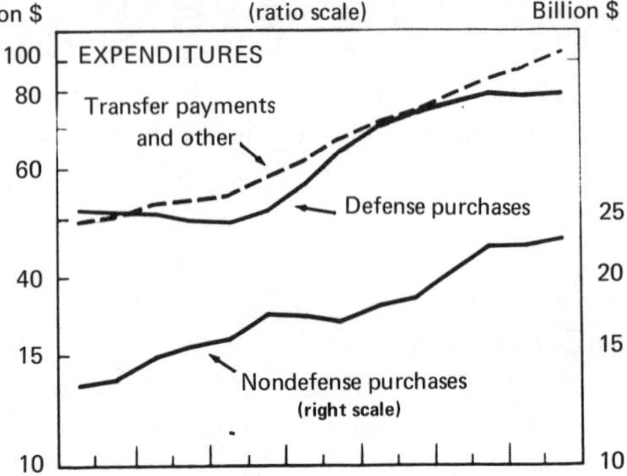

The growth of receipts, which had been boosted by imposition of the surcharge, slowed in the second half . . .

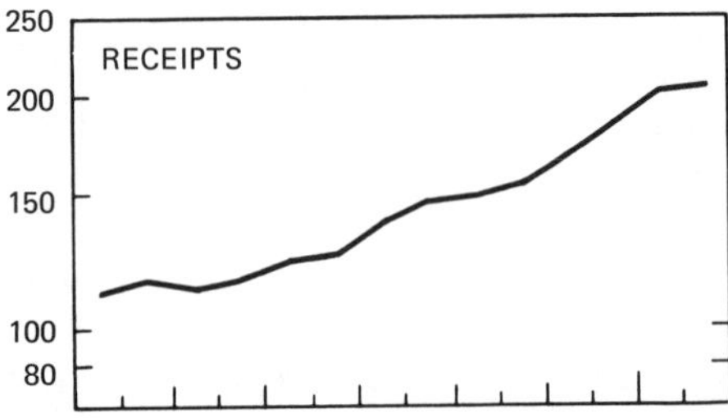

and the budget surplus shrank.

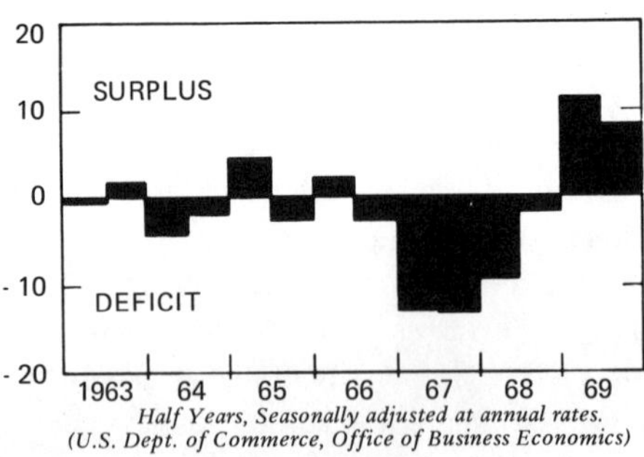

Half Years, Seasonally adjusted at annual rates.
(U.S. Dept. of Commerce, Office of Business Economics)

Some Federal budget figures on a national accounts basis. The upper panel shows three categories of expenditure, timed by when goods are delivered to the government rather than when they are paid for. The center panel shows receipts on the basis of when tax liability accrues rather than when taxes are collected. The bottom panel shows surplus or deficit by half years. A deficit tends to expand the private economy while a surplus tends to contract it.

sector of the national income and product accounts. This budget counts tax liabilities rather than tax collections in a specific year and also drops government expenditures not for current output, such as land purchases. It is felt by some economists that this national accounts budget more accurately measures the impact of the budget on economic activity than does the cash budget. The cash budget, of course, is what must actually be financed, either by taxes or borrowing.

Current and capital budgets.

Many countries make a distinction in their budgets between expenditures for current and for capital purposes. Salaries of government employees in regular departments would be a current expenditure, while construction cost of a dam for flood control, power, and irrigation might be a capital expenditure. Sometimes certain revenues are earmarked for one or the

Building an interstate highway in South Carolina. Federal taxes on gasoline and tires go into the highway trust fund. Interstate highways are then financed 90 percent from federal and 10 percent from local funds. The gasoline tax is virtually a user charge system of highway finance. Taxation on the benefit principle is an old concept in public finance. Special assessments on property along a street for improving the street would be another example.

other budgets. In Iran, for example, about 70 percent of all revenues from the export of petroleum products is earmarked for the capital budget.

The United States Government budget does not distinguish current from capital outlays. Relief expenditures are treated the same as costs of highway construction. Each year a part of the outlay which some Congressmen regularly decry as government spending is really in the nature of investments that will yield benefits over a long period of years. Some will even, in time, recover their costs and yield a profit to the public purse. The Panama Canal, for example, still continues to collect tolls on ships that transit its length, even though the cost of the Canal has been recovered long since.

Budget making in state and local governments does not differ essentially from the process in the Federal Government, although with smaller areas and less money involved, the process may be less formal and more simplified.Basically, however, the Governor of a state or the Mayor of a city has to present an annual budget to the state legislature or the city council. These bodies then examine the budget, cut it where they consider necessary, and pass the required appropriations legislation. This legislation constitutes the authority for government departments to operate and to make outlays during the coming year.

All budgets have to be made up well in advance of the year or other period they cover; consequently, their preparation involves forecasting. Since even legendary seers see the future only dimly, forecasting is subject to error.

The budget process usually makes provision for the correction of large but not necessarily of small errors. In the United States Government, for example, we have the deficiency or supplemental appropriation. Suppose war should break out in the middle of the fiscal year. Wars are seldom scheduled for a particular date and, under our system, advance budgeting is not made for them. If the United States were attacked, the Defense Department would quickly go to Congress, with the backing of the President, for a supplemental appropriation. This would probably be quickly voted if the urgency of the appropriation were apparent to the majority.

Less drastic than war, but perhaps deserving of a supplemental appropriation might be a special program for public works, should an unforeseen recession develop. Similarly if inflation needed to be met by price and wage controls, a deficiency appropriation would be sought to pay for the organization to operate these controls. Supplemental appropriations, in a word, are designed primarily to meet unforeseen developments that were not included in the ordinary budget-making process. The United States Congress generally dislikes these appropriations, since they can seldom be given the thorough review that normal budgetary requests get.

Nevertheless, supplemental appropriations are necessary and are in fact used almost every year for some purpose.

Once budgetary proposals have been converted into appropriations legislation, governmental agencies are not entirely free to obligate or spend the money. Appropriation laws are typically quite detailed, specifying how much can be used for individual line items, with only very limited authority to shift funds from one purpose to another. In the United States Government, the Office of Management and Budget exercises close surveillance after appropriations have been made, setting quarterly personnel ceilings, releasing funds for expenditure only in installments, and sometimes withholding appropriated funds if programs have not been fully worked out or are not progressing on schedule. Expenditure of public funds is hedged with many restrictions and formalities, some designed to frustrate fraud, others for purposes less plain.

Comprehensiveness.

An unresolved issue of budgetary practice is how comprehensive a budget should be, i.e., whether all activities of government should be covered or whether some, particularly of a business nature—where goods or services are sold to the public—should be outside the budget proper. In the United States Federal budget, for example, bank supervisory activities are extra budgetary because these activities are supported by fees charged the banks for their supervision.

Likewise, the activities of the central bank, the Federal Reserve System, are outside the budget because the Federal Reserve holds the reserves of commercial banks, on which it pays no interest, while it derives a large income from investing these reserves in United States Government securities, on which it receives the same interest that you or I would. Thus, the Federal Reserve each year can cover all its expenditures and still return a substantial sum to the Treasury—a refund of part of the interest the Treasury has paid to the central bank.

Mention has already been made of the trust funds which are fed from earmarked tax revenue and from which expenditure can be made under standing authority rather than from the authority of annual appropriation bills. The Social Security Trust Fund, for example, is fed from payroll taxes levied both on employers and employees. Old age pensions are paid from this trust fund to all who qualify under the Social Security Act in accordance with the terms of that legislation.

Earmarking of revenues for particular purposes is often considered a bad budgetary practice because it lets certain activities escape the budgetary review process. Over time an earmarked source of revenue will usually be either too large or too small for the activity it supports. The Social Security Trust Fund, for example, is too small on an actuarial basis for the liabilities it will someday be called upon to meet. Assistance from general revenue is inevitable if benefits already legislated are to be met; and benefits are regularly increased with each advance in living costs.

Ideally, all government activities ought to compete on an equal basis for appropriations, if proper priorities are to be set. When activities, such as road building, are supported from trust funds, they escape this competition. This may not always be a good thing.

Other countries often have relatively more extra-budgetary government activity than we do. This is especially true where government operates extensive business-type activities which earn their own operating revenues. In Costa Rica, for example, the government has a monopoly over the distilling, the banking, and the insurance businesses. All these are outside the budget, with one result being that the public gets very little information about how these businesses are operated—whether they make profits or accrue losses—what use is made of the profits if they exist—and other vital data.

The largest business operated by the United States Government is the Post Office. Formerly, when this was a government department, it was included in the budget on a net basis, i.e., the excess of expenditure over revenue was reported as an expenditure item. Now that the Post Office has been changed to a government corporation, both its receipts and expenditures are outside the budget proper.

The federal budget.

For perspective on the United States Government budget in a recent year, consider the following figures (in billions of dollars) for the fiscal year 1969:

FEDERAL BUDGET

Receipts	
Individual income taxes	80.9
Corporation income taxes	34.3
Excise taxes	14.7
Employment taxes	34.2
All other receipts	13.1
Total receipts	178.1

Expenditures

National defense	79.8
Social security and other trust funds	38.5
Other major social programs	20.8
Interest	14.4
All other	37.6
Less: intragovernmental payments	5.0
Total expenditures	186.1

You will note that this budget projected a deficit of $8 billion, to be covered by borrowing or by drawing upon cash balances. In reality, the government is borrowing continually, even in years when there is no deficit, because portions of the outstanding public debt are continually coming due and must be replaced.

Actually, the government borrows both on short- and long-term bases, and tries to gear its offerings to the preferences and needs of various financial institutions. It sells 91-day Treasury bills at auction each week; these securities are bought mainly by commercial banks who regard them as a kind of secondary reserve. On the other hand, the Treasury offers 20- and 30-year bonds which are bought mainly by pension funds that will not need to pay benefits for many years. The Treasury also offers all types of securities in between 6-month bills, 1- and 2-year certificates of indebtedness, 5-year notes, etc.

Even in a year when the budget is in surplus there will be refunding operations, or "roll overs" as they are known in the trade. Suppose a 10-year bond is coming due. The Treasury will offer a new security which holders of the maturing issue can take in trade. If they do not wish to exchange, they have the option to be paid in cash. If holders of 90 percent of a maturing issue accept the exchange offer, the remaining 10 percent is called "attrition," or loss from the standpoint of the borrower. Every refunding operation has some attrition, although efforts are often made to keep it as low as possible.

The business of rearranging and refinancing the public debt is known as "debt management." It used to be thought that debt management could be a positive tool for managing the economy and the monetary system. In all normal periods, long-term interest rates will be higher than short-term interest rates for equally good security. Thus, by borrowing as much as possible at short term, the debt managers can keep the carrying costs of the public debt relatively low. However, if too many short-term bills are offered, the banks will not want to buy them all. Prices will fall, which is merely another way of saying that short-term interest rates will rise.

At the same time, if not enough long-term bonds are offered, their prices will rise, which is another way of saying that long-term interest rates will fall. The yield curve on government securities, which normally rises as the term is extended, will get flatter. At times long-term rates fall below short-term rates, although this condition is unusual and generally strictly temporary.

In practice, debt management is mainly a process of guessing what the market will absorb and offering a proper mix of securities to appeal to all sectors of the potential buying group. Insofar as is consistent with their other objectives, the debt managers also try to keep the carrying cost of the debt down. But there are few opportunities, with a debt as large and as varied as our government's, to use refunding operations for positive economic objectives.

Expenditure priorities.

One of the most difficult problems in budget making or budget appraisal is properly evaluating expenditure claims, one against another. Should $1 billion more be spent to modernize aircraft for the Air Force, or should this $1 billion better be spent for retraining the hard-core unemployed? Decisions of this nature are constantly being forced on the Office of Management and Budget, or whoever else the responsible budget-making authority may be. The decisions are hard ones because the potential benefits from different programs are seldom directly comparable, while the claims of the advocates usually proceed from different premises. Nevertheless, decisions of this nature have to be made, often from inadequate data.

Few budget makers would claim to do their job perfectly, although they usually claim a rough-and-ready precision for their results. Whether more wisdom resides in the professional budget makers, or in the Congressional appropriations committee members who modify and then bless their results, would be hard to say. As elsewhere in our system of government, the final result is a product of checks and balances, of proposal, counterproposal, and compromise. Sometimes it seems that the final compromise contains the worst features of all the preliminary proposals!

The improvement most needed in the budgetary process of the United States Government is to get it done on time, so that agencies do not have to wait half the fiscal year to learn what their appropriations are. Better staff work for the Congressional appropriations committees is one possible answer. A joint staff, like the joint staff for internal revenue taxation, would seem an obvious possibility. Although this has been proposed a number of times, the appropriations committees themselves have never warmed to the idea. Increasing tardiness may eventually force them to it.

Some years ago much talk was heard about a *program and performance budget;* generally this reform has now been introduced into the United States system, although the practice of many other countries still lags. A program and performance budget is one that draws all costs of a given program together, so that expected results can be compared with budgeted costs. This would seem an obvious thing to do, although for many years the budget of the Federal Government did not follow this procedure, and instead dealt merely in object of expenditure categories such as salaries, travel, equipment, etc. Little or no connection was made between objects of expenditure and the purposes for which these expenditures were requested. You can see that this system made proper budget review extremely difficult.

The second major reform that seems to be needed in the United States Federal budgetary process is an end to the marginal concept of looking hard only at proposed increases. Instead, entire programs should be carefully examined. This is sometimes described as a *zero base program review,* as opposed to the system where last year's appropriation is taken as the base, and only the proposed increases are justified. Under the zero base system not all programs would be thoroughly reviewed each year, but all would be in the course of 3 or 4 years.

The difficulty with this system, which is the only way of getting rid entirely of obsolete programs, is that it conflicts with the objective of getting the budget work done on time. A thorough program review takes time, when the appropriations process is already lagging seriously behind schedule. Much of the program review could be delegated to staff, although Congress would have to make the final decisions.

As an example of how the marginal system of budget review fails to kill obsolete programs, the record of the United States Spruce Authority may be cited. Originally established late in World War I, to obtain spruce for aircraft, when they were still made of this material, the agency got started too late to be of any significant help to the war effort. Yet, because of both Congressional and executive branch oversight, it persisted until 1936 before finally being eliminated. Unfortunately, other examples of this type, perhaps slightly less ignominious, could be cited. If the spruce authority had been subjected to a thorough zero base program review within a few years of its establishment, its demise would not have been so long overdue.

In a very real sense, the budget of the United States Government must reflect, indeed must be the President's program. This is his only opportunity to set expenditure priorities to reflect his view of what the Federal Government should and should not do, and to what extent. If the President believes that preservation of the environment is our highest priority, his budget should reflect that fact and should assign lower priorities and lower expenditures to less essential programs.

When a new President takes office one problem he has is that a budget must be presented immediately. Naturally this budget was developed by the outgoing administration and reflects its priorities, which may differ substantially from those of the incoming administration. It is not until the second year of his term that a President really gets control of the budget and can use it actively to reflect his program.

Another fact about the budget is that many of the expenditure programs in it are not readily controllable, even if an administration wishes to change them. Veterans and social security pensions, interest on the public debt, pay and subsistence of minimum military forces are examples of contractual or morally-obligated expenditures that cannot readily be reduced. When these virtually uncontrollable obligations are deducted from total projected government expenditures, the discretionary or controllable portion of the budget is much smaller than generally realized. Fortunately, the spruce authorities do not bulk very large in total government outlay.

Another reason budgets are difficult to control is that authority to obligate funds often runs far ahead of actual expenditure. Basically, appropriations acts are authority to obligate. In the case of a new military airplane, it may be 5 years or more before all expenditures under that obligation authority are made. First comes research and development, then product testing, followed by acceptance, and then actual production contracts. Only some time later do completed aircraft begin rolling off assembly lines.

Likewise in the annual foreign aid budgetary exercise, an authorization bill must first be cleared before the actual budget proposals can advance. The authorization bill is usually full of exhortations about program direction, about doing more of this and less of that, extracting more self-help from the aid-receiving nations, etc. Most of the Congressional criticism, bombast, etc., about foreign aid is delivered in connection with the authorization bill. This means the appropriation bill is invariably the last such bill to be considered, gets only short shrift, and is usually not finally passed until adjournment day.

All this means less disruption to the foreign aid program than one would expect, since foreign aid expenditures run at least a year behind obligations. The wheat that goes to feed Pakistan today was covered by last year's foreign aid appropriation bill, or will be covered by a deficiency appropriation if the need was not foreseen.

The above are some of the reasons why a budget is not the precise instrument it perhaps should be. After all, most government programs are continuous; the practice of chopping them up into annual segments for budget purposes is to some extent artificial, and not entirely practical.

But Congress has traditionally been reluctant to make open-end appropriations. The power of the purse is a vital power, which the legislative branch of our government guards jealously.

Budgets as political documents.

Appropriation bills are often full of precise administrative directions—to do this and not that, to change this program in a particular way, etc. Often these administrative directions amount to unusual interference in the executive process—attempts by Congress not only to authorize and fund programs, but actually to operate them. Riders on appropriations bills have often been used for non fiscal purposes, such as limiting the number of government employees, etc.

One reason for the attachment of these non germane riders is that appropriation bills are normally considered veto proof. The President must, under our system, sign or reject an entire bill. Only rarely does he veto an appropriations bill, although this has been done. This situation has led many political scientists to suggest that the President should have what they call an item veto in connection with appropriations; this would be authority to veto individual items without having to reject the entire bill. While this suggestion would undoubtedly improve the budgetary process, it would strengthen the President's hand at the expense of Congress. Since the proposal would require legislation to become effective, it is not surprising that Congress has exhibited a noticeable lack of enthusiasm for passing the legislation.

The budgetary process illustrates very well the division of powers under our form of government. It exemplifies the old saying that the President proposes, but Congress disposes. While the President holds the veto power over all acts of Congress, he can use this only sparingly where appropriations are concerned. When President Nixon vetoed the Health, Education, and Welfare appropriation in 1970, he did so knowing that Congress would have to develop a new bill, because it would not want to accept the onus of stopping social security and welfare payments, or of not aiding hospitals, etc., all of which were provided for in the appropriations bill in question. For a less vital bill, he could not have been so certain of a substitute.

A word should be said about use of the budget as an active instrument of economic policy. This applies particularly to the Federal budget since those of the states and localities are not large enough to influence the level of economic activity significantly. The budget is a tool to produce either economic expansion or contraction. Remember that the surplus or deficit is the difference between receipts from the public and payments to the public. If payments exceed receipts, in other words if the budget is in deficit, this deficit is an expansive force so far as the private sector of the economy is concerned. It tends to increase employment, raise expenditures, and expand profits in the private sector. Just the opposite results occur when the budget is in surplus—when receipts from the public exceed payments to them.

In recent years budgetary surpluses and deficits have been recognized as powerful tools for influencing the level of economic activity. If a recession is impending, for example, a budget deficit will tend to offset the decline in employment, since government outlays are adding more to the expenditure stream than taxes are taking from it.

If the problem is inflation, on the other hand, a budget surplus is considered a good anti-inflationary weapon.

One difficulty with this kind of functional budgetary finance is that budget makers may misread economic trends, since budgets must be prepared well in advance. If a recession develops rather suddenly, expected tax revenues will probably not be realized. We shall note in connection with the income tax, for example, that revenues from this tax rise and fall more than proportionately to changes in aggregate personal income. A 1 percent fall in income may produce a 1-1/2 percent decline in income tax yield. Likewise in recession certain government expenditures, for example, unemployment compensation, rise automatically, simply because more people become unemployed. These tendencies for tax yields and expenditures to change as variations occur in economic activity are sometimes referred to as built-in fiscal stabilizers.

In the years before the great depression that began in 1929, it was normally taken as an axiom of conventional wisdom that budgets should be balanced every year, regardless of economic conditions. To think otherwise was considered fiscal heresy, quite deserving of banishment from orthodox citadels of monetary power. Now the conventional wisdom holds that budgets should be balanced only over the course of a complete business cycle, with deficits in years of high unemployment and surpluses in years of low unemployment. The Committee for Economic Development, an organization of big businessmen that makes pronouncements on economic policy, goes even further, advocating that the Federal budget should be balanced only when unemployment is 4 percent or less of the labor force, a figure synonymous in their opinion with full employment.

Thus conventional thinking about economic problems does change with the passage of time and the accumulation of experience. J.M. Keynes, the famous British economist, once rather cynically remarked that most businessmen are slaves of some defunct economist, meaning that their views were derived from obsolete economic doctrine. Whether Keynes was right or not is something of an unresolved question; like all aphorisms, his probably contained an element of truth.

It is not accidental that the United States budget is presented at about the same time as the annual economic report of the President. This latter document, prepared by the Council of Economic Advisers, tries to assess the state of the economy and to forecast its course during the year ahead. If their crystal ball reveals an impending recession, they will be looking for fiscal and monetary stimuli, to keep the economic machine functioning at near capacity. A budget deficit, a tax reduction, an expenditure expansion, or an easing of monetary policy would all be stimuli of the type believed necessary.

Similarly if the clear and present economic danger is thought to be not recession but inflation, the advisers will be looking for fiscal and monetary deterrents. Tax increases, tighter monetary policy, or a budget surplus would be deterrents of this type. Actually, budgetary policy and general economic policy have now been quite effectively integrated in the United States Government. This does not mean that the integrated policy is always correct. It is always possible to prepare for recession when inflation is what actually ensues. We do not always see the future clearly, even with the most elaborate econometric models.

Anyone who thinks that Federal forecasters are infallible, should read the history of Federal Reserve policy written after the fact. There one will find breast-beating and sackcloth-wearing for having done the right thing at the wrong time or the wrong thing at the right time.

At least the Federal Reserve is reasonably honest in its post mortems—perhaps more so than budget makers or Treasury officials find it expedient to be. After all, Federal board members have 14-year terms—they are only somewhat more vulnerable than federal judges, and certainly far less so than officials who serve at the pleasure of the President.

If there is one general thing to be said about budget making, it is that it is an art—one that is constantly evolving and developing. If we look at the way in which budgets were made 30 years ago, there has clearly been remarkable progress; but a lot more progress is still needed. Above all, the public needs to be better informed about what budget decisions mean, and how they affect the economy. It also needs to know how priorities are set, and whether these are proper in terms of where we want to go. The whole process needs speeding up, without loosening Congressional control or making its review less thorough.

A formidable agenda, you will say, and rightly so; but progress must be made if big government, growing larger each year, is not to get out of hand. The agenda of budget reform and improvement is an urgent one at all levels of government—federal, state, and local.

Budgets are the throttles of government programs; they cause them to

The Cleveland, Ohio city council during a budget session. The budget process in state and local governments is a smaller version of the process in the federal government. Estimates are proposed by the mayor and approved by the legislative body. In this photo the council members are seated at the three rows of desks, with spectators toward the rear.

move faster or slower. Sometimes budgets are also the brakes. Just as to drive a car successfully requires judicious application of the throttle and the brakes, each at the right time, so to pilot the ship of state requires sometimes stimulus and sometimes restraint. Budgets are one of the chief instruments for this type of fiscal regulation.

In the final analysis the budget of a government is not so different from the budget of a household, except that the former is much larger and consequently has more far-reaching ramifications. Someone once said that economics is basically housewifery applied to large organizations. If this analogy is apt, the budget director of a government is a kind of chief housekeeper, charged with managing the resources of the government and seeing they are used most effectively.

Chapter 12

THE POWER TO DESTROY—Taxation

David Ricardo, a retired stockbroker turned economist, wrote in 1817 that "the desire which every man has to keep his station in life, and to maintain his wealth at the height it has once attained, occasions most taxes, whether laid on capital or on income, to be paid from income."

To Ricardo, an eminently practical man, taxation was one of the most important topics for economic study. Many subsequent economists have shared this view.

Governments provide services for which someone must pay. To provide the necessary revenue, governments levy taxes, which may be defined as compulsory payments to government in accordance with revenue laws. In this country we have three levels of government—the federal, the state, and the local. All three levy taxes, sometimes on the same object or transaction. For example, personal incomes are taxed by the Federal Government, by most but not all states, and by some localities.

The weight of taxation is becoming increasingly heavy, now amounting to roughly 25 percent of gross national product. For the past decade most of the growth has been in state and local taxes. Federal taxes, although growing in absolute terms, have actually declined as a percentage of the GNP. War and national defense account for the largest part of federal expenditures; states invest heavily in education, in highways, and in social services; while localities must finance public schools, streets, garbage collection, police, and many other local services which citizens expect.

Taxes have existed as long as governments have existed; frequently they have been cause for controversy between the sovereign and the governed. The American Revolution was precipitated, in large part, by the stamp tax, the duty on tea, and other excises which the American colonists considered unjust and unfair. They objected not so much to the taxes themselves as to the fact that they (the colonists) had no say in their levy or collection.
unjust and unfair. They objected not so much to the taxes themselves as to the fact that they (the colonists) had no say in their levy or collection.

In the modern world, taxes come into being because a legislative body—the United States Contress, a state legislature, or the local city council—passes a bill levying these taxes on some definite basis. This bill also specifies how and when these taxes will be paid; they then become a legal obligation upon all citizens who meet the criteria, such as owning real estate or having an income above a specified minimum, laid down in the tax statute.

1971 TAX BITE IN THE 40 HOUR WEEK

The average wage worker must each week spend from Monday morning until Tuesday afternoon earning enough to pay all his taxes, Federal, state and local. Taxes are the largest item in his budget, more than food or housing. Many taxes are hidden in the prices of commodities and services. Others, such as income and property taxes, are visible. Taxes are likely to absorb an ever increasing portion of a worker's earnings because people demand more and more government services.
(Courtesy, Tax Foundation.)

Suppose the government of a locality, such as the city of Baltimore faced with expanding revenue needs, decides it must have a local income tax. The city council passes the necessary ordinance, which may or may not require ratification by the voters. Suppose the local income tax is to be of the "piggy back" type, essentially a rider on the Maryland income tax. The bill reads that each person shall compute his Maryland state income tax as before, but then add 25 percent to the liability, which surcharge will be paid directly to the city of Baltimore. This is a popular form of local income tax since it avoids all problems of defining income, specifying deductions, and so on. In the federal income tax these rules for arriving at taxable income are quite complex; they also require considerable checking of income tax returns.

The mainstay of local governments, so far as revenue is concerned, has always been, and still is, the property tax on land and buildings; but increasingly local governments are turning to new revenue sources, such as personal incomes, to meet their new and pressing revenue needs. Baltimore might have levied a local sales tax, or increased its business license taxes, instead of turning to the local income tax. One reason for relying on income taxes is that the yield from these taxes automatically rises and falls with the level of business activity.

Our purpose in this chapter is to examine, in some detail, the different types of taxes that governments use, to see what are the advantages and disadvantages of each, what their potential is for revenue, and what problems of administration and enforcement they raise. Let us begin with income taxation, which is the bulwark of the federal revenue system, and work our way through some of the other taxes that make up the revenue scene.

The income tax.

Today this tax is the mainstay of the federal revenue system; but we never had such a tax until the Civil War and the present one has been in continuous existence only since 1913. Historically, the income tax has been a war tax, an emergency measure to find the enormous revenue needed in time of war. England first adopted the income tax during the Napoleonic wars and has used this fiscal instrument continuously since 1844.

The income tax is a levy on the net income of individuals or corporations. The rates may be either flat or progressive. Usually, allowance is made for personal or family exemptions as well as for ordinary and necessary business expenses.

The first income tax we had during the Civil War was a simple statute less than two pages long. It allowed the deduction of rent as an expense—

a deduction no longer permitted, although certain costs of homeownership—mortgage interest and property taxes— are still deductible.

Today's income tax is a highly complex statute, requiring a 5-foot shelf of books to present all its nuances and variations. Rates of the early personal income taxes ranged from 1 to 5 percent, after generous family exemptions. Today's rates run from 14 to 70 percent; in addition there are state and sometimes city income taxes. Today's income taxes raise nearly $100 billion; the early ones raised a few million.

The income tax is a favorite fiscal instrument because it possesses certain characteristics dear to the hearts of governments and especially to those of finance ministers. One of the attributes is revenue flexibility. When total personal income rises, income tax yield rises more than proportionately, because of the progressive rates. This increase in tax yield is automatic, requiring no action by the Congress or Parliament.

In every year when economic activity is increasing there is therefore an automatic fiscal dividend or increase in revenue; this can be used to finance new government programs, for debt reduction, or for selective tax reduction, sometimes called fiscal incentives.

We have, or have had in the past, fiscal incentives to encourage mining, drilling for oil, investing in new equipment, building additional grain storage facilities, and other activities temporarily considered vital and in need of financial encouragement. People who do not like these incentives call them tax loopholes; but whether these allowances are called loopholes or necessary incentives, the income tax, as defined in the Internal Revenue Code, is interlarded with them. This is one reason it now takes a 5-foot shelf of books to explain the tax in all its complexity.

If you have held a summer job, you have already had some experience with the federal income tax, since you have had to file a return to get your refund of tax withheld. This withholding of tax from wages and salaries has been a prominent feature of this tax since World War II, when the income tax first became a mass tax.

Basically the federal income tax works as follows. It is on an annual basis. Husbands and wives usually file joint returns, including the incomes of each. Single taxpayers usually file separate returns; if a single person is the head of a household, it is normally better for him to file under this schedule.

After determining the proper schedule, the taxpayer lists all income from wages or salary, from interest and dividends, from rents, royalties, partnerships, and any other source. Certain exclusions, such as interest on municipal securities, social security pension payments, income earned while a bona fide resident of a foreign country, etc., are permitted at this stage.

After exclusions, the taxpayer is permitted to take certain deductions permitted by statute. These include traveling expenses (if unreimbursed) while on the employer's business, all ordinary and necessary business expenses (including depreciation, but not costs of going to and from work), interest, taxes, casualty losses, extraordinary medical expenses. All these deductions must be itemized and supported by adequate evidence in the form of receipts, canceled checks, etc. , so that they can be verified if an audit is made.

In lieu of itemizing deductions, the taxpayer may elect to use the "standard deduction," which is ordinarily 10 percent of "gross income" but which also has minimum and maximum limits. If you filed a return based on your summer earnings, you probably used the minimum standard deduction in arriving at your tax liability, if any.

After allowable deductions, gross has been reduced to "net income." From this latter figure, additional deductions, called "personal exemptions," are allowed. In 1971 the personal exemption was $675 per capita. Thus a man with a wife and two dependent children was allowed 4 times $675 or $2,700 personal exemption deductions from net income.

The net figure, after exclusions, deductions, and personal exemptions, is called "taxable income" and is the figure to which rates are applied to determine tax liability. At present the federal rates begin at 14 percent on the first slice of taxable income and rise to 70 percent on taxable income in excess of $100,000.

State income taxes depend on much the same sort of calculation to reduce gross to net income; but the rates are ordinarily much lower than the federal rates. A common state income tax might have rates ranging from 2 to 6 percent, but they rarely go much higher than this.

Local income taxes, as already noted, are commonly based directly on the state liability, and do not require a separate calculation of taxable net income.

The second most important revenue source for the United States Government, after the personal income tax, is the income tax on corporations. In structure this is quite similar to the personal income tax, with basically the same deductions allowed, except that there are no personal exemptions under the corporate tax. Also the corporate tax rate is basically flat rather than progressive, although there is a reduced rate on the first $25,000 of net income. In 1971 the first $25,000 of a corporation's profits were taxed at 22 percent, the remainder at 48 percent.

An old question concerning the corporate income tax is whether or not it is shifted and, if so, on whom the burden actually falls. Some economists feel the tax is largely shifted forward into final product prices; thus it falls, in the final analysis, on consumers. Others feel that the tax is not actually

GROWTH OF STATE INCOME TAX COLLECTIONS
1960–1970

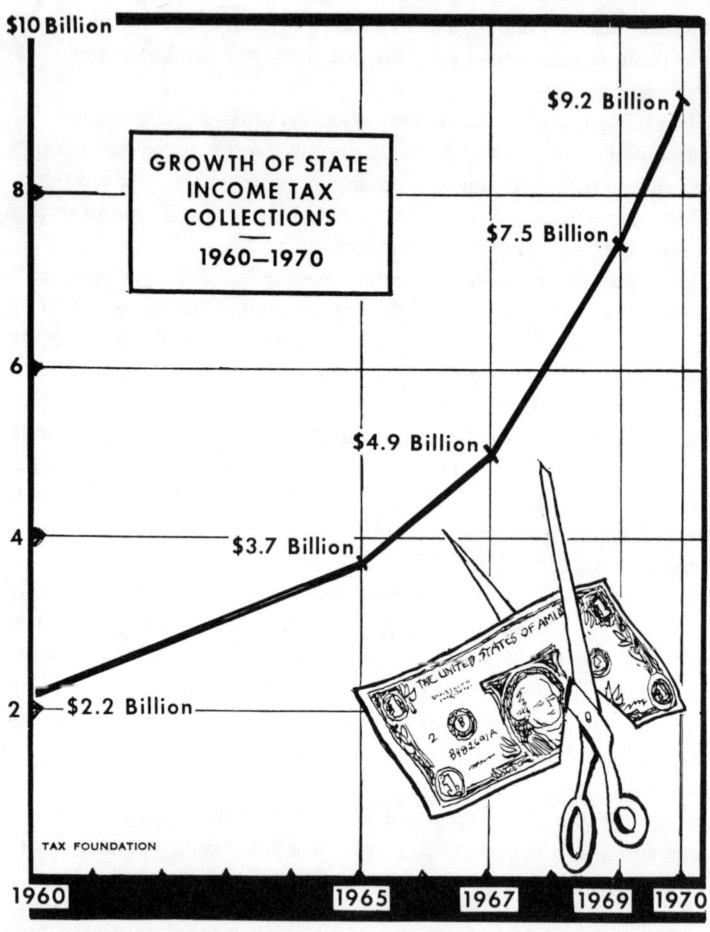

As the chart shows, state income tax yields more than quadrupled during the ten years 1960-70. State income tax rates are generally low, usually not in excess of 5 percent. They produce less than 10 percent of the federal income tax yield, but are next in importance to the sales tax as a state revenue source. More and more state income taxes are conforming to the federal rules, which facilitates the exchange of information and makes collection of state income taxes easier.

shifted but falls on the stockholders, who are the ultimate recipients of any profit a corporation makes. Actually the truth is probably somewhere in between. In part the corporate tax is probably shifted forward and in part it is probably a real burden on profits; in any case the American economy has become adjusted to having corporate profits taxed in the neighborhood of 50 percent.

Income taxes are direct taxes, in the sense they are levied on people rather than on transactions, as a sales tax is. Next in importance as direct taxes in the federal revenue structure are death and gift taxes.

Death and gift taxes.

We have seen that income taxes are the basis of the federal fiscal system in this country; other countries, France, for example, depend less heavily on income taxation than we do. Another set of taxes, of limited fiscal but substantial social significance, is imposed on transfers of wealth at death or by gift.

The federal government levies what is known as an estate tax; that is, the basis of the tax is the entire estate of a person who dies, rather than the individual shares received by his heirs. An inheritance tax, which is used by some states, is based on the share each heir receives.

The federal estate tax uses progressive rates ranging from 3 to 70 percent above a relatively high exemption, currently $60,000. In addition, a husband or wife can leave to the surviving spouse half of his or her total estate without tax. This provision, known as the marital deduction, dates from 1948; it is designed to equalize tax between residents of community property and noncommunity property states. In a community property state, primarily in the Southwest, a husband or wife is each considered to be a 50 percent owner of their combined property, even though one member may have accumulated all the wealth and may be the sole legal owner.

A progressive tax on wealth transferred at death is thought by some to be socially desirable in preventing the accumulation of large family fortunes that may enable succeeding generations to live without working. The present tax serves this purpose to some extent but can be quite easily avoided by various devices.

One such device is to will property in trust rather than outright. A person taking this route leaves his property to a trustee, such as a bank or law firm, to be used for the benefit of his children during their lifetimes and then distributed to his grandchildren. A tax is due when the donor dies and the property passes into trust; but no tax is due when the children die, since they had only a life interest in the property and not full ownership. Only when the trust dissolves and the property passes to the grandchildren will the second tax be due; one generation has been skipped tax free.

Another device used by wealthy individuals is to donate property to charitable or educational organizations or to establish foundations for philanthropic purposes. Such donations are deductions from the taxable estate and redound to the donor's credit. The Rockefeller, Carnegie, and Ford Foundations were set up partly with an eye to tax savings. If a millionaire is subject to a 50 percent estate tax rate, every $2 he leaves to charity will be $1 at the cost of his heirs and $1 at the expense of the revenue of the government. This may be regarded as a kind of cut-rate philanthropy.

The gift tax is a necessary adjunct to the estate tax designed to protect the revenue. Without the gift tax, deathbed gifts or gifts in contemplation of death could provide easy opportunities for estate tax avoidance. In the United States, federal gift tax rates are 75 percent of the corresponding estate tax rates. One reason for this discount is that the gift tax is paid earlier.

The gift tax carries both a lifetime exemption and an annual exclusion per donee. A wealthy man with 10 children could distribute a substantial amount of property to them tax free by systematic annual gifts below the exclusion, currently $3,000 per year per donee.

Gift and estate taxes were once quite controversial but seem now to have become well established as part of our tax system. Little agitation for major changes in these taxes is heard today.

Excise and sales taxes.

Among the indirect taxes used by the federal government are the excises, or taxes on specific commodities. Taxed objects include alcoholic beverages, tobacco, motor vehicles, and gasoline. The federal gasoline tax does not go into general revenue but into the highway trust fund; from here it is paid out to the states for roadbuilding. The interstate highway system is financed 90 percent from federal and 10 percent from state revenues.

The gasoline tax is based primarily on the benefit theory—the notion being that those who use the highways most should pay the largest share of their construction and maintenance. Taxing gasoline is one way to approximate this result.

Alcohol and tobacco are traditional objects of taxation; they are sometimes called sumptuary levies on the ground that the taxes serve both to raise revenue and to limit consumption of items that are harmful, or dangerous, or socially undesirable. While liquor and tobacco taxes do serve to limit consumption of these products somewhat, both products have basically inelastic demands in the eyes of consumers. Thus the taxes are largely shifted forward and in the final analysis borne by those who drink and smoke.

The federal government also has a number of other specific excise taxes on manufactured products such as phonographs and records, playing cards, and the like. These are mainly holdovers from World War II when many more excises were in force.

The United States Government has no sales tax; this is reserved by custom for use by the states.

One variant of the sales tax to which the federal government may eventually come is the "value-added" tax. This is essentially a business tax on the gross income of an enterprise. It is like a sales tax in that gross income is ordinarily derived from sales; but some sales taxes are imposed only at the retail level and do not apply to inter-business sales.

Tapping trees on a rubber plantation in Malaysia. Malaysia has a tax on exported rubber the rate of which varies with the price of rubber in world markets. Thus much of the profit from exporting rubber is taken by the government and used for general purposes or for economic development. One result of this system is that plantation owners have inadequate incentive to replant with higher yielding varieties of trees. Another result is that the budget of the Malaysian Government is highly sensitive to changes in the world economy.

A value-added tax would operate somewhat as follows. Each business firm, large or small, would report its gross income and from this would be allowed to deduct purchases from other business firms but nothing else. Therefore, the tax base would include wages and salaries, interest, and in fact all the distributive shares of income. It is contemplated that a value-added tax, if used in this country, would be levied at a low flat rate, such as 2 percent. Because the base of the value-added tax is essentially national income generated by the private sector, the revenue potential, even at a 2 percent rate, is very large.

France, the principal foreign country that makes extensive use of a value-added tax, does not use a flat rate, but a series of rates, inverse to the essentiality of the product or service. Thus bread is taxed at a low rate, while high fashion clothing takes a considerably higher rate. France uses this tax essentially as a substitute for income taxation, which has never been popular in that country. Should we come to value-added taxation here, it would probably be in addition to income taxation, rather than as a substitute for it.

Import duties.

In addition to direct taxes and the excises on specific goods, our Federal Government still taxes imports. Import duties, or tariffs or customs duties, are the oldest form of tax still in use in most countries. Historically, a new nation derives its first revenue from taxing imports, usually at low rates, but at higher rates when they become concerned about fostering manufacturing.

Import taxes at high rates are sometimes designed to be protective tariffs, i.e., not to raise revenue but to keep foreign manufactures out, so local companies can serve the home market without fear of foreign competition.

This is not the place for an extended discussion of protective tariffs. They will be taken up in the chapter on international economic relations and foreign trade policy. They have a long and varied history. Historically in this country the Republican Party has favored high tariffs and the Democratic Party somewhat lower tariffs; this division is no longer so sharp, however, since tariffs have become progressively less important in the federal revenue system.

State tax systems.

In state revenue systems, we find the sales tax to be a major instrument. In addition, most but not all states tax incomes and wealth-transfers at

RISE IN STATE SALES TAX COLLECTIONS
1950–1970

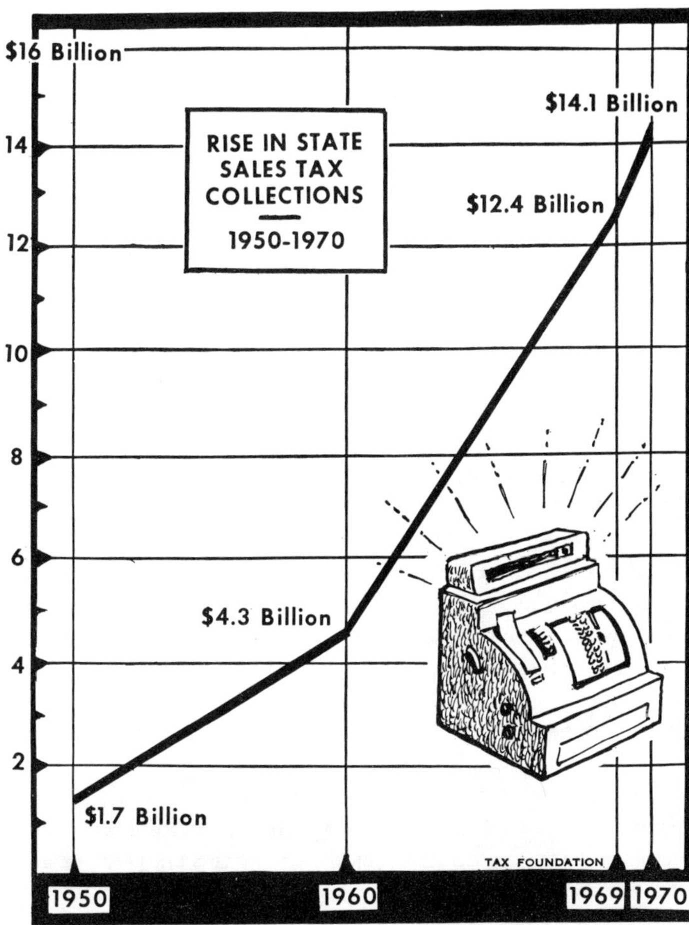

State sales tax collections have risen more than 7 fold in the 20 years between 1950 and 1970. This tax is now the bulwark of most state revenue systems. The sales tax is convenient because retail merchants do the collecting and turn the proceeds over to the states. The tax, however, is regressive in that it bears more heavily on small incomes than on larger ones, as do most flat rate taxes. In 1971 several states raised their sales taxes. Others will undoubtedly follow suit in 1972. Courtesy Tax Foundation Inc.

death. Some states still employ property taxes, on real estate and also personal property such as automobiles and household goods; but increasingly property taxation is being left to localities such as counties and cities.

The sales tax is usually levied at a flat rate such as 5 percent. Normally it applies only to sales at retail, and not at wholesale, or to materials and parts used in manufacturing. Retailers are charged with collecting the tax from consumers and remitting the proceeds to the state government.

One problem the states have with the sales tax is interstate sales, often by mail order. If you live in Ohio and buy a dress at a retail store in Ohio, the sales tax will be assessed. If you order the same dress from a mail order house in Chicago, while living in Ohio, the sales tax may or may not be assessed. The government of Ohio will be anxious to collect sales tax on all dutiable imports into the state, such as the dress in question, But, since the seller is in another state, and may have no office or place of business in Ohio, collecting the tax from the seller may be difficult. Collecting from the buyer would be even more difficult and expensive.

Thus interstate sales are a big hole and a problem in most state sales tax systems. How to resolve this problem without getting multiple collection of sales tax has yet to be determined. Two approaches to a solution are (1) a federal law that will lay down uniform jurisdictional rules the states would be obliged to follow in levying taxes on interstate commerce, and (2) a cooperative system to be based on agreement among the states, and enforcement by a body of the states' own creation. At this juncture one cannot state with certainty which system will become dominant; but some solution to the problem probably will be found before too many years have passed.

In addition to general sales and income taxes, most states have excises on certain products such as liquor, tobacco, and gasoline. They may also have franchise or capital stock taxes on corporations chartered by the state, and business license fees on real estate brokers, barbers, chiropractors, etc. In addition, many states tax motor vehicles, coupling this tax with the licensing operation. As already noted, some states still tax real estate.

A major problem with state revenue systems in recent years is that these systems have not been expansive enough for the burgeoning revenue needs of the states. Thus states have had to hunt for new revenue sources and to raise the rates on existing sources, such as the sales tax, to high and burdensome levels. In spite of tax increases, states have had to rely increasingly on grants-in-aid from the federal government, and on borrowing, to cover their fiscal deficits. Many states have constitutional limits on the size of their public debt or on the amount of borrowing they can do in a year.

One possible escape from the revenue pinch in which most states are

A vault in the Treasury Dept., Washington, D.C. Note the bags of coins below and the packages of paper currency above. One needs to distinguish between money, which is a stock, and revenue, which is a flow. If revenue sharing becomes effective, the Federal Government will return to the states and localities a portion of the tax revenue collected. Money, as shown here, is used chiefly for hand to hand payments. It is much less important than payments by check, which are far larger in amount.

caught is "revenue sharing," an idea being more and more discussed. As usually contemplated under this plan, the federal government would share some of the revenue it obtains, usually from personal income taxation, with the states on an unrestricted basis. For example, 5 percent of all income tax revenue obtained by the federal government might be paid back to the states, on the basis of the residence of the taxpayer.

In addition to relieving the states' fiscal problems, revenue sharing is normally considered to have other advantages. The plan could be devised, for example, to require all states to conform their income taxes to the definitions and methods of calculation used for the federal income tax. This would be an important simplification for taxpayers. Revenue-sharing plans also sometimes base a state's share on revenue effort, or effort the state makes to expand its own tax collections. This is to prevent a state from merely substituting federal money for money it now collects for itself or should collect.

Much more will be heard about revenue sharing in the next few years; some system for this purpose may well come into being. The Nixon administration sponsored a bill in Congress to make a token beginning on such a system; the bill has not attracted much Congressional support.

Local revenue systems.

Turning now from the states to purely local government such as cities or counties, we find that these governments, like the states, have been extremely hard pressed to finance their needs. Traditionally local government has depended primarily on the property tax on real estate to finance the bulk of its needs. Increasingly, however, local governments are turning to sales, use, and income taxes to supplement property tax revenue.

The property tax is not easy to administer. It requires a complete register of property and who owns it; it depends on periodic assessments to keep valuations uniform and up to date; normally it incorporates an appeals procedure for those who consider their assessments unfair or too high; appeals are time consuming and never wholly satisfactory.

Property tax rates are normally set by comparing the budget of a local government with the total assessed value of property; thus the rate may work out to 2.3 percent of assessed valuation; it is subject to change every year as costs increase and more and more property comes on the tax rolls. Generally property tax rates, like other rates, have been creeping upward. Sometimes the creep has seemed to the harassed taxpayer more like a gallop.

If a locality turns to sales taxation, it usually finds even greater difficulty than states do in reaching imports with its tax. It is quite easy to go outside the city to shop and to avoid the tax on mail order purchases. If a city turns to income taxation, it must either set up its own enforcement and collection machinery, a difficult and expensive process, or piggy back the state income tax. The latter course is normally followed.

You can see from the preceding pages that there are a limited number of taxes governments find it expedient to use to raise the revenues they need. In earlier times there were many more excises, on such items as carriages, windows in the home, tea, stamps to be affixed to such documents as checks, mortgages, and notes. These would all be inadequate to today's larger revenue needs; the emphasis today is on broad-based taxes, such as income, sales, or value-added taxes. These broad-based taxes make taxpayers of everybody, allowing no one to escape.

The old saying that nothing in life is certain except death and taxes might be rephrased to read: it is virtually certain that in the course of time taxes will increase. The reason is simply that the public demands more and more public services, and these are necessarily more costly in an urban society. When people live on farms, there is no problem of garbage disposal; it is simply fed to the hogs. In an urban society the waste must be collected and hauled to a central point, treated by chemical or other means, certain items salvaged for re-cycling, and the remainder finally buried or otherwise disposed of. Talk to the mayor of any town. He will tell you his greatest problem is refuse and what to do with it.

Similarly most other public services—police protection, welfare, roads, sewer and water facilities, grow geometrically in cost as we shift from a rural to an urban society. For this reason alone, the cost of government increases. Reflect further that in 1900 we had no social security, no unemployment insurance, no highway patrols, virtually no public hospitals, and you realize how the demand for public services is constantly growing. Even the staunchest conservatives know that, realistically, they can turn the clock back only a few moments.

Big government and meddlesome government are here to stay. They are likely to become more rather than less pervasive; more rather than less involved with the ordinary citizen who must pay for them. Much as he may groan at the payment, he would groan even more at the absence of government services he has come to expect.

Public borrowing.

The only alternative to taxes for financing government is borrowing—an expedient resorted to by all governments at some time. Governments borrow by selling securities to the public, such as notes, bonds, and treasury bills. If government securities are not bought by the public out of savings, but by the banks out of credit expansion, government finance may be an important engine of inflation. In fact, most of the hyperinflations the world has experienced, such as the German inflation of 1923, or the Greek inflation following World War II, have occurred because the tax collection process was inadequate or had broken down, forcing the government to resort to credit creation, or the actual expedient of printing paper currency to finance its operations. In the United States over the past several decades, we have had relatively few years in which the budget of the United States Government has not been somewhat in deficit. Thus, our public debt has gradually risen.

Public debt is a basic item in the financial structure of a well-developed country such as the United States. In certain periods before the Civil War we had no public debt; the country was on a pay-as-we-went basis, despite its lack of income taxes and dependence on import duties and some excises for revenue; however, services and hence costs of government were much lower in those days.

As already noted, this country first used an income tax during the Civil War. This tax continued into the 1870's when it was ruled unconstitutional by the Supreme Court. Basic to the decision was the fact that the income tax was a direct tax, and a clause in the Constitution said that direct taxes must be levied in accordance with population. A poll tax would have filled this bill; but an income tax did not.

It was only after the Constitution was amended, specifically to permit income taxation, that the tax was reimposed in 1913. We have had it in continuous operation since that time—for nearly 60 years. It is unlikely to disappear any time soon. You may as well learn to live with it.

When in 1819 the Supreme Court declared that the power to tax is the power to destroy (McCulloch vs. Maryland), they so stated in denying the power of the State of Maryland to tax a branch of the Bank of the United States. To permit such a tax, the Court said, would be to deny the supremacy of the federal power over that of the states. The point is an important one because taxation is one of the inherent prerogatives of sovereignty. Whoever exercises sovereignty in fact possesses the power to tax, which is essential to maintenance of that sovereignty.

Likewise the debt of a government to one who holds its securities in good faith is above and beyond any temporary political differences. The British Government, during the American Revolution, regularly paid George Washington interest on the British bonds he owned, despite the fact that he was officially a traitor in the eyes of the British Government.

As John Locke long ago affirmed, and Jefferson reaffirmed in the Declaration of Independence, governments are instituted among men with the consent of the governed. This consent, however, need not extend to specific acts of the government, such as the levying of a particular tax. Citizens have repeatedly sought to express their disapproval of certain acts of government by refusing to pay taxes for that purpose. In our own time, for example, those who disapprove of the war in Vietnam have sought to withhold from their tax payments some percentage which they calculate is used to defray the cost of this war. Such protests have uniformly failed. It is a well-settled principle of law that taxes shall be uniform among people similarly situated. None can escape—including an anarchist who, disbelieving in any government, gives no consent to any of its acts. Taxes are truly compulsory levies. You cannot escape them; but you can learn to live with them as well as possible—to know and take advantage of their intricacies, to arrange your affairs so the tax impact on them will be minimal.

Today we have a large industry—accountants, attorneys, and advisers, whose main business is to advise people and corporations how to minimize their taxes. This profession has been steadily growing and bids fair to continue to grow as taxes become more and more complex and burdensome.

If the power to tax is the power to destroy, it is also the power to create new public programs: for the aged, for the preservation of the environment, for the alleviation of poverty, and for other purposes we cannot yet envision.

Chapter **13**

TO WHOM SHALL BE GIVEN—Distribution of Income

In 1859, on the eve of the American Civil War, Karl Marx, concerned with the philosophy of revolution and discontent, wrote that political economy is the study of the anatomy of society. As Marx saw it, men entered into a social relationship for production, but as production increased, this social relationship became increasingly hampered and inappropriate. To change the social relationship would require a political revolution in which the old structure based on property relations would give way to a new one.

Laboring for years in the British Museum, while his family suffered privation, Marx was a profound and original student of economic literature. He saw in economic writings what other students did not see, and what the writers themselves probably had not intended. Where others saw harmony, he saw discord; where they saw stability, he saw upheaval; where they saw justice, he saw injustice.

Whether Marx the student and interpreter was right or wrong is basically irrelevant. History has judged him to have been at least 87 percent wrong. What is important is what Marx considered the central problem of economics, namely that the system did not properly distribute the results of production to those who had contributed to it.

In his concern with distribution Marx was a classical economist, although the answers he found were anticlassical. By insisting that the distribution of income and wealth is the core of the economic process, he was formally consistent with other economists of his time. Today, economists see the distribution of income as merely one aspect of the pricing process which governs allocation of resources in the private sector of the economy.

We have seen in an earlier chapter that the pricing process is a mechanism for determing what shall be produced and in what quantities. It also operates to determine what incomes people will derive from their participation in the production process. It is this latter aspect to the price system that concerns us here.

There are two significant aspects to income distribution. The first, called the functional distribution of income, is the process in which payments to the factors of production are determined. The second, called the size distribution of income, is concerned primarily with inequality of incomes among people and families, with the measurement of this inequality, and with social policies to change this inequality, usually by reducing it somewhat.

This latter aspect of income distribution belongs in the area of normative or welfare economics. Functional distribution, on the other hand, is a part of the analytical sector of economics, more particularly a part of value and distribution analysis, or the study of the price system in action. To this subject of functional distribution of income let us now turn our attention.

Functional distribution of income.

The distribution of income is a price process in which factors of production (land, labor, capital, and entrepreneurship) and the owners of these factors are compensated for their contributions to the productive process. The compensation may be fair or unfair, niggardly or generous. Our concern is not with the ethics of the income distribution process, but with its mechanics, the way it actually works. Although it is primarily a pricing process, there are some limitations on the freedom of this pricing process. Minimum wage legislation, for example, is one such limitation.

For a small individual business, the prices it must pay to hire factors of production are market determined and largely outside its own control. To attract and hold labor it must offer at least prevailing wage rates for the area and the industry. If the labor the firm needs is organized, a contract with the union has to be negotiated.

The cost of labor to the employer will be more than simply the wages paid. It will include the employer's contribution to social security, any amenities furnished the labor force such as cafeterias, washrooms, and lockers, and any other fringe benefits that may be covered in the union contract or provided voluntarily as a contribution to employee efficiency and morale.

By land as a factor of production, we mean chiefly space and location. A farmer is concerned with the fertility of the soil, with the water supply, and the climate; but for a plant or business site the concern is merely for adequate space and for an advantageous location with respect to transport and markets. In another place I have mentioned some of the factors that determine whether a location will be advantageous for a particular business purpose, and how important this can be to the success of the business.

Business premises may be either leased or rented. Merchants commonly lease their stores, as do professional men their offices. A manufacturer, needing special facilities, will often own the land on which his plant is situated. In many businesses, owning or renting land is an option, a choice to be made.

Land values and rents are determined primarily by the pressure of population and by location in relation to past and future growth patterns. Land

A contrast in land values. Land in Manhattan (upper photo) is extremely valuable, in some cases as much as $100 per sq. ft. Land in Montana (lower photo) on the other hand is worth relatively little, in some cases as little as $100 per acre. The difference in value is of course attributable to location. The only way to use land in Manhattan more intensively is to build taller buildings. The land in Montana, being remote, is useful only for farming or grazing.

on Fifth Avenue at 50th Street in New York City is extremely valuable and is sold by the square foot, because it is in the commercial heart of our largest city. Land in northern Nevada is cheap and is sold by the acre because it is near nothing, except perhaps nuclear test sites.

Land is unique among the factors of production in that its supply is virtually fixed. We do fill an occasional ravine and perhaps reclaim a marsh from the sea; but we cannot make more Fifth Avenue; we can merely make more intensive use of what is already there, as, for example, by building taller buildings.

Land values and rents therefore reflect primarily scarcity value. As population increases, land values in the direction of population advance inevitably increase also. This is why land, historically, has been a good investment and still is, provided one properly anticipates the geographic pattern of growth.

Undeveloped land is one thing; fully developed land is quite a different and more valuable thing. To be fully developed for nonagricultural purposes, land requires a large investment in what is sometimes pretentiously called infrastructure–in streets and other transport systems, in water and sewage disposal systems, in power and gas, and finally in buildings. This capital invested in land is partly privately and partly publicly financed, *i.e.*, local government supplies the streets, utility companies the gas and electricity, and private capital the buildings.

To operate a business requires, besides land, capital which must also be compensated. This capital will consist both of equity capital, the investment of the proprietor or the stockholders, and borrowed capital or debt, represented perhaps by bonds or notes. In general, the reward of borrowed capital is interest; that of equity capital is dividends and profit; a proprietor may also compensate himself in wages of management, *i.e.*, payment for the services he performs for the business in addition to the capital he provides.

Interest rates are market determined, and determined in a market which is highly developed and interrelated. A small businessman in a small town may have no place to borrow except his local bank; but a large national corporation has many options. It may borrow from banks, or insurance companies, or sell commercial paper (its own notes) or perhaps float a bond issue using the services of an investment banking syndicate.

The cost of these various options will depend on how well the company is established and how good its prospects are; also on how long the loan will run, and on the current condition of the capital market, whether it is easy or tight.

Normally, there is considerable competition for loan capital; lenders are able to choose those situations that promise the least risk and the greatest reward. Financial capital grows out of savings, which at any given time may be more or less adequate to the prevailing demand. Thus the cost of capital fluctuates.

Equity capital is generally more expensive than loan capital because it bears a higher risk. The supplier of equity capital is not a debtor but an owner; his security fluctuates with the ups and downs of the business. If it costs 6 percent to borrow money on a bond issue, the comparable cost of equity capital may be 8 or even 10 percent, depending on how the risk is assessed by potential capital suppliers.

Annual meeting of a corporation. This meeting, open to all stockholders, is the occasion for electing officers and directors as well as reviewing events of the past year and prospects for the future. Stockholders who are unable to attend in person may send in their proxies to be voted by management or some other group. Voting is by number of shares held, either outright or by proxy. Between annual meetings the affairs of the corporation are handled by the management and the board of directors. The man standing in this photo is collecting proxies.

Once financial capital is raised, by either the debt or equity method, it must be invested in equipment essential for the business: in machinery, motor trucks, stocks of materials, buildings, and whatever else may be needed. Some capital must be kept in money, to pay wages and other purchases, to carry work in process, and to meet other needs before income from sales is actually realized. These liquid funds are the working capital necessary to support a growing operation.

Working capital can also be borrowed for short terms from banks and other institutions with the expectation that payment will not be long delayed. A merchant, for example, borrows from a bank to stock his store with a new fall line; he expects to repay the bank with proceeds from the sale of this merchandise.

Finally, we come to profit, that distributive share which claims all that is left over after the other factors of production have been compensated in accordance with their contractual terms. Profit can often be zero or negative, if miscalculations have been made or expectations are unfulfilled. Basically, profit is a payment for accepting risk and uncertainty, for organizing the production process, for anticipating wants, and providing for their fulfillment. These are the functions of entrepreneurship.

Because profit is an uncertain distributive share, it fluctuates more than the other shares do. In an expanding and rising market profit will increase faster than wages, or interest rates. In a declining market profit will fall faster.

The entrepreneur is largely oriented toward growth and toward new products and processes. His reward depends heavily on how good an innovator he is, and how well he anticipates future trends. To increase inventory heavily just at the beginning of a boom may be a smart move; to do so at the beginning of a recession may be to court disaster.

Profit is thus a payment for foresight and goes largely to those who correctly sense the future. Obviously, in business it is better to be right, perhaps for the wrong reasons, than to be wrong for the right reasons.

Wage theory.

Wage rates are determined by supply and demand, by the productivity of workers and by their relative scarcity. We have seen that a prudent employer hires workers up to the point where the marginal value product of labor is equal to the marginal cost of employment, for this is the condition consistent with profit maximization.

The demand for labor, in a local labor market area such as Indianapolis, Indiana, is made up of the separate demands of all the employers in the area, who together may need 80,000 workers with a particular array of skills and aptitudes. There may be only 70,000 potential workers in the area, so the balance may have to be drawn from outside this particular labor market area, *i.e.*, from small towns and the countryside within commuting distance of Indianapolis.

One function served by the local labor market is to match available skills with the demand for them. If there is a shortage of, say, toolmakers, the employers may have to reach out to other areas or possibly organize a training course for toolmakers whose graduates will supply their need.

Local labor markets are essentially unstructured, although governments may provide some assistance in getting employers and employees together. The United States Employment Service, for example, operates local offices which function both to find jobs and to distribute unemployment insurance payments when jobs are not available. The Labor Department also partially supports many retraining programs. In Massachusetts, for example, many textile workers were left jobless when the mills in which they had been employed moved South; workers with the proper aptitudes received training in electronics, a growing trade in the area. Thus a potentially serious unemployment problem was averted.

If unions are strong in a local labor market, they will undertake to supply employers with the workers they need, all good union members, naturally. The union may also operate an apprenticeship training program. Trades such as bricklaying, plumbing, and steamfitting are still entered largely through training programs conducted by or under the control of local unions.

To fill jobs in the higher skill categories—top secretaries, engineers, foremen, and production managers—employers may search quite a broad area for suitable candidates, often advertising in general or trade media, and carefully screening the candidates who respond. Bargaining over wages, working conditions, and perquisites is largely an individual matter in these cases. The employer is concerned to hire within his established wage structure, but to obtain the best qualified candidate he can consistent with that structure. For an especially desirable candidate he may stretch his wage structure, or provide inducements in the form of moving allowances, company cars, or other perquisites.

In the chapter on organized labor, the collective bargaining process will be discussed, in which wages are set for all the workers represented by a given union, such as the United Auto Workers. This bargaining process is becoming steadily more formal and broader in coverage as more and more fringe benefits are included in the negotiable package.

The old system in which the individual worker asked for a raise and was either given it or not is steadily being replaced by more standardized structures such as annual salary reviews, rating systems which carry automatic wage increases, and the like. These steps are obvious ones as businesses grow larger, employing more and more workers. Informal wage determination is still the rule, however, in small businesses.

Worker productivity is an extremely important factor in wage determination. The old saw about paying a worker what he is worth is testimony to the importance of productivity. Some years ago, in the 1920's, for example, there was a substantial move toward putting wages on a piecework basis, *i.e.*, so much per shirt sewn in a shirt factory, or per ton of coal mined in a mine.

This system is still to be found in some factory operations. One of its disadvantages is that it encourages quick and sloppy work and is therefore not too suitable for a precision operation such as assembling electronic components. Piecework produces too many television tubes that don't operate or cameras that are not lightproof.

Whether wages are on a piecework basis or an hourly, weekly, monthly, or annual basis, they reflect the relative scarcity of the skills being employed, and the value of these skills to the business. Common labor is paid poorly because no special skills are required—merely a strong back. Nuclear physicists and physicians are paid well because a long, expensive training period is required to become proficient in these arts, and because the supply of well-trained and experienced people is not large. Most wage differentials can be explained in these terms of relative scarcity and specific productivity.

A tobacco auction in North Carolina. The crop is grown mainly by small farmers and sold chiefly to large companies that manufacture cigarettes, pipe tobacco, etc. The leaf varies in quality and in characteristics and hence is sold by lot at auction for blending with other imported and domestic leaf. The auction method of selling is a good one in this case because it disposes of the entire crop that farmers wish to sell. It also relieves them of bargaining individually with the tobacco companies.

Since wage rates are market determined, they fluctuate, although perhaps not so rapidly as would be consistent with maximum economic efficiency. Should there be a surplus of bricklayers in a particular area, some of them would be unemployed; employers will feel safe in reducing wage rates, knowing there is a surplus in this trade. Some bricklayers may migrate to other areas where work is more plentiful and wages are higher. Migration, however, is a big step involving moving, finding new housing, changing schools and many other family adjustments. Workers will not relocate unless they think employment prospects in their present locale will remain poor for some time, or are enough better elsewhere to offset the time, trouble, and expense of moving.

Labor mobility, in a word, is neither swift nor complete. There are coal miners living in West Virginia, for example, who know the mines are unlikely to reopen, yet are unwilling or unable to seek work elsewhere. To the extent that labor mobility does operate, it tends to equalize wages geographically within a given skill group. If mobility for any reason does not operate, geographic wage differentials will persist.

Manufacturing television sets in the Netherlands. The productivity of workers in this plant is high, enabling good wages to be paid and yet the finished product sold at competitive prices. Note that the work is chiefly detailed hand assembly with virtually no automated machinery. Note also that the plant is clean and well lighted. Each worker has a rack of parts at hand which he assembles on the chassis before him.

The largest wage differentials are attributable to differences in skill and training, which determine the supply of workers qualified for a particular task. Studies that have been made of the earnings potential attributable to various forms of training show that specialized training is usually an extremely good investment.

You may wonder, for example, whether going to college is a good idea. The cost is heavy, usually upwards of $10,000, to which should be added the loss of possible earnings, which we might put, for purposes of illustration, at $20,000. Thus going to college involves a capital cost of $30,000.

Suppose your working life is 30 years. As a college graduate your annual earnings will be far in excess of $1,000 per year more than if you had not attended college. Most studies indicate the rate of return on an investment in college is at least 10 percent or $3,000 per year, if not more. Very few investments consistently yield annual returns in excess of ten percent. Education is apparently one that does.

If you remember the distribution of national income by type of income which was given in an earlier chapter, you know that compensation of employees is some 70 percent of total national income. It is thus by far the largest of the distributive shares, in part because the number of salaried workers is greater than the number of landlords or recipients of dividends and interest. For most of us, our wages or salary *are* our income. Although we may receive small amounts of other distributive shares, such as interest on a savings and loan account, what we earn from labor is most of what we receive.

In general, it is clear that the productive worker earns more than the unproductive one; the trained more than the untrained; the highly educated more than the less highly educated; the skilled more than the unskilled. As our economy becomes more and more technologically oriented (and this trend seems a constant and irreversible one), it is clear that skill and competence will be more and more in demand and will command high earnings. Lack of skill and lack of fundamental education, on the other hand, will continue to be in oversupply and to command only low earnings.

Of all the possible types of capital investment, investment in human beings, in their education and training, is perhaps the most productive of all, both for the individual and for the society in which he lives.

Theory of interest.

As the distributive share accruing to capital, interest has been explained in numerous ways. To some, it is the reward for saving; to others, a payment for parting with liquidity; to still others, a reward for waiting; to some, simply a market price for money, like any other market price.

All of these explanations have their relevance. Obviously, someone must save in order to accumulate capital; and capital in one sense is merely accumulated past saving. But saving is not all, because people must be ready to part with capital at the proper moment to take advantage of future options that may arise. Waiting and saving are closely related because a saver waits for future satisfaction instead of consuming now.

Interest rates are determined in money and capital markets, which are highly organized and interconnected. By convention we refer to short-term loans, normally one year or less, as being negotiated in the money market, and to long-term loans and equity investments as clearing through the capital markets. In reality, the two markets are not actually distinct but merge into one another, with many of the same institutions being participants in both.

Frequent reference is made to the structure of interest rates, because rates are obviously not all the same. The principal factor causing one interest rate to be higher than another is risk; one borrower is required to pay 8 percent while another is charged only 6 percent because the risk in the first loan is judged to be greater than in the second. By the same token, long-term loans bear higher rates than short-term loans on equally good security because uncertainty is greater in a 5-year loan than in one for only 90 days. Lenders establish the structure of interest rates because they have the option of making this loan and refusing that one, and because they are sensitive to ways in which money may be employed, and also to the factors

Workers at a credit union in their plant. Such credit unions are formed to encourage thrift among workers and to make loans at reasonable interest rates for buying a car, appliances, or other purposes. Credit unions serve a purpose where workers are unfamiliar with banks and are forced to borrow from finance companies or loan sharks. Credit unions are cooperatives, just as savings and loan associations and mutual savings banks are.

that determine whether money is easy or tight.

In the structure of interest rates prevailing at any given time, the base or lowest rate is that prevailing on 91-day Treasury bills, which are obligations of the United States Government. These bills are sold weekly on an autction basis; their yield is extremely sensitive to monetary policy, rising when this policy is tight and falling when it is loose.

Rates on other United States Government securities scale upward from this bill rate. Rates for private borrowing command quite well-standardized premiums over the rate for government borrowing of the same maturity.

Securities which are obligations of states and municipalities command a low rate because the interest on them is exempt from federal income tax, making these securities peculiarly attractive to individuals with large incomes and high marginal tax rates. To a person subject to a 50 percent tax rate, a five percent municipal bond is the equivalent of a 10 percent taxable bond.

The interest rates least sensitive to market forces are those where the borrower has the fewest alternatives, such as small loans and installment accounts. Even in times when credit is abundant, these rates are high, in part because the risk is high and because a substantial administrative cost is involved in servicing small loans.

Theory of rent.

In contemporary economics this subject is not felt worthy of much attention; but in classical economics of the early 19th century, rent theory was considered part of the basic core of economic analysis. David Ricardo, a stockbroker who made a fortune at an early age and then retired to become a serious student of economics, read in a letter from Malthus that political economy should be defined as an inquiry into the nature and causes of wealth. To this, Ricardo was moved to reply that, "it should rather be called an inquiry into the laws which determine the division of the produce of industry among the classes that concur in its formation."

To Ricardo distribution was important; he was especially concerned to elucidate how the rent of land was determined. His explanation, the Ricardian theory of rent, was for many years a cornerstone of classical distribution theory. Remember that this theory was developed in 1817, when England was the principal industrial society, and the United States still almost exclusively an agricultural nation.

Ricardo's theory of rent explained differential rents commanded by different pieces of land as attributable to differences in fertility and location. Clearly some land is more valuable than other land because it is more productive for agricultural purposes or better situated for industrial, commercial, or residential purposes.

Ricardo, however, endeavored to go farther than merely explaining differential rent. He saw all rent as a kind of surplus, attributable to the pressure of population, and not to any contribution of land to the value of production. He was led to this rather odd conclusion because he held a cost-of-production theory of value, in which labor and capital were thought to be remunerated in accordance with their costs of reproduction. As land could not be increased, it had no cost of reproduction and hence no intrinsic value.

Since present-day economics no longer believes in a cost-of-production theory of value, this part of Ricardian rent theory has become obsolete. It is interesting, nevertheless, than in 150 years we have been unable to improve substantially on the Ricardian explanation of differential rent.

Ricardo's theory that rent was not a cost of production was, in its day, a strong blow against the British landowning aristocracy in favor of the rising industrial class. It grew out of intense involvement with the political and social issues of the day. As always, developments in economic thought have occurred primarily because people thought deeply about the issues of their time and attempted to analyze them.

Techniques of analysis have often survived the problems that led to their development. This is one reason for the penetrating remark of Lord Keynes that businessmen are generally the intellectual slaves of some defunct economist.

Theory of profit.

Profit is the return to entrepreneurship, or the reward for accepting risk and uncertainty. How well a businessman anticipates future developments will largely determine whether or not he realizes profit. Monopoly situations, featuring a high degree of control over a given market, may also be a source of profit; but such profits are constantly threatened by potential competition.

Classical economists saw profit less as a distributive share in the aggregate than as a distribution of rewards among successful and unsuccessful businessmen. While not denying that some businessmen would always make profits, the classicists thought these profits were largely balanced by the losses sustained by other businessmen.

In a stationary state, which was an economic condition characterized by no growth and an unchanging general price level, such economists as John Stuart Mill hypothesized (in 1848) that aggregate profits would be zero. Of course, the stationary state was not a real economic condition but a philosophical abstraction; the fact that profits existed was proof that economic life actually had some dynamic elements and was not really in a stationary state.

Those economists who held to a labor theory of value, as did Adam Smith for example, saw profit as something produced by workers but somehow appropriated from them. The so-called scientific socialists, and particularly Karl Marx, thought that profit represented part of the surplus value produced by labor and extracted from labor by the exploitative owners of the means of production. This kind of thinking antedated the marginal productivity theory of distribution, and rested on a cruder notion sometimes described as labor's right to the whole product of its employment.

Today we see this doctrine to be a crude kind of fallacy, not worthy of serious intellectual attention. Labor does not create the whole social product; this is done by all the factors of production, appropriately combined and directed. Consequently, labor is not entitled to the whole product but merely to the largest portion thereof; its claim is on a par with that of owners of all other productive factors.

Characteristic of Marxian economics also was a principle labeled that of the constantly falling rate of profit, which would pave the way for the destruction of capitalism and its replacement by the socialist or communist form of organization. According to the Marxists, profits would fall because the workers would resist exploitation and because the capitalists themselves would compete through lower prices and increased output.

The Marxian theory of the falling rate of profit was less a principle based on extensive observation than a slogan of social dynamics, which its perpetrators hoped to use to hasten the end to which they were committed, namely the replacement of capitalism by the system of economic organization they wanted.

As is well known, Marxism took over in Russia in the revolution of 1917. Its practical development as a system of organization in the 50 odd years since that time has been far from consistent with classical Marxian precepts, being much more centralized, authoritarian, and capitalist in spirit than classical Marxism envisioned.

In countries that have remained capitalist, the falling rate of profit has hardly appeared as an inevitable tendency.

Profit in the sense here being discussed naturally excludes wages of management, or payment for the services performed by the entrepreneur or owner of the means of production. In the modern corporation, management is essentially performed by a professional class, basically divorced from ownership, but compensated by salaries plus bonuses and perhaps stock ownership through options. Profit as such accrues to the stockholders but obviously includes an element of interest on equity capital provided by the stockholders.

In the small proprietorship, on the other hand, where one family contributes all the capital and also the management, the distinction between interest, management compensation, and profit is not clear-cut, since all accrue to basically the same people.

In economics, profit is an elusive thing, constantly sought after but not always found. The search for profit is a leading element of dynamism in the private enterprise system—it causes adjustments to be made that direct the use of economic resources into the most lucrative channels. Without profit and its private appropriation, the economy would be sluggish in its response to basic changes in conditions or consumer tastes.

One problem with the state-directed economics of socialist countries is that they overproduce item A while underproducing item B; in the absence of a free price and profit system, signals of this over and underproduction are not necessarily received at central planning headquarters. In the private enterprise economy, item A would quickly become unprofitable.

What this chapter has presented is naturally the merest skeletal indication of the theory of distribution and of the actual pricing process that controls it. There is much more to the process than this. Among the frictions and interferences in the processes of pricing factors of production are minimum wage legislation and standards, conventional interest rate differentials between large and small loans, conventional leasing techniques, and tax saving methods of management compensation. These are institutional aspects of the process of distribution and income determination. To describe them fully would take much space and would also be of limited permanent value, because they are constantly evolving and changing.

Likewise, size distribution of income will be discussed in another place, where we are examining the causes and consequences of income inequality and whether social policy should aim at reducing that inequality.

The thing above all to remember about value and distribution in economics is that the same pricing process that determines the relative prices or exchange values of goods and services also determines who will receive what incomes from participation in the production process. Pricing goods and distributing incomes are opposite sides of a coin, codetermined as it were, rather than being independent, unrelated processes. Incomes arise from participation in production; in this process the whole product is exhausted in the sense of becoming someone's income.

In 1866, Proudhon, a French philosophic anarchist best remembered for his remark "property is theft," wrote that property may be said no longer to exist when agriculture and industry are carried on by numerous small producers. In this condition of "social mutualism," the state would disappear. Proudhon's view of economics was a peculiar one. He saw economic development going backward not forward. What he failed to see was that the pricing process governs the distribution of income.

Chapter 14

WORTHY OF HIS HIRE—Labor Problems and Labor History

In 1755 Richard Cantillon, considered by many the best systematic economist before Adam Smith, wrote that the value of labor is found in the amount of land needed to support the worker's sustenance, plus an equal amount for the rearing of two children up to the age at which they can work. Two children were specified because in the 18th century half the children born died before age 17.

Cantillon's remarks were an early statement of the subsistence theory or iron law of wages. For the next 100 years or more, economists generally believed the doctrine that wages could not for long rise above a minimum subsistence level. This was one of the gloomy forecasts that helped make economics the "dismal science."

History has disproved the subsistence theory, but labor's struggle to win higher wages has nevertheless been a long and bitter one. Let us notice a few landmarks in this struggle.

To work, to put forth effort, whether it be physical or mental, skilled or unskilled, is what makes the economy go. Too often it has been assumed that people work only for money. The economic man, that oversimplified stereotype, has been portrayed as calculating very coldly whether an extra hour is balanced by an extra few dollars or not. In fact we all know, not excluding even the economists who constructed the stereotype, that motivations to work are much more complex than this.

Most of us work, of course, in order to live; but we hope at least for a little more than this. The Bible tells us that man does not live by bread alone, but for other satisfactions, psychic as well as economic. In the gloomy days of Malthus and threatened overpopulation, much was heard about the iron law of wages, which held that wages could never rise much above the level of bare subsistence, because, if they did, population would increase and drive wages down again because too many workers would be seeking employment.

The iron law of wages was a convenient rationalization for the owners of the first factories in the industrial revolution, where wages were virtually a pittance and working conditions atrocious. Perhaps in urban ghettos the iron law can still be observed at work; today, though, the trouble is a lack of skill in an economy that is steadily becoming more technological, where the demand is no longer for strong backs but for skilled hands and more skillful minds.

Motivation for work.

If men worked only for money, it would be hard to explain those business executives who put in long hours of intense effort when their marginal income tax rate is 60 or 70 percent; when they have only a minority interest in additional income. Yet toil they do. They are motivated more by power than by dollars. To be head of a giant corporation, to give orders to thousands of workers, to confront and defeat rivals in business competition, these are the motivations that drive them.

Many workers derive inner satisfaction from a job well done. This is particularly true of craftsmen, who shape materials with their hands, and who see a finished product emerge that is useful and functional and hence beautiful. It is also true of a bookkeeper who derives satisfaction from a neatly ruled ledger, a trial balance with no errors, and a bank statement that reconciles on the first try. In our mass production economy, however, craftsmen and others who actually complete a job are fast disappearing. The average factory workman does not finish a job; he merely fastens on a fender or installs a sub-assembly before passing the uncompleted product on to the next station in the assembly line.

Samuel Gompers, 1850-1924. The cigarmaker who founded the American Federation of Labor. He was also instrumental in establishing the International Labor Organization. An advocate of business unionism or not getting involved in partisan politics.

For some people, work is a creative experience because it means solving problems, developing new concepts, or keeping a machine or an organization running smoothly. The engineer, the computer programmer, the professional manager may derive this kind of satisfaction as well as money from their efforts.

We can hardly discuss motivation for work without also discussing compensation systems; these are designed both to motivate people and to reward effort. One thing clear about business compensation systems is that payment is largely for responsibility. The president of a company is paid more than his chief engineer not because he works harder or has more skill or ability, but merely because he bears a higher responsibility for the success or failure of the organization. He is judged by the results not of his own efforts, but of the efforts of all who come under his control. Those who bear less responsibility are judged by narrower standards and are less well compensated.

Most of you will spend a good share of your lives working, either because you must, or because you want to make some use of your training, or merely because you would like more money than you can have by not working. Even some people who are independently wealthy and could live without working often prefer to have an occupation, to be useful, to be a part of the world. Diplomacy, the arts, philanthropy provide outlets for such feelings.

People, then, do not work just for money. They are driven by a variety of motives, such as power, service, and influence, of which money is only one, and often not the most powerful. Thorstein Veblen, a rather unconventional economist of some years ago, wrote a book about the instinct of workmanship, in which he described this "instinct" in its various manifestations. Veblen was objecting to the stereotype of the economic man, who was no more true to life in Veblen's day than he is in our own.

Psychologists and psychiatrists tell us that human motivations are always complex; we are all a mixture of loves and hates, of desires and repressions, of wishes fulfilled and unfulfilled. Since work is a part of life, and a large part, amounting to one-third or more of our adult existence, it is clear that motivations to work are complex also.

Under the feudal system of the Middle Ages life was much simpler. One was born to a certain station in life and that determined one's occupation and one's life pattern. If your father was a tanner, you would be a tanner too, marry a tanner's daughter from a neighboring village, and raise a crop of third generation tanners.

The rise of the capitalist system with its emphasis on change, on the growth of factories, and on urbanization, put an end to the feudal system of status and tradition. Under capitalism the emphasis was on social mobility, on rising as far as one could by one's own efforts.

You are too young to remember the dime novels of Horatio Alger, but your fathers and grandfathers had their exposure to this literary fare. The theme was always the same. A poor boy, by extraordinary effort, saving and sacrifice, ultimately becomes head of a big business, rich, famous and respected, and all because of his own efforts and a little bit of luck, usually in the form of a wealthy patron whose fancy he strikes. In these novels motivations to work and succeed were simplistic.

Today's motivations to work are probably more complex than ever; we are told that today's generation is more idealistic and less materialistic than earlier generations. In part this viewpoint is a function of age. Voltaire wrote that if a young man was not radical, something was wrong with his heart; if an old man was not conservative, something was wrong with his head. Voltaire's rather cynical proverb may or may not be apt today; it is, however, typical of many viewpoints both past and present. A person does not continue to grow in life without work that is challenging, stimulating, and rewarding—whether the rewards be monetary, or the approval of his fellow men.

Some wise men have said that, if one pursues money as a sole objective, he will probably not attain it; but if one pursues a worthwhile objective with the sole intent of excelling in it beyond all others, the money will probably come as a by-product. This is a thought to ponder.

The workingman—organized or not?

Those of you who work for a living—as an employee of some business or organization, which most of us are—will be concerned during your working career with many things; to mention a few, your wages or salary, your opportunities for promotion and advancement, your working conditions, your fringe benefits in the form of pension plans, vacations, insurance, and even parking facilities. These terms and conditions of employment will be determined by negotiation between you and your employer, either individual negotiation, in which you are the only employee covered, or collective bargaining, if you are a member of a labor union that bargains on behalf of all the employees in a plant or company.

If you remain an employee for long, the chances are good you will have to decide whether or not to join a labor union. It is estimated that some 24 percent of all employees today are union members. Union membership today extends far beyond blue collar workers to include clerks, secretaries, and even executives.

If you become a professional worker you will probably belong to a professional association such as the American Bar Association or the American Medical Association. While not strictly trade unions, since many of the members are self-employed in independent professional practice, these associations use many of the tactics that trade unions have developed; for example, they often limit entry into the trade or profession.

In the United States labor unions have waged a long and uphill battle to

CHART OF EMPLOYMENT AND UNEMPLOYMENT

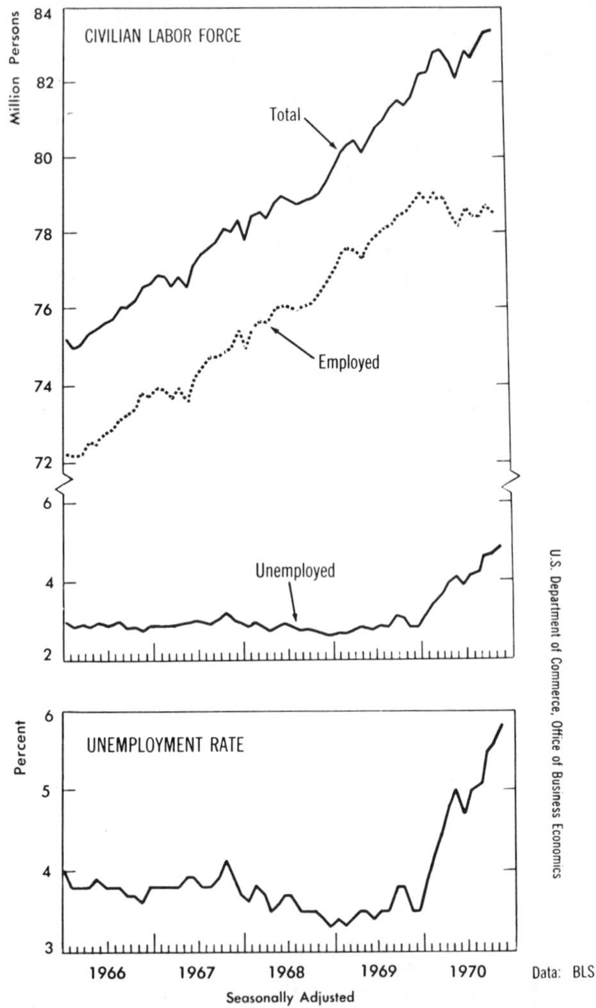

Movements in the civilian labor force and in the employed and unemployed components thereof. The civilian labor force grows with population, but participation rates vary with the availability of job opportunities. More women, for example, seek jobs when jobs are more abundant. Notice that the unemployment rate (lower panel) was generally at or below 4 percent through 1969, but rose rapidly in 1970. In late 1971 the rate was still near 6 percent. A major objective of current economic programs is to reduce unemployment once more to 4 percent.

become recognized, to gain sufficient membership to exert real economic strength, and to get the best possible terms of employment for their members. The struggle has had many setbacks but also many gains.

Generally unions are strong when the economy is growing and when jobs are plentiful; wartime especially has brought marked gains to organized labor. On the other hand, when the economy is receding and jobs are relatively scarce, union membership drops off and organized labor is necessarily less forceful in its demands on employers. In the brief sketch of American labor history that follows, you can get some idea of the problems the American labor movement has faced.

Labor unions—their general nature.

Today when labor unions are common, it is difficult to remember the long struggle needed to win the right to organize and to bargain collectively. In the 19th century it was common for trade union membership to be cause for immediate dismissal and for employers to refuse to bargain with unions. Only after the great depression of the 1930's did trade union membership and influence become strong in this country.

Trade unions are of two general types, the craft union and the industry-wide union. Examples of craft unions are those of the carpenters, masons, and steamfitters; these craft unions are still strong in the building trades or the construction industry. On the other hand, the United Mine Workers, the Automobile Workers, and the Steelworkers are industrial unions that embrace all crafts to be found in their respective industries.

Formerly the American Federation of Labor was primarily a group of craft unions while the Congress of Industrial Organizations (CIO) was composed chiefly of industrial unions. Now that the two groups are merged into the AFL-CIO the distinction is no longer so sharp.

There was formerly also a difference in labor union tactics. The advocates of "business unionism," the intellectual descendants of Samuel Gompers, believed in sticking strictly to bread and butter problems and bargaining solely for improvements in wages, hours, and working conditions. The other group, largely the industrial unionists, believed in political action as well as in the details of wage negotiation.

Collective bargaining is the term used when the officials of a union, now largely paid full-time workers, bargain on behalf of their members with an employer—such as General Motors—or a group of employers—such as the coal mine operators. Today's labor negotiations are complex proceedings covering not only wages, hours, and working conditions, but pensions, vacations, seniority, and other matters commonly called fringe benefits.

The theory of collective bargaining is largely one of countervailing power.

It is claimed that a union, representing hundreds or thousands of workers, can make a fairer and better employment contract than could individual workers bargaining directly with their employer, who may be a large corporation. Many employers now see the advantages to them of collective bargaining and are happy to deal with union representatives. Most labor contracts now run for several years, sometimes with wage formulas built in.

When a contract is about to expire, the union representatives will present the employer with a set of demands—for higher wages and perhaps some additional fringe benefits. The employer will counter these demands with an offer of his own. The demands and the employer's offer then become the basis for bargaining between the two parties. Labor's weapon to enforce its demands is often the threat of a strike. The employer may resist the demands because they are too costly, or because worker productivity has not risen enough to make the demands practical, or for some other reason.

If the bargaining can be concluded successfully, a new contract is written and ratified by the union members. If the negotiations break down, mediators, sometimes representing the Department of Labor, may be called in to keep the talks going until a settlement is reached. In a labor negotiation, the union's ultimate weapon is always the threat to call a strike; management's ultimate weapon is the threat to close a plant if it can no longer be operated profitably.

If a strike is called both sides will lose heavily—the workers in lost wages and the employer in lost production and perhaps lost customers. Both sides will, during the strike, make efforts to convince the public that their view is the more reasonable. The outcome of a strike, particularly a lengthy one, often turns on public opinion which gradually will turn against one party or the other.

Most strikes result in a permanent loss to both the workers and the employer; consequently it is not surprising that extensive government efforts are made to prevent strikes and to settle them once they actually begin. Some people feel that compulsory arbitration proceedings should be invoked whenever strikes occur; both organized labor and employers have generally resisted any forced appeal to arbitration. It is felt that arbitration merely splits the difference between the parties, producing often unsatisfactory compromises.

Trade union history.

Some local craft unions were organized in this country before 1800; a few local strikes were also called before that date. In their early attempts at collective bargaining, unions were often hampered by court actions brought by employers. Under an old English common law doctrine, combinations of workingmen for the purpose of raising wages could be held illegal as a conspiracy in restraint of trade and against the public. Controversy over this conspiracy doctrine continued for much of the 19th century; but gradually the courts ceased to apply it to the activities of organized labor.

The early labor unions were purely local affairs, limited to the largest cities such as Philadelphia, Boston, and New York. These early unions devoted much time and energy to local politics, endeavoring to elect candidated friendly to labor, and campaigning for such labor standards as the 10-hour day.

Working hours in the early factories were often from sunup to sundown, frequently for women and children as well as men. By 1850 the 10-hour day had been generally established for skilled artisans in large cities; but the workday was still 11 or 12 hours for unskilled labor and for labor in nonmetropolitan areas.

The Civil War greatly increased the demand for labor and multiplied the number of local trade unions. By 1864 some 300 of these local unions were functioning in the 10 Northern states.

The 15 years following the Civil War were a period both of rapid growth and decline for the American labor movement. By 1872 union membership had grown to 300,000. In the following years of depression it fell to 50,000 by 1878. During these years several attempts were made to start national trade unions, but never with any permanent success.

The most promising of these efforts was the National Labor Union, which lasted from 1866 to 1872. This union devoted much of its effort to starting consumer cooperatives and to working with farm and other groups in an effort to elect "Greenback" politicians, whose program was abundant money and credit and low interest rates, a frankly inflationary program calculated to appeal to debtors.

In general the 1870's were a period of labor unrest, sometimes marked by strikes and violence. In 1877 a series of railroad strikes spread throughout the country, bringing martial law, riots, intervention of both Federal troops and state militia, and some fatalities. A group of radical workers in Pennsylvania, known as "Molly Maguires," employed terroristic tactics against employers and strikebreakers until the Maguires were finally broken up by the arrest of their ringleaders. In spite of the violence during this decade, unskilled workers began to look to unions as the chief method of bettering their lot. Until this time, union activity had been confined almost entirely to skilled craftsmen.

The first important union of national scope was the Knights of Labor, founded in 1869. In a decade its membership grew to 10,000; in another decade it claimed 700,000 members, although this estimate was probably inflated.

The Knights had a broad political program calling for cooperatives, the 8-hour day, equal pay for women, abolition of child and convict labor, and public ownership of utilities. They were less interested in bargaining with employers than in pushing their political objectives.

In the 1880's this philosophy came in conflict with that of the American Federation of Labor, which espoused "practical unionism," i.e., better wages, hours, and working conditions.By 1890 membership in the Knights had fallen to 100,000; thereafter it declined rapidly in both membership and influence as the Federation rose.

The American Federation of Labor (AF of L) had its genesis in a confederation of six strong craft unions—the printers, iron and steel workers, moulders, cigar makers, carpenters, and glassmakers; this confederation was formed in 1881.First known as the Federation of Organized Trades and Labor Unions (FOTLU), this group originally had about 45,000 members. Its leader was Samuel Gompers of the cigar makers; he was destined for a long and distinguished career as a labor leader.

In 1886 a group of craft unions in the Knights of Labor, dissatisfied with the political program of the Knights, withdrew and merged with the FOTLU. The merged group then adopted the name American Federation of Labor and elected Gompers as its first president. Membership after the merger was about 138,000, a figure which slowly doubled in about 12 years.

As the Knights of Labor declined, the AF of L grew steadily in membership and influence over the next several decades. It was the principal national labor organization in the United States and was, as the name implies, a federation of craft unions. The Federation's program was for the most part "business unionism," i.e., working strictly through collective bargaining to improve the lot of its members, with minimum involvement in political activity. Mr. Gompers continued to lead the Federation until his death in 1924.

Although the trade union movement grew steadily in this country from 1890 until World War I, the period was marked by strong employer resistance and some violent strikes. In 1892 the steel workers struck the Carnegie works at Homestead, Pa. The company imported strikebreakers and Pinkerton detectives who clashed with the striking workers in a pitched battle in which ten were killed before the National Guard restored order.

In 1894 the railway workers, led by Eugene V. Debs, later to be Socialist candidate for President, struck the Pullman Co. near Chicago. The strike quickly spread to other railroads using the Chicago terminals. Courts issued injunctions against the strikers; but violence flared in which some 25 were killed and many more injured.

Around 1900 the attitude of employers was generally one of trying to smash the unions rather than to cooperate with them. In this smashing effort court orders were extensively employed as were strikebreakers and the militia whenever possible. In overcoming this employer opposition, the conservative leadership of the AF of L, and the organization's non-partisan political posture of "rewarding labor's friends and defeating its enemies" played a large role.

In the period from 1890 until World War I, although the AF of L was the backbone of the American labor movement, several rivals, generally with more radical programs, rose to challenge it. Foremost among these groups was the Industrial Workers of the World (IWW) formed in 1905 to

An I.W.W. rally in Union Square, New York City in 1914. At this time the I.W.W. had already begun to decline in power and influence because of its radical program. It was never very strong in the cities, but achieved its greatest influence in the west in lumber camps and among agricultural workers.

organize the great mass of unskilled and casual labor. Organizing on an industrial rather than a craft basis, the IWW had considerable success for a time in wheat fields, mines, and lumber camps, primarily in the West. Its militant tactics and radical sounding program brought public disfavor and caused several states to outlaw the organization. After 1913 its influence rapidly declined.

During World War I the sharp rise in industrial activity brought substantial gains in union membership. The AF of L cooperated quite well with the government during this period and in return made some significant gains. A National War Labor Board was established for labor-management cooperation. Its charter set forth, for the first time in United States Federal law, labor's right to organize and to bargain collectively. An 8-hour day for railway workers was established by Federal law in 1916. Thereafter the 8-hour day spread rapidly to other industries.

As a result of economic expansion and the efforts of organized labor, average hourly earnings of all workers in manufacturing rose from about 15 cents in 1890 to 48 cents in 1919. Average hours worked per week declined from 60 in 1890 to 49 in 1914.

While these wages are low and hours long by today's standards, they do reflect significant progress during the period. Prices were also much lower then than they are today.

Trade unionism since World War I.

Trade unionism made remarkable gains during World War I; but after the war a reaction set in. First came several unsuccessful strikes in 1919 and 1920.

In 1921 the country suffered a sharp recession in economic activity. Union membership dropped. The War Labor Board, with its guarantee of the right to organize, was allowed to lapse. Many employers once more became strongly anti-union and took active measures to discourage union activity.

Many company unions were formed. Dominated by the employer, these gave employees the shadow but not the substance of collective bargaining. Many employers forced workers to sign "yellow dog" contracts in which the workers agreed not to join a union as a condition of employment.

Between 1920 and 1923 union membership declined from 5 million to nearly 3 1/2 million. It remained close to this latter figure for the rest of the decade. In 1929 came the stock market crash and the beginning of the great depression. Union membership declined again to about 3 million but held near this figure, in spite of widespread unemployment during the depth of the depression.

Labor's gains during the 1930's came less from successful collective bargaining than from the passage of Federal legislation favorable to labor. First came the Norris LaGuardia Act of 1932. It severely restricted use of injunctions in labor disputes and outlawed the yellow dog contract. Next came the National Recovery Act (NRA) which guaranteed labor the right to organize and to bargain collectively. When the Supreme Court voted the NRA unconstitutional in 1935, the labor sections were incorporated in the

A daily scene in a commercial bank. Although views differ as to whether changes in banking and credit cause business cycles, virtually all analysts agree that the money and credit processes play an important role in the mechanism of the cycle. By their ability to expand or contract credit, banks can influence interest rates and can encourage or discourage business expansion. Banking is a closely regulated industry because of its importance and its ability to influence cyclical processes.

Wagner Labor Relations Act passed the same year. This act also created the National Labor Relations Board, which survives as a government agency today.

The Board can take action against employers for unfair labor practices. It also holds representation elections to determine which union has the right to represent workers in a given plant or company; the company is obliged to recognize the union certified.

Labor also gained important benefits from the Social Security Act of 1935 and the wage and hour act of 1938. Both these laws were parts of President Roosevelt's "new deal" program.

As business gradually recovered during the latter 1930's, union membership began to pick up. Intensified efforts were made to organize workers, particularly in the mass production industries. The AF of L issued new charters to industrial rather than craft type unions, because the mass production industries had few skilled craftsmen. Still some union leaders felt these industries were not being organized rapidly enough.

Headquarters of the AFL-CIO in Washington, D.C. Since reunification in 1955, this organization has dominated the American Labor Movement. Currently headed by George Meany, a former plumber, the organization conducts a varied program of information, lobbying, and nationwide bargaining from this headquarters.

Following the AF of L national convention in 1935, a group of six unions split off from the parent and formed the Congress of Industrial Organizations (CIO). Led by John L. Lewis, president of the United Mine Workers, which had long been an industrial type union, this new organization embarked on an aggressive organizing campaign. Four AF of L unions subsequently joined the six.

The AF of L and the CIO continued as dual national labor organizations for 20 years, until they were finally reunited in 1955.

With two organizations competing, union membership again rose rapidly late in the 1930's. By the time of Pearl Harbor it had reached a figure of between 10 and 11 million. The 1930's saw the first use of the sitdown strike, and also a concerted effort by Communist agents to penetrate labor unions and to use them for their own political purposes. Most unions successfully beat down this attempt at subversion from within.

World War II meant another period of comparative labor peace and further gains for labor through legislation. Another War Labor Board was established and authorized to settle labor management disputes relating to the war effort. With the establishment of general price controls, this Board also became an instrument for the stabilization of wages. With wages controlled, labor obtained more and more fringe benefits such as pension plans, health insurance, and vacations.

At the end of the war, another period of labor unrest, featured by numerous strikes, occurred. With the loss of overtime and the rapid run up of prices, organized labor demanded substantial increases in wage rates. This led to some public reaction, including passage of the Taft-Hartley Act in 1947. Originally vetoed by President Truman, this act was repassed over his veto.

Taft-Hartley outlawed the closed shop under which all employees in a plant were required to be union members. It also provided special rules which applied to threatened strikes thought to imperil the national health or safety. In these cases the President has the power to order an 80-day cooling off period, and to appoint a fact-finding panel to recommend a settlement of the dispute.

Despite substantial opposition during its early years, the Taft-Hartley Act continues to function today with a fair degree of apparent success.

The international labor organization.

This institution, whose primary mission is to raise labor standards throughout the world by international cooperation, was started in 1919, right after World War I. It was then a specialized agency under the old League of Nations, which was established to carry out President Woodrow Wilson's 14 points for peace. As is well known, Wilson's dream failed and the United States never joined the League.

The League nevertheless functioned throughout the 1920's and into the 1930's although it never became fully effective as a peace-keeping agency. It failed, for example, to organize effective deterrents to Mussolini's invasion of Ethiopia in 1935.

With the outbreak of World War II, the League as such simply disappeared. The International Labor Organization (ILO) however, moved to Canada for the duration of the war and continued to function in a limited way.

Following the peace treaties after World War II and the establishment of the United Nations, the ILO became a specialized agency under the UN umbrella. With a membership of more than 100 countries, it has continued to work from its headquarters in Geneva, Switzerland, for more than 50 years for improved labor standards.

In this lifetime more than 125 conventions, dealing with such matters as limits on the workday for women, working conditions for merchant seamen, and health and safety in mines, have been developed by international negotiation and submitted to the member countries for ratification.

In recent years, with the rise in international efforts to aid in the development of emerging countries, the ILO has been active in organizing all kinds of worker training programs in various countries.

The ILO is interesting both because it is the sole surviving remnant of the original League of Nations, and because of its unique tripartite structure. To each of its meetings, each member country sends a three-man delegation, one representing the government, one the employers of the country, and one the workers. The employers' and workers' delegates are selected by their own respective organizations, and the government representative has no control over their views or votes. Thus, a government representative may be, and frequently is, outvoted by his own countrymen.

The survival and growing influence of the ILO is a tribute to the vigor of organized labor and its sustained effort to raise labor conditions whereever men (and women) work. Despite technological progress, we have not yet been able to abolish work; nor are we likely to do so in the foreseeable future. Its character is changing and will continue to alter; but it will still be in store for most of us for most of our lives.

Labor and its income.

Since most of us are employees, wages are our most important source of income. In 1969, for example, out of a total national income, or aggregate of payments to the factors of production, of $771 billion, wages accounted for almost $510 billion, and supplements to wages and salaries, largely social security and other pension contributions, accounted for another $54 billion. In contrast aggregate corporate profits (before taxes) were only $94 billion, and interest received by individuals only $30 billion. Rental income of persons was only $21 billion.

The national income measures essentially the incomes earned by persons from participation in productive activity. It does not include the pension incomes of retired persons, or receipts from unemployment compensation, or other receipts of this type which are called transfer payments; nor does it include payments for reasons other than current productive activity.

Official statistics show that, at the end of 1969, out of a total United States population of more than 203 million persons, nearly 138 million were over 16 years of age and outside of institutions, such as prisons, hospitals etc. Of this 138 million, 84 million or a little over 60 per cent were in what is known as the labor force; that is, they either had a job, were looking for work, or were in the armed forces. With 3.5 million persons in the armed forces, the civilian labor force was just over 79 million persons. Of this group 2.4 million or 3.5 percent were unemployed, while the rest were employed. With the business recession in early 1970, unemployment has risen somewhat, reaching 5 percent by mid-1970 (still a low figure in comparison, say, with the 1930's).

The distribution of employees among different types of activity is interesting, and is shown in the following table for 1929 and 1969, 40 years apart. From this table you can get some idea of how employment has grown and changed over the last four decades.

WAGE AND SALARY WORKERS IN
NONAGRICULTURAL ESTABLISHMENTS
(Millions of persons)

	1929	1969
Manufacturing	10.7	20.1
Mining	1.1	.6
Contract construction	1.5	3.4
Transportation and public utilities	3.9	4.4
Wholesale and retail trade	6.1	14.6
Finance, insurance, real estate	1.5	3.6
Services	3.4	11.1
Federal government	.5	2.8
State and local government	2.5	9.5
Totals	31.3	70.1

Source: United States Bureau of Labor Statistics

As you can see from this table, the number of jobs has more than doubled in the 40-year period, with the largest relative increases being in services and in government. This increase in employment is a reflection of both population growth and economic growth, as well as an indication of rising living standards. It is characteristic of a relatively affluent society that a rising fraction of income is spent for services, and that public outlays also rise because governments take on more and more functions and programs.

The growth in wages over the past 40 years has been even more rapid than the growth in employment. In 1929, average gross hourly earnings in manufacturing were 56 cents. In 1969 they averaged $3.19. Similarly, gross

Workers leaving a shift at a steel plant. In the past 50 years the welfare of labor has improved greatly, partly because of unionism and partly because of legislation and economic growth. Wages are higher, working conditions better, and hours shorter. Pension and welfare benefits have also improved markedly. Yet much factory work is still monotonous, dirty, and dangerous. Workers with little skill are still subject to periodic unemployment and chronically low earnings.

weekly earnings in manufacturing in 1929 were under $25. In 1969, the average was $134.

A large part of this increase has been dissipated by higher prices; even expressed in constant prices of 1957-1959, the gain has been substantial but not remarkable. From 1947, when average weekly earnings revalued in 1957-1959 prices were $58, the rise by 1969 was to $89, or more than $30 per week of real income.

These labor income figures show that, although considerable progress has been made, we are far from being an affluent society so far as the majority of factory workers are concerned.

Pensions.

Important features in employment contracts are the pension benefits that typically accrue for each year of an employee's service; these credits are intended to yield a life income at retirement.

The most important pension scheme is, of course, the Federal Social Security system. The bulk of employees are now covered under the Social Security program, although there are exceptions—some physicians and some migratory workers are still uncovered, for example.

Under the Social Security program, employees pay a specified percentage of their wages as payroll tax and employers are assessed an equal percentage. These payments go into a Social Security trust fund and are invested in special issues of United States Government securities. From this trust fund, benefits are paid to retired workers, based on number of years in covered employment and on wages received. There are minimum and maximum benefits and also provisions for survivors and for dependent children's benefits.

In addition to Social Security, which is a public program, many private employers have pension plans of their own. These plans have varied features; some depend on insurance whereas others are known as trusteed plans. In an insured plan the contributions are used to purchase annuities from an insurance company, under either a group contract or individual contracts for each employee. In a trusteed plan contributions are paid to a trustee such as a bank. The trustee invests the proceeds and pays the benefits to retired workers.

Pension plans are also contributory and noncontributory. To the former both employees and the employer contribute in accordance with a fixed formula. To the latter only the employer contributes.

Noncontributory plans are also vested or nonvested. In a vested plan an employee has certain rights to the contributions made on his behalf in the event he should leave the company for another job. In a nonvested plan the departing employee would forfeit his rights and the contributions made for him would accrue to the other employees who remain with the company until retirement. A nonvested retirement plan may be an effective device for reducing employee turnover; it is often opposed by organized labor on the ground that it limits labor mobility.

In a contributory plan the employee will usually have a vested right to at least his own contributions, and perhaps to something more.

Pension plans have grown rapidly in scope and in amount of assets in the last several decades. The Social Security system, which became effective in the 1930's, has contributed importantly to this development. Many corporate pension plans are designed to supplement Social Security and to provide a more adequate retirement income than Social Security alone does.

Pension funds enjoy a special tax status in keeping with their social purpose. Contributions made by an employer to a pension plan are deductible for tax purposes as a business expense, provided the plan is a qualified one that covers all employees in a nondiscriminatory manner. Contributions by employees are not tax deductible but are considered an investment. Earnings of the pension assets are not taxed.

When an employee begins to receive retirement benefits, he is entitled to exclude from his taxable income his own past contributions to the pension scheme since these contributions were made out of taxable income. There is also a special retirement income credit in the Federal income tax law. Social Security pension payments are not taxed.

Pension programs have made an important contribution to easing the economic problems of older people and to reducing the dependency of older people on children and other family members.

A special problem exists in connection with pensions during an extended period of inflation. As pension benefits are generally fixed in amount at the time of retirement, their purchasing power diminishes with subsequent inflation. Social Security benefits, for example, have been raised several times by legislation on essentially a cost of living basis. Private pension benefits often cannot be escalated in this manner without supplementary contributions by the employer.

In collective bargaining between an employer and the labor union representing the employees, pension benefits may be an important item in the bargaining package. Pension and other benefits are known as "fringe benefits" to distinguish them from cash wages. In recent wage negotiations these fringe benefits have often been as important and as costly as the actual cash wage increases secured.

In 1824 Daniel Webster said in a speech that "labor in this country is independent and proud." The history of the American labor movement bears Webster out.

Chapter 15

STOP MAKING THOSE WAVES—Business Cycles

In 1803 J. B. Say, a French economist whose greatest achievement was helping to bury the labor theory of value, which held that the value of commodities was determined primarily by the amount of labor embodied in them, propounded an ingenious law of markets. This law held that every commodity put on the market creates its own demand, and that every demand exerted in the market creates its own supply. Hence, general overproduction is impossible.

Say's law is an outstanding example of economic thought taking a wrong turn or going down a blind alley. For the next 100 years his law was a standard ingredient of accepted economic doctrine, despite repeated demonstrations by events that it was neither true nor useful as an analytical construct.

Economists have always been concerned about crises—breakdowns of the economic system featured by unemployment, falling production, and financial panics. These were commonly seen as disturbances originating from without the system, from wars, or natural disasters, or financial excesses. Only gradually did economists come to see that crises originated in factors within the system: from over or underinvestment, from monetary surfeit or deficiency.

From this it was but a step to the position held early in this century that business cycles were inevitable, and that little could be done to interrupt or change their rhythm.

The modern position, as the following pages will show, is that industrial fluctuations, while perhaps inevitable, are to a substantial degree controllable. Much of current economic policy is concerned with this control.

For a long time economists have observed that industrial activity has its ups and downs, that it does not always stay on an even keel but fluctuates. Good times are succeeded by bad times, which in their turn give way to good times again. There is no regularity in these movements, although the most ingenious efforts have been exerted to find a regular pattern that could be used for prediction.

Nor do economists even agree about the causes of industrial fluctuations; on the contrary, directly conflicting explanations have often been advanced. There is substantial agreement, however, about what happens during different phases of the business cycle, and to these standard patterns or sequences we may first turn our attention. To describe a typical business cycle is quite easy. To diagnose its root cause and to prescribe its cure is a much more difficult matter. Similarly, it may be easy to recognize a case of smallpox, but not so easy to cure it.

Business cycle sequences.

Business cycles are irregular, wavelike fluctuations in total economic activity, as measured by comprehensive indexes such as industrial production, gross national product, or factory employment. Cycles are usually seen as consisting of several different phases or sequences that may be described in different ways. One such rudimentary description would be as follows.

Starting from the end of a downward phase, we would have a period of recovery in which employment would increase, prices would rise but only moderately, profits would expand, investment would increase, and existing capacity would be utilized more fully. This recovery might then be followed by a boom or inflationary phase in which prices would rise more rapidly, wages would increase, interest rates would advance, and output might press against capacity. Business costs would be pushed up and speculation would intensify.

Then would come an upper turning point at which the boom would break down to be followed by a recession. The turning point might be triggered by a break in the stock market or an important business failure. Confidence would disappear and speculators would hurry to cover their commitments and perhaps to sell securities or commodities short. As the recession developed, unemployment would increase, inventories would be liquidated, investment plans would be cut back; the federal budget might move into deficit because of the shortage of tax receipts below expectations. Retailers would have more distress sales with prices marked down; manufacturers would slow down production and order less from their suppliers. Pessimism would increase.

Eventually, a lower turning point would be reached when costs had fallen so low that profit opportunities began to reappear. The stock market would have reached its lowest before the actual economic turning point and would be rising in anticipation of recovery. During the recession, prices might or might not fall. In old-style recessions there were almost always some price reductions. In the new style, when government takes vigorous counter measures, there may be little or no price reduction. Following this lower turning point the economy would begin a new period of recovery.

None of these phases of the cycle takes a fixed length of time; indeed, the pattern varies from one cycle to the next. For example, we had a continuous upward phase of the cycle for nearly 9 years, from 1961 until late in 1969. Similarly, the downward phase of the cycle that began in September, 1929 with the great bear market on Wall Street lasted well into 1933.

Economists used to devote a great deal of attention to describing typical sequences of events during a representative cycle. During the downward phase prices fell, unemployment increased, wages were reduced but profits were reduced even more, interest rates fell, and so on. During the upward phase prices rose, wages also rose but lagged behind prices, profits rose more than either wages or prices, interest rates advanced, etc. What these older economists were describing was essentially an unmanaged cycle, in which few, if any, efforts were made by government to intervene; rather, economic forces were left to work themselves out.

In this process a good deal of hardship ensued in the form of unemployment, forced liquidations, foreclosures, and the like; but this was seen as a necessary curative process, like taking a dose of castor oil. Depressions were regarded as a result of the excesses of the preceding boom, and as a necessary purgative process to prepare for the next expansion. One is rather reminded of the ancient medical practice of regularly bleeding an ill patient.

Today we are accustomed to all sorts of interferences in an effort to smooth out the business cycle, or at least to lengthen expansion phases and to shorten contraction phases. In an expansion the central bank will tighten credit to discourage inflation and to dampen investment; pressure will be brought to bear on labor unions not to demand such large wage increases, and on businesses not to raise selling prices so rapidly. Taxes may be increased, a surplus of government receipts over expenditures may be encouraged, and the proceeds used to retire outstanding debt. Consumers may be urged to be more cautious in their spending and to borrow less for buying durable goods. All of this is essentially a call for voluntary action to keep an expansion phase from coming to a premature end.

During a contraction phase there will be exhortations to maintain production in the face of declining demand, to reduce prices while maintaining wages, to move ahead faster with public works, and to both cut taxes and expand public expenditures. The central bank will supply bank reserves liberally and interest rates will fall. Consumers will be urged to "buy now."

One reason business cycles are more irregular in their timing now is that we interfere more with them. Even when government policy was not consciously contracyclical, however, cycles were not predictable in either duration or amplitude.

Under the old gold standard, depressions tended to be transmitted from one country to another. If one country lost gold reserves, it had to submit to deflation at home; this caused its export prices to fall, making other countries follow suit to maintain their competitive positions. Each country had little independence to manage an independent monetary policy. Now that currencies are less rigidly tied to gold, there is not so great a tendency to export depression to other countries. Nevertheless, a country that is heavily involved in foreign trade—England, Japan, or the Netherlands, for example—will still find it extremely difficult to isolate its domestic economy from the world economy and from trends in world trade.

Some economists have seen the sequences observable during business cycles to be the very essence of the cycle itself. They have avoided theories or fundamental explanations of the cycle in favor of the fact that it is itself a self-perpetuating process. The excesses, the lags and leads that develop during an expansion phase, cause the boom to break down and degenerate into a contraction. Similarly, the corrective forces that operate during a downswing inevitably cause a lower turning point to be reached. This mechanical explanation of the cycle is associated with name of Wesley C. Mitchell in this country, for he was one of the foremost advocates.

An echo of his work today may be seen in the publication of leading, lagging, and coincident indicators—series which have been observed in the past to have this cyclical timing. A *leading indicator,* such as the number of hours worked per week in factories, is supposed, when it rises, to presage an upturn in business. It is called a leading indicator because it typically moves before industrial production or gross national product. The leading indicator method is a pragmatic approach to business cycles. What is important is accurate prediction above all else, never mind whether or not we know why the economy turns up or down.

Economists who have theorized about the business cycle have advanced a wide range of explanations for this phenomenon. Let us notice a few of these explanations.

Business cycle theories.

Business cycles have been explained by everything from sunspots to alternating waves of optimism and pessimism among people. We may call the former a "natural phenomenon" theory and the latter a "psychological" theory. Neither deserves to be taken too seriously.

One of the more ingenious business cycle theories, associated with the name of Schumpeter, is the "innovation" theory. According to Schumpeter, innovations, based on inventions, tend to cluster in time. A cluster of innovations, with a host of imitators following in hot pursuit, brings on a rash of new investment and hence a boom in business activity. After a while the investment based on these innovations tapers off. If new innovations are not in evidence, investment may actually decline, leading to a recession or a depression. Eventually a new group of innovations will appear, starting a new investment boom.

The evidence for innovations appearing in clusters is rather fragmentary, but granted that they do, the rest of the theory follows logically from this fact.

Since this and a number of other theories make fluctuations in investment a central point, mention should be made at this stage of two investment characteristics, namely the *multiplier* and the *acceleration* principle. The multiplier is based on the fact that an initial increase in demand will generate additional incomes which in turn will be spent on consumption, leading to a second round of income increases and so on. Thus if an additional $1 million is invested, the multiplier may cause $3 million of additional income to be generated. The multiplier in this case is 3. In other cases it might be 4 or only 2. The multiplier was a concept used by J.M. Keynes in 1936 and generally familiar to economists since that time. Actually the concept is much older, although not previously called by that name.

The acceleration principle is based on the fact that investment is related to the change in consumer demand rather than to the level of that demand. If consumer demand has been increasing 1 percent per year, a certain level of investment will be geared to that normal increase. If consumer demand should increase by 1.5 percent per year, this might cause a 50 percent increase in investment. In other words, investment demand is derived from the change in consumer demand and fluctuates more than that underlying demand. Small changes in consumer demand may, via the acceleration principle, lead to large changes in investment demand. These large changes in investment are characteristic of different phases of the business cycle.

The multiplier and the acceleration principles are not actually theories of the business cycle but mechanisms that are incorporated in various theories, particularly those that are concerned largely with fluctuations in investment.

Underconsumption theories of the cycle have a periodic vogue and keep recurring in spite of the discrediting of earlier versions. Underconsumption theories have been associated with the name of Hobson in England and Foster and Catchings in the United States. Perhaps the most notorious underconsumptionist of all was Karl Marx. According to Marx, exploitation of the workers by capitalists, who drained away surplus value into profit, left too little purchasing power in the workers' hands to buy the results of productive activity, so the capitalist system would break down into periodic crises or depressions. The Marxian theory of crises was actually one of the strongest parts of Marx's intellectual system. One of the boasts of communist systems today is that they do not have depressions or unemployment.

The underconsumptionist view generally held that saving meant a loss

Some of the statistical material necessary to measure the structure of American business. The Census of Business is ordinarily taken every five years and gives details concerning the number, size, location, and nature of all business enterprises in the United States. The other volumes are published more frequently and give less detailed but more nearly current information on business trends and problems. Data such as these are basic to following cylical fluctuations and forecasting future prospects.

from the income stream that left this stream unable to buy all the goods produced. What the underconsumptionists often lose sight of is that investment, which is only possible because of saving, is quite as much a purchase of current output as is consumption. Hence there is no loss from the income stream but merely a diversion of some demand into investment goods, which are quite as necessary as consumption goods.

Underconsumption theories have ranged from naive to quite sophisticated. They have usually been based on the premise that the existing distribution of income is unfair, or inefficient, or wrong in some way. Usually they have sought to reduce inequality in the size distribution of income.

Another group of theories have seen the basic cause of the business cycle in the investment process. They feel that investment gets distorted or out of kilter during a boom and that this improper structure causes the boom to break down and a recession to ensue. Usually these theories make abundant use of the multiplier and the acceleration principle to explain how investment gets distorted, and why this distortion cannot be sustained. Some of these investment theories are extremely elaborate.

One reason there are so many different theories of the business cycle is that cycles differ greatly from one another in their sequences and in their characteristics. One cycle will see a strong investment boom, while in another rising consumer expenditure will appear to be the main driving force. Prices at one time will rise strongly while at another time the advance will be more measured. The role of government and of international factors will be different from one cycle to another. Likewise, the role played by banking and monetary conditions has often varied. In older cycles depressions used to be touched off by financial panics. Today we have the monetary system under much better control.

The business cycle was once regarded as a kind of inevitability. Today we hold the view that it can and will be controlled. The Employment Act of 1946, which created the Council of Economic Advisers, is the chief vehicle for this business cycle control. Its activity is not phrased in terms of controlling the business cycle, but in terms of maintaining full employment or keeping expansion going. The tools for this purpose are primarily monetary and fiscal policy, including within the latter, budgetary policy.

Control over the cycle implies some theory of the cyclical process. The doctrine of the Council of Economic Advisers may be described as latter day Keynesianism, meaning that its intellectual parent is the *General Theory* published in 1936. In this book Keynes made the case for relieving unemployment by massive doses of public expenditure, designed to get an expansion process going. This doctrine replaced the previous conventional budgetary wisdom, which held that government expenditures should be reduced during a depression. Today we are nearly all Keynesians, at least as far as government expenditure policy is concerned.

We also have a group of essentially monetary theories of the cycle. According to this view it is the instability of the credit creation process which causes the ebb and flow of business. During an expansion, because profit opportunities seem lush and loan demand is strong, banks create too much money. Their reserves decline and eventually press on the required levels. Banks expand credit in close step with one another because they compete strongly for loans and because any bank that expanded too rapidly would lose reserves to its fellow banks. Thus they all create too much credit together.

According to the monetary theorists the boom will break down primarily because of financial stringency. When banks reach their limit and can no longer go on creating credit, businesses will fail or be forced to retrench for want of funds. Business prospects will then worsen and loan demand will fall off. The downward phase will see credit contraction rather than expansion, and falling interest rates as loan demand shrinks. Banks will accentuate the downward phase by contracting credit too much, just as they expanded it too much during the boom.

Monetary forces certainly play a role in the mechanism of business cycles, whether or not they are the root cause. Indeed, most monetary theories do not contend that changes in credit are the sole factor in cycles; they merely see these credit changes interacting with confidence and other factors in causing the swings in business that constitute the cycle.

Monetary theories often took the position that a certain amount of liquidation, cost cutting, and disinflation was necessary during a contraction to lay the basis for a new expansion. They often took the view that interfering with this corrective mechanism during a recession merely prolonged the process and prevented a sound expansion from developing. This may be described as the cathartic theory of recession or depression.

Business cycle therapy.

Regardless of their theoretical stance, economists have reached a good deal of agreement on measures to be taken during various phases of the cycle in an effort to manage the economy. During an expansion period the main emphasis is on monetary restraint; that is, supplying only limited reserves to the commercial banks. The banks find loan demand to be strong; if they have secondary reserves in the form of United States Government securities, they may sell these to expand their reserve funds. Since this selling expands bank reserves, the Federal Reserve may be selling on its own account to counteract this expansion.

The appropriate fiscal policy during an expansion is usually seen now in terms of letting a robust budget surplus develop. This may be accomplished either by raising taxes, or allowing the fiscal dividend, the growth in tax revenues at existing rates, to develop without being appropriated by additional expenditure claims. This is also the time to reduce government expenditures by postponing programs and scrutinizing requests for appropriations very carefully. If a budget surplus does develop, it will be a restraining factor on the economy as well as an anti-inflationary force.

An expansion is also the time for incomes policy to be effective, for restraint to be put on prices and wages. We do this presently by informal action, chiefly putting the light of publicity on wage or price rises that are considered to be excessive. Realistically, all that "jawboning" does is to slow down the price and wage advance somewhat, but slowing down can be an advantage when one is trying to keep an expansion running as long as possible.

The policy watchword today is to get expansion without inflation. This is not easy to accomplish. When there is unemployment of more than 4 percent of the labor force, the emphasis is usually put on reducing that unemployment, even at the expense of some additional inflation. Many economists feel that our contracyclical policies are biased on the side of inflation by the continuous desire to keep unemployment down.

Once the upper turning point has been passed and it is clear that a recession is developing, the policy prescriptions become the reverse of what they have been during the boom. Instead of a budget surplus, we now want a deficit, so that the government will be putting more into the income stream than it takes out.

Instead of monetary restraint, we want ease, meaning that the central bank will be supplying reserves on net balance instead of extinguishing them. Businesses reduce their inventories in anticipation of price declines; the demand for bank loans of all types falls, and banks begin switching from loans into investments, chiefly government securities. Governments will begin talking about public works projects, construction, which perhaps they have postponed during the previous boom when construction costs were rising rapidly.

In a word, policy measures seek to expand demand by all available means instead of restraining it. Government spokesmen will utter ringing pronouncements to the effect that prosperity is just around the corner or that all we need is confidence for the economy to resume its expansion. Sometimes these pronouncements, like Herbert Hoover's in 1929, read rather hollowly when viewed historically.

If your view of economics in later years is chiefly that of a concerned citizen, most of what you will hear and read of economic discourse will be about contracyclical policy measures, both those in force and those under consideration. Economists are constantly inventing new contracyclical weapons and urging their adoption. Congress will also be occupied in the economic sphere chiefly with legislation to expand demand and employment if we are in a recession, or to restrain demand if inflation is the main problem. Our policy bias against unemployment carries over into legislation; no Congressman wants to cast votes in favor of unemployment however much he may talk about fiscal irresponsibility or the need to restrain the advance in prices. Deflation is still bitter medicine and always will be. About the only group to benefit from it are retired people living on fixed incomes; and politically their clout is limited.

Despite the fact that government contracyclical policy is today both more powerful and more precise than it once was, the causes and cure of cyclical fluctuations in economic activity reside primarily in the private sector. Business still responds to expanding demand by producing more and to contracting demand by producing less. No individual business firm can for long take contracyclical action on its own; to do so would mean loss of profits, inappropriate inventories, and plant expansions at the wrong time.

In addition to its own contracyclical policies, government can help chiefly by publishing factual information about the current economic situation and about its own policies, so that business may know how best to react. This is the area where the indicative economic planning used in France gives business an important advantage. Government is forced to quantify its policy plans and to make them consistent with the plans being formulated by business. As already noted, however, we are not likely to see the

The Lincoln Center for the Performing Arts under construction in New York City. Construction is one industry peculiarly susceptible to business cycles because of the long time involved and the sensitiveness to interest rates on borrowed money. Construction costs have also been steadily increasing because of rising wages rates and relatively small increases in productivity. In cities rising land values are also a factor in determining the volume and nature of construction.

adoption of this system in the United States during the foreseeable future.

Within the private sector of the economy, the severity of cyclical fluctuations will vary considerably from industry to industry. In the capital goods industries, producing machinery, generating equipment, etc., fluctuations are quite severe. Construction is also cyclically unstable. In some consumer goods industries, producing food, for example, cycles are much more mild. People will continue to eat even during a depression, although their eating habits will change as their incomes decline. Likewise certain of the service industries, such as medical care, barber shops, etc., will show only modest cyclical fluctuations. A few industries, such as gold mining, are actually contracyclical. This is because the selling price for gold is fixed, whereas mining costs will be lower when the rest of the economy is depressed. So if you become unemployed during the next depression, try panning gold.

The differential impact of cycles on different industries makes policy

Making cellulose ceiling tile at a factory in Ontario. The tile, made from pulpwood, is used both in new construction and remodelling. Demand for building materials is cyclical, as construction responds both to aggregate demand and to interest rates. In the operation shown here the ceiling tiles are being cut to final size and boxed for shipment. Note the inventory of large sheets stacked in the rear awaiting final cutting.

prescriptions for counter cyclical action difficult because policy measures also have a differential impact and not always the one that is desired. A tight monetary policy, for example, bears with special severity on housing at a time when the construction industry may be just recovering from a downturn that struck it more severely than other industries. Thus, in a sense, housing labors under the double burden of being one of the first industries to feel a decline and one of the first to be repressed by measures to restrain a boom. When we consider that housing is also one of the technologically most backward of all industries, with numerous built-in resistances to changing methods, largely because of the jurisdictional claims of strong craft unions, we see that macroeconomic policy measures, on which we depend for contracyclical action, may have their shortcomings.

This is not to suggest that a counter cyclical policy could be tailored separately for a number of industries and applied separately. Such a policy bundle would be too cumbersome, too inherently inequitable, and too slow both to apply and to unwind. One of the greatest problems in business cycle policy is to know when to apply the medicine and in what strength. There is always the danger of too much too soon or too little too late. When Goldilocks tasted the porridge she had to try all the bowls before she found one just right. Economic policy experiments are too big and too costly to afford much opportunity for trial and error. In an economy as large and complex as ours, tinkering may be worse than no policy measures at all.

It can be said on balance about economic policy measures that they are getting better and more precise all the time, and will undoubtedly continue

A modern electronic computer. These are used for many purposes, including business, scientific, and research. One application is the manipulation of econometric models for forecasting and analyzing data. Computer inputs may be punched cards, magnetic tape, or direct input as shown here. Outputs may be printed on sheets of paper, on tape, or may go direct to memory drums in another machine. The chief advantage of computers is the speed with which they can perform calculations.

to improve. Whether we shall ever succeed in eliminating the cycle altogether is questionable, but the fine tuning should at least give us a more stable picture. The economy is, after,all, a large and intricate machine, not centrally directed but responding to a mass of stimuli, both internal and external. Were it less interconnected and less delicately balanced cyclical swings might be smaller; but the whole system would be far less productive and our national product would be much smaller. It is not surprising for a large and intricate machine, such as a big computer, occasionally to get out of order, even to develop neuroses. The American economy is a much bigger and more intricate machine than any computer. So it occasionally suffers from malaise. We call this recession. Although our efforts to control it are continually being refined, we still have a good way to go.

Forecasting.

We have seen in the preceding pages that contracyclical policy requires the application of various instruments, such as monetary or fiscal restraint, before a serious disruption in business activity has developed. We have also seen that no two cycles are precisely the same, and that boom or recession phases do not run for a certain, predetermined length of time. The question that remains is—are cyclical fluctuations sufficiently predictable so that the right policy prescriptions can be applied at the right time? The answer to this is no, if 100 percent precision in timing is considered mandatory. On the other hand, if one expects only reasonably accurate results, and is content to operate within a margin of error, the answer is that forecasting is *often* accurate enough to serve as a guide to proper policy measures; but not always.

We need to notice, although not to explore, some of the techniques that are used for forecasting economic activity. One is reliance on leading indicators—statistical series that have been observed in the past to move before general series, such as gross national product. Some empirical forecasters rely primarily on these leading series to predict the timing if not the magnitude of cyclical swings.

Another forecasting technique might be called the projection of past relationships. This depends on the observance of certain relatively stable relationships in the past and their extrapolation into the future. For example, if one has observed that consumers tend to save about 7 percent of their disposable income and to spend 93 percent on consumption, this relationship might be projected to a different level of disposable income than we have had in the past for a rough reading of what saving might be. The estimate, naturally would be no better than the projection of disposable income on which it was based; this figure in turn may have been derived from a relationship to some other series such as employment.

What one can say about the relationship technique is that it gives one an internally consistent forecast that will be as good or bad as the controlling assumptions on which it is based. Alfred Marshall once remarked that nature makes no jumps. The import of this for economics is that most observed relationships between or among economic variables are, in fact, reasonably stable and not subject to erratic fluctuations. Those who forecast largely on the basis of past relationships are relying heavily on this relationship stability.

More and more, forecasting today is based on econometric models, i.e., quantitative systems of relationships that can be manipulated simultaneously by computer calculations. In the days before computers, economic models had to be calculated laboriously; this tended to keep them relatively simple. Now, since the computer can solve 100 simultaneous equations, the tendency is to bring in more and more relationships in an effort to add precision to the results. Sometimes this works; at others, it does not. Even a highly complex model, with dozens of variables, sometimes gives no better results than a simple model with four or five variables. Clearly it is not the number of variables that is important, but the precision and stability of the relationships among the variables, plus the underlying assumptions, that make all the difference. Just as the late Rube Goldberg used to invent incredibly complex machines to perform simple tasks, so some latter-day model builders seem more interested in the intracy of their apparatus than in its efficiency. There is, after all, a very simple pragmatic test. That system is best which produces the most accurate results—which calls the turn at the right time, or predicts how long a cumulative process will run before it reverses itself.

There is, finally, a forecasting technique, essentially judgmental, that relies on identifying and weighing those factors that dominate a particular situation and largely determine how economic time series will move. The controlling factors will vary from period to period. At one time it may be the course of the war in Vietnam, at another business intentions concerning capital spending, at a third, expectations of price behavior, which determine what will happen to costs, profits, and wages.

Most economists use the critical factor approach to some extent, although they may combine this with formal model building or with a close watch on the leading and lagging series. We are back at the old point, made in an earlier chapter, that since in economics everything is related to everything else, it is necessary to pick out those few relationships that are most significant. The critical factor approach is an effort to do just that, with the difference that the critical factors are not stable but themselves continuously changing. What was critical in the last cycle may not be in this one; what is critical now may not be so in the next cycle five years hence.

You have by now grasped the notion that forecasting is not a precise art but a pragmatic one. It relies heavily on observation of facts and trends, on judgment, and on intuition. Were you to talk to a group of professional forecasters, you would observe that they frequently have visceral feelings that a trend will continue or that it will not, that a certain relationship will hold or change, that a cloud on the horizon, now no bigger than a man's hand, will either blow up a storm or pass unnoticed.

Because forecasting is so imprecise, and recognized to be, policy makers often rely on the consensus of many different forecasts, on the theory that errors will be offsetting. This has two consequences. First, since a consensus is like an average, it rules out the extremes. Thus, consensus forecasts tend to underestimate change. Policy measures based on them run the risk of being too little and too late. Second, forecasters are gregarious creatures; like buffalo, they tend to move in herds; they talk to and convince one another until they all come to believe much the same thing; they are often wrong together.

If there were a golden rule for forecasters, it might be—speak not to your colleague lest you be influenced by his misconceptions. Like juggling or sword swallowing, forecasting takes a lot of practice. It is not like parachute jumping which one must expect to do perfectly the first time. As long as we have contracyclical policy, and we are not likely to back away from it, we shall continue to depend on forecasters. Let us hope that, like glassblowing, the art will improve with use.

In 1835 Alexis De Tocqueville, after touring the United States, wrote that "democratic nations care but little for what has been, but they are haunted by visions of what will be. ...Democracy, which shuts the past against the poet, opens the future before him."

Unfortunately, De Tocqueville did not tell us how to see more of the future.

Chapter 16

THE SILKS OF CATHAY—International Trade and Finance

When Marco Polo set out on his fabulous journey many centuries ago, he was following a profession already well established. His father, a merchant and international trader, desired to open commerce with Cathay (China) in hopes of gaining profits. Although Polo is remembered today chiefly for his literary efforts, it was trade that prompted and financed his journey.

Trade among nations takes place for the same reasons as trade within a nation, namely to increase total product by specialization and division of labor. Virtually no coffee is produced in the United States, but a great deal is consumed here; we import it from Brazil, Colombia, and other Latin

Spinning wool at a textile mill in New Zealand. New Zealand has a comparative advantage in growing and spinning wool. Wool exports are an important part of the country's export trade. One method of increasing export earnings is to do more processing. Formerly most of New Zealand's wool was exported in raw form. Today more and more of it is processed into yarn or even finished cloth.

American countries. They can produce it better and cheaper than we can. In return we sell them automobiles, machinery, and other products we can make better and cheaper than they can.

A country that produces a particular product well and cheaply is said to have a comparative advantage in the production of that commodity. Costa Rica has one in bananas, Cuba in sugar, Russia in furs, Pakistan in jute, and so on. These commodities are therefore prominent in the exports of these countries because it pays to specialize in them. A comparative advantage may arise from natural factors such as climate or soil, from accumulated experience, as in the case of Harris tweeds made on the Hebrides Islands, or from technological leadership, as in the case of the United States and computers.

Extension of the market.

Obviously a country can specialize more when it sells its products in the world market than when it is limited to its own national market. Also all countries must import some products they cannot grow or make themselves to good advantage or in sufficient quantities. Exports provide the wherewithal to pay for imports. We have virtually no nickel in this country but must use substantial quantities for alloying steel and other purposes; consequently we import it, primarily from Canada, which has extensive nickelbearing ores.

The relation between a country's total exports and total imports is known as its *balance of trade.* If exports exceed imports, the trade balance is said to be favorable or active. If imports exceed exports, it is said to be unfavorable or passive.

In addition to foreign trade in merchandise, a country will have foreign payments to make and will receive income from abroad due to so-called invisible items–shipping and insurance charges, tourist expenditures, interest on indebtedness, and earnings from overseas investments. These items, as well as the trade items, enter into what is known as the country's *balance of international payments.* When an American business firm exports goods, it is paid in dollars owned by foreigners; these may have been earned by shipping services furnished by foreign shipping companies, from the expenditure of American tourists in Europe, or from our imports from these foreign countries.

Foreign exchange.

Payments to individuals or business firms in other countries are known as foreign exchange transactions since they involve the exchange of one national currency for another. A bill in Great Britain must be paid in pounds sterling, one in Switzerland in Swiss francs, and so on. Banks handle the making and receipt of these payments through their foreign exchange departments. They pay the seller in his local currency and acquire a corresponding claim in some foreign currency. A bank with too many Swiss francs may exchange some for Italian lira, or Indian rupees, whatever they need. There are organized markets in foreign exchange for just this purpose.

International payments involve what are known as foreign exchange rates. The British pound is worth $2.40 United States and there are 4.76 Indian rupees to the United States dollar. The Malayan dollar is only 33 cents United States, and the Lebanese pound is about 30 to the United States dollar.

Foreign exchange rates are determined partly by supply and demand, partly by official parities defined by the different countries, and partly by official controls exercised by some countries (usually poor ones) over foreign payments. Those countries that belong to the International Monetary Fund, as most countries outside the Soviet bloc do, undertake an obligation in that fund to define a par value for their currency and to maintain actual exchange rates within 1 per cent of that par value. This definition of par value may be in terms of a gold content or merely in relation to a reserve currency.

The United States dollar was officially defined as 1/35 of a troy ounce of gold, which simply means that the United States Treasury had a standing offer to buy or sell gold to foreign governments or central banks at $35 per ounce. If we were to raise this price to $40, we would be devaluing the dollar to 1/40 of an ounce of gold. A bill is now before Congress to redefine the dollar as 1/38 of an ounce of gold.

The United States dollar is a reserve currency because foreign governments and banks are willing to hold all or part of their monetary reserves in the form of dollars, usually in a deposit account with the Federal Reserve Bank of New York. Instead of holding gold which must be stored and earns no interest, the Colombian Government, for example, merely keeps its monetary reserves in a dollar account in New York. This account may be drawn on or converted into gold at will. Meanwhile, if Colombia wishes, the Federal Reserve will invest part of these reserves in United States treasury bills on which the Colombian treasury will draw interest.

Transactions in a country's balance of international payments may be divided into current and capital transactions. Imports of coffee from Brazil are current account transactions giving rise to current payments. On the other hand, if an American company were to establish a branch in Brazil, this would give rise to an export of capital from the United States. In subsequent years, if the factory is successful, dividends would flow back to the

American parent as an invisible income or current item.

If a country's balance of payments is in surplus (that is, if in-payments exceed out-payments), that country will be accumulating liquid claims abroad in the form of deposits payable in foreign currency. Or this increase in claims may be converted into gold which can be brought home (i.e., sent to the United States and sold to the Treasury) or held abroad under earmark (i.e., in the custody of a foreign central bank). Conversely, if a country's international accounts are in deficit, foreign liquid claims against its currency will accumulate.

UNITED STATES BALANCE OF PAYMENTS

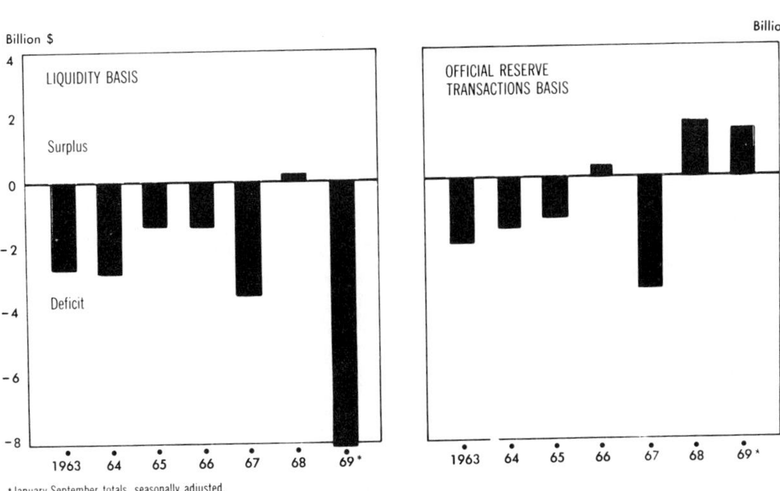

*January-September totals, seasonally adjusted.

U.S. Department of Commerce, Office of Business Economics

Two concepts of the United States balance of international payments. The liquidity basis (left panel) includes changes in liquid liabilities of private foreign individuals. If German corporations hold more dollars, this adds to the United States deficit on a liquidity basis. The official reserve transactions basis (right panel) measures only changes in official dollar holdings, such as by foreign governments or foreign central banks. Notice that in most years the United States deficit is considerably larger on the liquidity than on the official settlements basis. This means private foreign holdings of dollars have generally increased during the 1960's.

Virtually for 20 years the United States balance of payments has been in continuous deficit. This means that foreign claims against United States dollars have grown rapidly. We have also had some gold outflow, although not an unusually large amount. Foreign banks and governments have been content merely to hold dollar balances. If confidence in the dollar were to be seriously shaken, all our gold reserves could disappear quite quickly, since foreign claims on dollars substantially exceed the gold reserve stored at Fort Knox. For two decades the United States has been supplying liquidity to the rest of the world through its balance of payments deficits. This has helped greatly to finance a growing volume of world trade and payments. The United States has been, in effect, banker to the rest of the world. During the 19th century, Britain served this function as primary financial power and international banker.

The only reason that trade between the United States and Britain seems more complex than trade between Illinois and Indiana is that these two states are part of a common market with a common currency whereas the United States and the United Kingdom are not. States in this country are prohibited by the constitution from erecting tariff barriers against one another, whereas different countries have no such limitation. In addition to tariff barriers in the sense of border taxes, many countries have other barriers, often called nontariff barriers to trade, which inhibit the free flow of commerce.

The communist countries, of course, use trade as an instrument of national policy to gain political advantages in countries with whom they are doing business. Hence it is difficult to analyze communist trade patterns on a purely economic basis.

How foreign trade develops.

In a country such as the United States, foreign trade takes place because individual business firms seek out and develop sales and purchase opportunities abroad. An American manufacturer of computers undertakes to sell these in foreign countries just as he would in this country. He finds the export business more complicated because, not only are different currencies involved, but also customs of doing business differ in various countries. But if the foreign market is potentially lucrative enough, these difficulties will be surmounted.

We have noticed that a country which can produce something well and cheaply has a comparative advantage in the production of that commodity. This advantage may be attributable to natural factors such as climate or soil, plus accumulated experience. Brazil can grow coffee cheaply because it has the right soil and climate and because it has specialized in this crop for a long time. The United States and Canada are both wheat exporters because we have the right growing conditions and the right agricultural methods to grow wheat more cheaply than many other countries.

International trade, in a word, arises from international specialization

Ships engaged in international trade at anchor in the harbor of Montevideo, Uruguay. The bulk of international trade still moves by ship but some high value commodities are now shipped by air and some by truck, for example between Canada and the United States. Notice the warehouse buildings alongside the loading zones and the rail spurs leading to the warehouse areas.

and from concentration on the most profitable and productive activities within each country.

For a country to aspire to be self-sufficient in everything would be like a family returning to self-sufficient farming when all other farmers were specializing and using the exchange process to satisfy their wants. One of the prices a country aiming at self-sufficiency or autarky would pay for this policy would be a lower standard of living than if it allowed more specialized production to develop. Switzerland is poor in natural resources and small in area; but it has become rich by specializing in manufactured items where the value added is high, such as watches, and because it has demonstrated an ability to make these products better and cheaper than any other country in the world.

Trade barriers.

One reason international trade is not more developed and extensive than it is, is the tariff or nontariff barriers most countries have erected to limit this trade. Tariffs have a long history, often being intertwined with a country's past efforts to develop its home industry. For the past several decades the United States and some other countries as well have made determined efforts to reduce tariff barriers and to expand the volume of world trade.

In the 1930's the United States had a policy, often associated with the name of Cordell Hull, Secretary of State under Franklin Roosevelt, of negotiating bilateral trade agreements providing for tariff reduction. We would agree to reduce tariffs on a list of items if the other country would agree to reduce tariffs on another list of potentially equal value. Though effective, this bilateral program proceeded slowly since it required many agreements with individual countries. Use was made of what is known as the *most favored nation principle* under which, if we reduced duties on French perfumes, and thus made France the most favored nation so far as United States tariffs on perfumes were concerned, this reduction would also be extended to all other countries with whom we had agreements and who also exported perfume. By use of the most favored nation principle, inequities in tariff reduction could be prevented from remaining in effect for long periods.

Following World War II, the major trading countries of the world negotiated an international agreement known as the General Agreement on Tariffs and Trade (GATT). Under this agreement, to which the United States is a party, the countries pledged not to engage in certain practices, such as subsidizing exports, and to consult together before making extensive changes in tariffs or other trade barriers. The GATT has a small international staff and is, in effect, now a specialized agency under the auspices of the United Nations. It has been reasonably effective in expanding world trade and in preventing "beggar your neighbor" trade practices.

In recent years what has come to be known as the Kennedy round of negotiated general tariff reductions was conducted under GATT auspices. In this round the United States made substantial reductions in duties on a number of products as did other countries. These tariff negotiations differed from earlier ones in that bargaining was by groups of commodities rather than by individual items. Thus the agreement could achieve tariff reduction on a much broader front.

The whole question of tariffs and other trade restrictions is a difficult one because the entire matter has in the past been more political than economic. For much of the 19th century the tariff was one of the main national political issues in this country. Generally the representatives of manufacturing states and interests favored high tariffs, whereas the representatives of agricultural interests favored low tariffs. Thus the tariff was a sectional issue with the Northeast quadrant of the country being high tariff and the South and West being low tariff.

Now that the United States is fully developed industrially, the tariff is no longer such a burning political issue. It is still an issue, however. Indeed, legislation is now pending in Congress that would limit imports into the United States of textiles and leather products. The case being made for the legislation is the old one that American industries are being injured by foreign competition. These industries are undoubtedly being injured by imports, but largely because they have become technologically backward; with high wages, they find it harder and harder to meet foreign competition which has largely caught up with our technology. Our industries have, in brief, lost most of their comparative advantage. The legislation under consideration would not raise tariffs on textiles and leather products but would impose quotas, setting absolute limits to the quantities of these products that might be imported. Quotas are an example of nontariff trade barriers.

When speaking of tariffs or border taxes, it is necessary to distinguish between those for *revenue* and those for *protection.* A revenue tariff is less than the cost differential between countries and hence does not stop trade, but merely taxes it, producing some revenue. A protective tariff, on the other hand, is more than the cost differential so that trade is halted and no revenue produced. If we put a tariff of $1 on some product which Japan could make for 75 cents and we could make for $1.25, that would be a protective tariff since the Japanese product could not compete in the United States market after shouldering the tariff.

Tariffs, whether for revenue or protection, are of two kinds, called *ad valorem* and *specific.* An ad valorem duty, as the name implies, would be a certain percentage of the import price. A specific duty would be so much per unit, as 10 cents per gallon on a certain chemical. Ad valorem duties keep up with price changes in internationally traded commodities. Specific duties can get badly out of date. If the price of a product doubles and the specific duty remains unchanged, for example, this is equivalent to halving the tariff rate. Some tariffs are complex, with both specific and ad valorem duties being levied on the same item.

In the United States, import taxes are collected by the United States Customs Service, a branch of the Treasury Department. You are most likely to encounter customs officers if you return from a foreign trip. As a traveler you are allowed to bring in $100 worth of foreign products duty free; if you have more than this amount you must pay some tariff. The great majority of customs officers do not deal with travelers but with business firms that import merchandise for resale. Imported merchandise is unloaded from ships into bonded warehouses; it may be withdrawn from these warehouses only after duties have been paid and other customs formalities complied with. Plant matter, for example, must be examined by agents of the Department of Agriculture to make certain it is free from disease.

The gains from trade.

Trade among nations is a powerful force for peace; many people go so far as to claim it accomplishes more than all the aid programs that have yet been devised. Some years ago many European countries used the slogan "trade not aid," indicating they preferred trade opportunities in the United States to loans or grants. Use of this slogan helped the campaign to reduce United States trade barriers.

Although our political relations with the USSR are not always smooth, we do trade with them regularly, importing furs and minerals and exporting machinery and other items. For a number of years we have had export controls limiting the sale of strategic items to communist countries. Recently these controls have been relaxed to the point where they are not too limiting except in the case of Red China.

It may be interesting to see some of the items that enter into United States foreign trade. The following summary table shows exports and imports by product groups for 1967. The figures are in billions of dollars:

	U. S. Exports	U. S. Imports
Food and live animals	4.1	4.0
Beverages and tobacco	.6	.7
Crude inedible materials	3.2	3.0
Mineral fuels	1.1	2.3
Animal and vegetable fats and oils	.3	.1
Chemicals	2.8	1.0
Machinery and transport equipment	12.6	5.8
Other manufactured goods	5.4	9.0

You will notice in the table above that some categories come close to balancing, although in reality the products exported and imported are quite different. In the food and live animals category, for example, we import cattle but export wheat and other grains. In the mineral fuels category, we export coal but import petroleum. In the machinery and transportation equipment category, we export aircraft but import foreign-made automobiles, such as Volkswagens.

Because the United States is a large country with a well-developed home

UNITED STATES EXPORTS AND IMPORTS
BY MAJOR COMMODITY CATEGORY

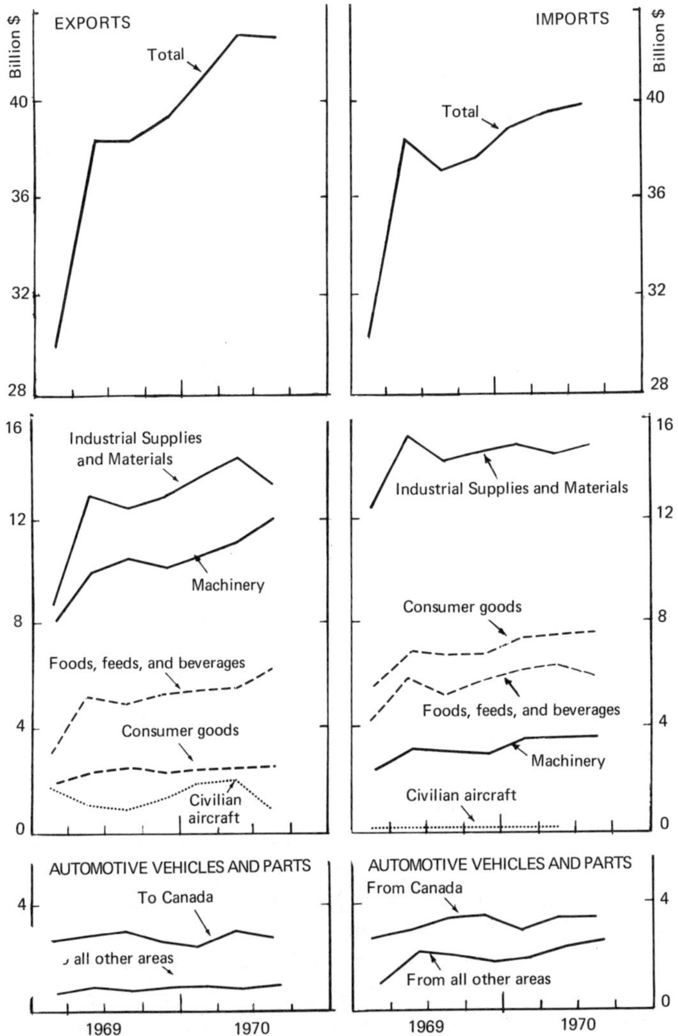

Major categories of United States exports and imports. Notice that although some of the categories nearly balance, the products exported and imported are quite different. For example in industrial materials we export coal and import oil. In foods we export wheat and import cattle. In 1971, not shown on the charts, imports increased rapidly while exports increased more slowly. The 10 per cent import surcharge imposed on August 15, 1971 slowed the growth in imports somewhat as did the defacto devaluation of the United States dollar.

market that is a free trade area, our foreign trade is relatively small in relation to our GNP, in fact only about 3 percent. Smaller countries, such as England and Japan, depend much more heavily on foreign trade, which may amount to 30 percent or more of their respective GNP's. Japan, which has comparatively few natural resources, has become a prosperous country by importing materials and exporting finished manufactured products. The value added by manufacture is a major bulwark of the Japanese economy.

England also lives in the world economy largely by importing materials and exporting manufactured products. An interruption to world trade, for example due to a war, is far more harmful to small countries dependent on commerce than it is to a large country such as the United States. In World War II, for example, the British went hungry because they were dependent on food imports. In the United States we are self-sufficient in most foodstuffs, although not in such items as coffee and tea, which are largely imported.

We have noticed that one reason the United States is relatively less dependent on foreign trade than some other countries is the existence of a large common market in this country, without tariff barriers or other trade restrictions. Other countries, realizing the advantage of a large free trade, are moving in that direction. We now have, for example, the European Common Market, composed of six countries that have virtually abolished tariff barriers among themselves, while preserving them against other countries. One recent question of considerable importance was whether England would be allowed to join the European Common Market and if so on what terms. Until recently a French veto kept the United Kingdom outside the fold. Early in 1972 England and several other countries formally joined the Common Market.

In recent years world trade has grown very considerably in value. One question to which this has given rise is whether there is sufficient international liquidity to finance this growing volume of trade and other payments. World trade has grown much faster than world gold production. By international liquidity we mean essentially money that is internationally acceptable. This may be gold or a reserve currency such as the United States dollar. By our persistent balance of payments deficits over the last two decades, the United States has provided liquidity to the rest of the world. But we cannot do this indefinitely and indeed have a program, not yet successful, to balance our international accounts.

Through the International Monetary Fund (the IMF), the leading industrial countries of the world have moved to help solve the international liquidity problem by establishing special drawing rights (SDR's) sometimes popularly known as paper gold. These rights are in effect a new kind of international currency, bank created, as it were, to accommodate international payments. Just as banks create money within a country, so countries, by agreeing to accept credits in the IMF as money, have added to the international monetary stock. Under the agreement creating SDR's, the volume of these instruments will gradually rise over a period of years. This may be regarded as a first step toward making the IMF a true international central bank.

United States trade.

We have noticed that a country's balance of payments is the result not only of merchandise exports and imports but also of invisible and capital items as well. Let us look at some actual figures. In 1967 the United States exported goods worth $45.8 billion and imported goods worth $41 billion. We had a surplus on goods and services account of $4.8 billion. Against this, however, we had net outpayments of $1.1 billion for remittances and pensions, $4.2 billion for government grants and aid, $3.3 billion for direct investment in foreign countries, and $.5 billion for other items. Even though there was some offset to these items in the form of investments by foreigners in the United States, our net payments deficit, on a liquidity basis, was $3.6 billion. This meant essentially that foreign claims against the dollar increased by this amount.

Since 1967 our trade surplus has grown much smaller. In 1971 for the first time in more than 80 years the United States experienced a foreign trade deficit. United States exports have continued to increase, but imports have increased much more rapidly. Although our foreign aid expenditures have decreased and controls have been placed over direct investment abroad, our international accounts are still in deficit. We may finally turn to import restriction to reduce this payments deficit. This is perhaps the least desirable way to solve the problem since, if we restrict imports, we invite other countries to retaliate by limiting their imports from us. This is beggar your neighbor with a vengence.

The classic remedy for a country with a persistent balance of payments deficit is devaluation. Reducing the par value of a currency makes imports more expensive and encourages exports, which are now cheaper in the currencies of other countries. The United States does not have the devaluation option to the same degree as other countries because the dollar is the world's most important reserve currency. If we devalued the dollar, many other countries might follow suit, leaving us no better off vis-a-vis them than we were before. Instead of devaluation, the cure for our balance of payments deficit until recently was sought in control of capital outflow from this country, and in efforts to keep prices and wages from rising as rapidly as these rise in other countries.

PERCENT CHANGE IN UNITED STATES GNP AND PERCENT CHANGE IN UNITED STATES IMPORTS

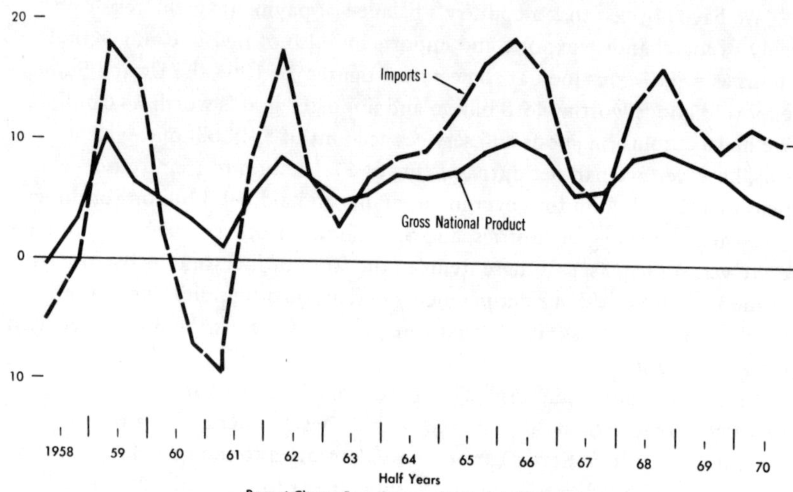

1. U.S. imports are adjusted to exclude automotive shipments from Canada to the United States and effects of major U.S. strikes and initial effects of closure of Suez Canal in 1967.

U.S. Department of Commerce, Office of Business Economics

Percent changes in United States imports and in United States GNP compared. Note that the two series follow the same general pattern but that changes in imports are relatively larger. Imports are only a small percentage of GNP, so the smaller aggregate moves relatively more. A similar pattern can be found for other countries, meaning that United States exports respond to the GNP's of our principal customer countries. A recession in Europe, for example, would be damaging to United States export prospects.

our exports become more competitive relative to those of Germany in world markets.

In December 1971 the United States did informally devalue its dollar in agreement with other countries, some of whom, such as Japan and Germany, revalued their currencies upward. Thus the dollar is now about 10 per cent cheaper in terms of other major currencies. This will stimulate our exports and restrict our imports.

If a country has a currency that is acceptable internationally, there is no need for its bilateral accounts with any other single country to balance. Much of international trade is triangular or even more complex. For many years we sold more to Japan than we bought from them; we used part of this surplus to purchase coffee and tea, while Japan made up her deficit with us by surpluses with other countries. If American banks accumulated too much Japanese yen from American exports to Japan, they could trade this yen for Brazilian or other currency in the foreign exchange market. The analogy would be an American business firm that had bank accounts in a number of states. If it had too much in Illinois and too little in New Jersey it could shift some funds from Illinois to New Jersey. This is precisely what banks do by means of the foreign exchange market.

Exchange controls.

Mention has been made of the fact that one type of interference with international trade is exchange controls within particular countries. Countries with exchange control ration their supply of foreign exchange by allowing only certain types of foreign payments in certain amounts to be made. Other transactions are prohibited. Countries that control their foreign exchange are in effect trying to maintain an artificially high value for their currency in international markets. If payments were unrestricted, their currency would sink, just as it does in devaluation. Put another way, foreign currencies would become more expensive since their relative scarcity would be increased.

When a country's currency is controlled, there will usually be a free or black market in that currency. This rate will measure what the currency is actually worth much more accurately than the official rate, which is maintained by the controls. The IMF makes a practice of urging its member countries to abandon exchange controls whenever they can and to define realistic parities for their currencies. This usually involves, in the first instance, some devaluation.

Countries that have exchange controls usually first adopted them during a period of emergency, such as a war. Controls are superficially attractive because they keep the cost of imports from rising, although the

Warehouses and port facilities in Lagos, Nigeria. Like many emerging countries, Nigeria is an exporter chiefly of products of tropical agriculture and an importer of manufactured products. In recent years with the discovery of oil, Nigeria has become an important exporter of petroleum products. Note the ships in the roadstead in the background. Note also the office buildings under construction at the left.

quantity of imports gets scarcer and scarcer. The longer controls are maintained the more unrealistic the exchange rate tends to get. Sometimes, when a country abandons its exchange control, the best course is to allow its exchange rate to float or seek its own level for a while, before attempting to define a new parity. Floating exchange rates are set by relative purchasing power within and without a given country.

Some countries do not even try to fix a par value for their currency but are content to let it fluctuate in the foreign exchange market. Canada has followed such a policy for years. At times the Canadian dollar will be at a premium compared to the American dollar; at other times it will be at a discount. Demand for the Canadian dollar in the foreign exchange market determines its value.

Floating exchange rates have an important advantage in that they constitute an automatic adjustment process in foreign trade and payments. When the Canadian dollar is scarce and it goes to a premium, exports from Canada are discouraged since they must be paid for in more expensive dollars. Imports into Canada are encouraged since the Canadian dollar will buy more of other currencies. The combination of fewer exports and more imports will increase the supply of Canadian dollars in the foreign exchange market and thus reduce the premium. If the Canadian dollar were to fall to a discount, the opposite mechanism would operate.

Thus floating rates tend to be always close to the purchasing power parity of a currency in terms of other currencies. This explains why such a system is advantageous for Canada. It would not do for the United States to follow such a policy, however, since the United States dollar is an important reserve currency. If its price were to fluctuate, foreigners would find it much less desirable to keep reserves in United States dollars. They would demand gold or would switch to a more stable currency such as Swiss francs or German marks. All currencies cannot float against one another. There need to be some fixed anchors. The dollar is such an anchor in the present world.

In the new economic policy of President Nixon, announced in mid-August of 1971, the United States has taken several backward steps so far as international trade and finance are concerned. First we have imposed a 10 per cent import surcharge on all foreign products previously subject to United States tariffs. This will make imports more expensive. Second we have cut the tie between gold and the United States dollar by placing an embargo on gold exports or closing the gold window. This means foreign countries holding dollar balances can no longer convert these into gold. For the time being the dollar is being allowed to float in relation to other currencies until more realistic rates of exchange can be established. Certain currencies, such as the Japanese yen, the German mark, and the Swiss franc are undervalued while the dollar is overvalued.

While the United States recently formally devalued the dollar to 1/38th ounce of gold, we have not yet resumed purchases and sales of gold at this new higher price. Other countries are still in process of revaluing their currencies also, some upward in terms of the dollar. The final result will undoubted by a compromise in which a whole new system of foreign exchange rates will be set. Instead of the yen being 360 to the U.S. dollar, it is now about 329. The German mark, formerly worth about 25 cents U.S., is now about 31 cents. The British pound, formerly worth $2.40 U.S., is now about $2.61. Additional changes in exchange rates can be expected. In the Smithsonian agreement in December, 1971, new parities were agreed upon for some currencies and the United States 10 percent import surcharge was removed.

These American moves were clearly dictated by inability to live longer with a large and growing balance of payments deficit. In 1972, imports into the United States exceeded exports, for the first time in many years. We are still committed to heavy offshore expenditures to support troops in Vietnam and in Europe in support of NATO. Tourist expenditures continue to drain our earnings in foreign currencies.

The long run consequences of these steps may well prove unfortunate. Foreign countries may retaliate against the United States import surcharge by raising their own tariffs, cutting off some of our exports. They may sell the dollar short in foreign exchange markets, causing it to drop more in terms of other currencies than it otherwise would. They may turn to other currencies as reserve assets, reducing the dollar's acceptability for this purpose.

It now appears the dollar's status will be settled only after a prolonged and difficult negotiation. In this process some far reaching changes in the world monetary system as we have known it since Bretton Woods are likely to be made. The nature of these changes cannot at this juncture be anticipated. Nor do we know whether our immediate objective to end our balance of payments deficits will be achieved. The only thing certain is that international monetary cooperation will be needed more than ever but will be harder to achieve because of our sudden and unilateral change in the rules of the game.

Trade policy.

Mention should be made of one controversy that concerns United States trade and tariff policy at the present time. It is contended by some that we are at a disadvantage in trading with other countries because of our tax system. The problem is this: the United States depends heavily on income taxes, whereas other countries use sales and excise taxes more extensively than we do. When goods are exported, it is customary to rebate the sales or excise taxes because these are imposed by the importing country. If we tax not sales but income, however, we have nothing to rebate, since to rebate income taxes is considered a subsidy and contrary to the GATT rules. Hence, it is contended, United States products are taxed abroad, without any corresponding rebate in this country, and therefore are at a tax disadvantage in competing with foreign products.

The implicit assumption in this argument is that income taxes are passed forward as a cost into the price of products, and hence that these products are priced higher than they would be without income taxes. If, however, income taxes are not passed forward into selling prices, but instead fall on profits, prices are not higher and American products are not at a tax disadvantage.

This argument is usually made by those who would like to replace the the corporate profits tax with a tax on value added. A value-added tax, being like a sales tax, would be rebated on exports and imposed on imports.

This is what the French do with their value-added tax, for example. This line of argument has some merit, although not all that its proponents claim for it but it seems unlikely we will choose to change our tax system to improve its effect on foreign trade, when foreign trade is only 3 per cent of our GNP. If we were more dependent on foreign trade, we might find it desirable to accommodate our tax system somewhat to this reality.

Another topic that has been much discussed in recent years concerns trade between the less and the more developed countries. The less developed or emerging countries claim that the terms of trade have moved steadily against their products, which are largely raw materials and products of tropical agriculture, in favor of the manufactured goods they must import. They have also claimed that the tariffs imposed by advanced countries discriminate against their raw materials.

The complaints of the less developed countries have been voiced largely through the United Nations Conference on Trade and Development (UNCTAD) a specialized United Nations agency for trade and development matters. While GATT has been regarded primarily as the agency of the advanced countries, UNCTAD has been the forum for the emerging countries.

What the poorer countries want is tariff preferences for their products in the advanced countries. They claim this would make them less dependent on foreign aid and would enable them to finance more of their own economic development. While this demand conflicts with the most favored nation principle, basic to trade negotiations for many years, the advanced countries may find it expedient before too long to move in this direction.

A growing volume of international trade is essential to economic growth and is a significant measure of economic advancement. The less developed countries want to graduate from their status of exporters of raw materials and become exporters of manufactured products, instead of strictly importers of these. In the economic development plans of many countries, substantial efforts are being made to create new exporting industries. Sometimes, however, these plans are not wholly realistic.

Egypt, for example, wanted to create a steel industry, although it had none of the materials, for example, coal and iron ore, from which steel is made. Consequently their costs in steelmaking cannot be competitive with those of other countries. Their only prospect of exporting steel would be to subsidize it heavily. Other countries have also made unfortunate choices about the export industries they wished to develop.

The most sensible choice is to build on the existing export industries but to add one or more stages of processing to get more value added. For example, Pakistan, instead of exporting raw jute, should process it into bags, thus exporting a finished product instead of a raw material. Building on an existing comparative advantage is usually better and more successful than trying to create an entirely new one.

It is interesting that the more a country develops industrially, the more it trades with its fellow countries that are also well developed. United States trade with Japan, for example, has grown rapidly as Japan has progressed industrially. Whereas some years ago many of our imports from Japan were handicraft and cheap copies of American products, now we import sophisticated electronic gear, automobiles, and other products of a well-developed manufacturing society. Our trade with Japan is much bigger today in both directions.

With the growth in trade has come another development, namely the growth of the international business firm. These firms, usually large, have facilities in many countries, including sales offices, manufacturing plants, and service facilities. Today typewriters may be manufactured by an American company from a plant in Sweden, or Spain, or Holland, whereas British and German companies may have plants in this country. Some people have expressed fears that locating manufacturing facilities abroad may reduce the volume of world trade. On the contrary, it has increased it. Manufacturing abroad is merely another step toward specialization that has spurred trade wherever and in whatever form it has been practiced.

Today's multinational business firm manufacturers wherever it can do so cheapest and to best advantage. Branches and subsidiaries are established abroad simply because it is good business to do so. Yesterday's business firm served only a local market; today's business regards the whole world as its market. It may serve that market from 50 different plants located in a dozen different countries. It employes thousands of people, of many nationalities. They all have better wages and working conditions than if they were employed by purely local firms.

The large business corporation is a creature of the modern industrial state; it operates across international boundaries as several decades ago smaller corporations operated over state boundaries.

Summary.

In brief, international trade is a manifestation of more complex and interdependent national economies. It arises from specialization and is stimulated by economic growth. Countries specialize in making those products in which they have comparative advantages, and exchange them for other things they need.

Banks finance international trade by supplying the necessary foreign currency to make payments and remittances of all types. The market for foreign exchange is a well-organized one in which rates of exchange for currencies against one another are determined. Those currencies that have par values are kept close to par in the foreign exchange market by gold shipments or by movement of reserve balances from one country to another.

Most countries have taxes or tariffs on imports. Sometimes these taxes are designed to raise revenue; at other times, to keep imports out. These latter are known as protective tariffs. Trade restriction by tariffs has a long history, and has been a frequently used device to foster economic development; in today's complex economy this is less likely to work. The modern trend is toward tariff reduction and removal of nontrade barriers so that world trade can continue to grow. This is not, however, the rule for all countries or for all times within a given country. The United States, for example, is presently in danger of reversing some of its liberal trade policies and embarking on a new course of protectionism. If we follow this course, other countries will retaliate against us. In the end we shall all suffer.

In 1824 Lord Macaulay, the British historian whose style Winston Churchill copied, wrote that, "free trade, one of the greatest blessings which a government can confer on a people, is in almost every country unpopular."

The unpopularity is there, Lord M., but it is variable and cyclical. At the moment we seem to be gaining a little.

Chapter 17

ALWAYS TO BE TOPICAL—Current Topics in Economics

Eli Heckscher, the Swedish historian of those 16th and 17th century economic doctrines known as mercantilism, regarded these doctrines essentially as a phase in the development of economic policy. They were designed mainly to secure political unification and national power, when these were scarce conditions.

If mercantilist doctrines frequently contained a strong element of beggar your neighbor, and they usually did, they were nevertheless intended to strengthen nations against medieval factions at home and commercial rivals abroad. In this effort they were often temporarily successful.

Economic policies grow out of contemporary events and are shaped largely by these events. In the 1930's economics was strongly depression oriented. In the 1940's it was war oriented. Today the orientation is largely toward maintaining full employment without inflation—a neat trick if we can turn it.

We have seen in earlier chapters that most of the advances in economic thought have come about because economists were trying to solve some great big social problem, such as poverty, unemployment, or the business cycle. As a discipline, economics is always topical. It is related to current events, which it seeks to analyze and explain. It never lacks for subject matter because our society never lacks for problems.

This season the main problem may be inflation; next season it will be unemployment or an unfavorable balance of payments; the season after that may bring fears about international competitiveness or the upward creep of wages in advance of productivity. The list is endless because society is always changing and because change does not come smoothly. Some groups are always benefited and other disadvantaged. Prosperity, it seems, is never shared evenly. A growing national product may be a source of national pride, but it conceals what is happening differentially to people.

In the study of economics, one of the first lessons to be learned is that redistribution, of wealth, of income, or of opportunity, is not the answer to social problems. If one seized all the wealth of millionaires in this country and gave the proceeds to the poor, the latter would benefit very little. They would get at best a few dollars each which would not alleviate their position except momentarily; moreover we would have destroyed wealth that serves a productive purpose, that supports industries, and educational institutions, and other necessary features of our society. The notion, often entertained by socialists, that equality of wealth or income would solve some of our social problems is a myth—the Robin Hood myth if you will—

as fictional as the tale of that benign outlaw who broke the law for the public good.

My purpose, however, is not to explode myths, although a considerable part of economics is devoted to just that objective, but to illustrate the fact that economics is a topical subject. The topics that are discussed today are not the same as those which will receive attention tomorrow. We cannot predict what tomorrow's topics will be, except that they will be large problems concerning the human condition. Rather, my purpose is to discuss briefly a few of today's topics, so you will appreciate a little better the changing nature of the subject matter of economics. The topics discussed here are by no means an exhaustive list. They are merely a few illustrations of what economists have been thinking and talking about in recent years.

With each topic you will get only the barest outline of what it is about, not all the controversy and all the complications. But this is an introduction to economic reasoning, not a fully developed exercise in the art. To reach that latter stage you must keep reading and studying. Mastery of a complex discipline, which economics is, is not available in capsule form.

Let us turn then to a few topics.

Economic planning.

Planning covers a broad range of activities, usually related in some way to controlling the path of economic development or deciding on the composition of output. Less developed countries work out development plans in some detail, in an effort to decide where foreign assistance will be invested or their own resources put to use to achieve agreed objectives. Communist countries plan production in even greater detail since they do not have free markets, and hence do not obtain from these markets signals, in the form of price advances and declines, telling what commodities are more and less intensively wanted. In the free enterprise system such central planning is unnecessary since the price system controls resource allocation.

In France, although the price system works and there is no official central planning, an exercise called indicative planning is carried through on a regular basis. In this process government and business officials meet together on regular occasions to work out consensus targets, usually in the form of input-output tables. These show what each industry is likely to buy from and sell to each other industry detailed in the table.

While such plans when finally coordinated are unofficial and nonbinding, in the sense that no penalties are assessed for failure to meet targets, the exercise is considered helpful by all parties, since they all know what to expect of one another. In the United States we do not use this tool of economic policy since business would very likely object to the central direction that is implicit in the program.

We do have a kind of planning exercise in that the Council of Economic Advisers works out each year an expectation for the year ahead, and then advises the President on economic policies it considers necessary to maintain full employment during the coming year. The President is free to accept or reject these recommendations, as the Congress is free to deal with the President's recommendations. This whole exercise, however, is concerned with a macro plan for the whole economy and not a detailed plan for individual industries and individual businesses.

Planning is also a business activity that is receiving ever more attention. Such planning is concerned with setting and working toward business objectives rather than attempting to plan for the whole economy or a sector of it. Business plans address themselves to such questions as when and where to expand, how to increase a company's market share, and how to finance expanded activities.

In the 1930's, following the great depression, there was a vogue of support for economic planning in this country; but this vogue passed in a few years when it became clear that a planned economy was not demonstrably more efficient than an unplanned one; the Russian experience showed, for example, that the planned economy was often highly inefficient. The vogue for planning was also short-lived because it soon became clear that planning meant the creation of a large and cumbersome bureaucracy that would proliferate controls and rob the economy of much of its dynamism. Today advocates of more extensive planning for advanced industrial countries are few, and not in great favor, except in France.

One reason why detailed economic planning has not been more successful is that it requires a great mass of statistics; also decisions made in one sector of the economy have ramifications that influence many other sectors. Thus a plan always runs the danger of being internally inconsistent, and unlikely of fulfillment because of these inconsistencies. Also comprehensive plans are likely to be rigid and incapable of swift response to changing economic circumstances. The price system is much more swiftly and appropriately responsive than is a central plan.

Emerging countries will undoubtedly stick with their development plans as these are more and more being made a requirement by lending institutions such as the World Bank.

Development of the emerging countries.

A broad problem of considerable significance since World War II has been how to assist the less developed countries of the world to speed up their modernization and their economic growth. This has been both a political and an economic problem. In the political sphere Russian style socialism and Western style capitalism have been competing intensively for the ideological conquest of the third or uncommitted world. Both systems have experienced successes and failures in different areas.

Substantial aid has been given by both superpowers, ostensibly to finance economic development; but much of this aid has been wasted in that it has not resulted in starting the cumulative process of growth originally expected. What we have discovered, after more than 20 years of the foreign aid and technical assistance business, is that getting a growth process started in a fundamentally backward economy is more difficult and

The Economic and Social Council of the United Nations in session. The Economic and Social Council is one of the United Nations subgroups similar to a Committee of the United States Congress. Notice the delegates from different countries seated at the horseshoe shaped table. Notice also the booths behind glass at the left which are occupied by translators. Each delegate can, through an earphone, hear the proceedings in his own language.

time consuming than we thought. Numerous preconditions for economic development—fundamental education, changing the traditional basis of agriculture, and instilling incentives to work—are necessary before economic growth can be expected to take root.

Country after country has also demonstrated a fundamental inability to finance development on its own without ruinous inflation, or foreign exchange crises, or political turmoil. While some countries have done well for a time, initial growth has often been followed by a period of relative stagnation in which much of the early momentum has been lost. Aspirations that income levels in emerging countries would begin to catch up with those of more developed countries have been thwarted. Poor countries have failed, even relatively, to keep pace with richer countries. The gap in incomes has widened rather than narrowed. This is a potent source of discontent and political unrest in the world today.

A hydroelectric project under construction in Brazil. Typical of a project designed to help the economic development of a country. This project, the largest of its type yet undertaken in Latin America, was assisted by a loan from the World Bank. Photo courtesy World Bank.

One problem emerging countries have encountered in attempting to program their entry into the modern world is a desire to do things for which they are not yet prepared—to start factories without an efficient transport or distribution network—to use the latest in modern machinery when they lack repair and maintenance services—and to make other leaps forward in technology in only a part of the economy.

Countries have also been prone to invest their resources in social services—in medical facilities, community centers, and the like. Desirable as these services may be in adding to the amenities of life, they contribute only indirectly and in the long run to such essentials as raising export earnings.

Because development is so slow, and so fraught with pitfalls, we are now in the process of establishing more reasonable expectations for this activity and for our efforts to assist it.

Less developed countries have usually wanted to start manufacturing industries, often to replace imports. What they have discovered is that these new manufacturing plants have been unable to compete with imports in price and still earn a profit. Too often the new industries have needed tariff protection, subsidization, and other forms of assistance. With attention centered on import replacement, too little effort has been devoted to expanding and improving exports. This upgrading of exports is necessary to finance the greatly enlarged volume of foreign payments occasioned by a development effort.

An electric power plant under construction in Argentina. The dockside location will make possible the delivery of fuel by water transport. This is typical of the kind of project needed to support a modern, industrial economy. Photo courtesy World Bank.

Irrigating wheat in Oklahoma. Such irrigation, supplementing light rainfall, greatly increases yields per acre. Other factors increasing grain yields are better seeds, fertilizer, and proper tillage. In recent years the so called green revolution has much increased crop yields, making some countries self sufficient in food and feed for the first time, and giving other countries exportable surpluses of agricultural products. An increase in agricultural productivity is one of the first and most important factors leading to economic growth in the less developed countries of the world.

Thus the developing countries have often encountered foreign exchange crises, from which they have had to be rescued either by foreign aid or by cutting back on imports for consumption. Often consumers in these countries have balked at these import restrictions, because the benefits of economic development are deferred while its costs are immediate.

Another fact the developing countries have discovered is that agricultural development must precede industrial development. It was thought initially by the aid-giving countries that agricultural development would come very slowly, because peasant cultivators were hard to reach and were extremely resistant to changing methods. But with high yielding varieties of seeds and plants, it has been discovered that small farmers will change their methods quickly when they see convincing demonstrations of what better seeds and fertilizers will do.

Change is now coming more quickly in agriculture; many countries which could not formerly do so now are near to feeding themselves. This is the most promising development to occur in less developed countries in many years. Better nutrition has much to do with the willingness and ability of people to work at development.

War economics.

A war economy is a forced draft sort of situation, in which time means more than money and the whole idea is to maximize production regardless of the cost. At least past wars have meant this because time has permitted the mobilization of resources and the production of war equipment after hostilities have broken out. Wars of the future, which may be opened by nuclear strikes and counter strikes, are likely to be much shorter. The equipment in being when war breaks out may be all we are permitted to use.

A war does illustrate some of the problems and policies of total mobilization, and the resiliences and bottlenecks of an economic system. The price system gets replaced by a complex series of mobilization orders, priorities, price and wage controls, and other fiats designed to shift resources from civilian to war output. Whole industries, such as the automobile industry, are converted to make tanks and aircraft; housewives join assembly lines or become riveters; men are called into uniform.

War finance is a special problem. Government expenditures increase enormously, while tax yields rise only moderately. New taxes are imposed but these never catch up with the rise in expenditures; a large part of war costs have to be financed by borrowing. Financial institutions are tapped and there are patriotic appeals to citizens, sometimes verging on compulsion, to buy bonds.

Inflation under these circumstances is inevitable; even if it is temporarily held in check by wage and price controls, it spills over later when these controls are dismantled. The transportation network is strained with the movement of goods and people needed to mount the war effort.

In World War II we had a remarkable demonstration of just how much idle capacity the American economy contained. The 1930's had been a decade of underemployment and limited economic growth. War provided the impetus to reach full capacity, and to stretch our resources beyond what many believed possible.

War also brought many innovations and improvements in technology, some of which were already known but were not used because demand was inadequate. War brought many geographic changes as new defense plants and military installations were built, and as people changed jobs to do higher priority work.

We managed in this country to redeploy the civilian population largely

A factory producing anti-aircraft guns during World War II. This is probably a converted automobile or other plant that shifted to war production. In past wars we have had time to mobilize manpower and make munitions after hostilities started. In future wars, which will probably begin with nuclear strikes and counterstrikes, we may not have this time. Note the substantial number of woman workers.

by financial incentives, higher wages and the like. Other countries, Britain for example, had to use some compulsion with regard to where people would live and work. Women were drafted for farm work; families were evacuated to the country.

There is always a question about financial incentives versus compulsion during war time. Generally in this country, apart from manpower for the actual armed forces, we have used little compulsion on the remainder of the people. Largely this has been because we were removed from the battle. A country that is invaded, or under continual bombardment, necessarily uses more compulsion.

One thing that makes war economics interesting is that it speeds up and carries to extreme limits economic adjustments that normally would take much longer and be much smaller. We know, for example, that the labor force normally expands somewhat when job opportunities are more numerous. Housewives think more often of going to work when more work is available. During wartime the demand for labor expands enormously, and the labor force expands substantially also. One mistake the Germans made in World War II was in not mobilizing women; most women remained at home, and extensive use was made instead of slave labor from occupied European territory. This labor often sabotaged and slowed down German war production.

Bad as the financial problems are during wartime, their principal impact is delayed until after the hostilities. The great inflations have occurred not during but after wars, particularly in countries where wars were lost. The destruction accompanying a lost war reduces production to a fraction of its former level, while needs for relief, reconstruction, etc., make it impossible to reduce government expenditures; hence the resort to the printing press, or forced loans, or taxation in kind. War provides the classic fuel for uncontrolled inflation—too much money.

Limited wars, such as Vietnam, are a different and, in some ways, a more difficult problem. Apart from the draft of manpower, we have used very little compulsion in mobilizing for this war. A few priority orders have been issued for materials, such as copper, directly used in military production; but these orders have been temporary and have not forced postponement of civilian production to any substantial extent. There has been sufficient productive capacity in the economy so that both war and civilian orders could be accommodated; very few plants have shifted exclusively to war production.

Some concern has been expressed about what might happen to the economy when and if Vietnam is over. With the war already winding down and becoming increasingly unpopular, we may have a settlement before too long. It will probably be a very unfavorable settlement with most of our war objectives unaccomplished; but sentiment is apparently swinging toward a settlement at any price.

What concerns those who have been speculating about the post Vietnam scene is the possibility of another depression such as we expected but did not get after World War II. This likelihood, while not to be totally discounted, seems remote because there are so many other federal programs waiting to take up any slack in public expenditures that an end to hostilities in Vietnam might produce. At the present level of forces and hostilities, Vietnam is costing only about $20 billion per year, a sum that could easily be expended in programs for health, education, and increased social services.

Moreover, we cannot reduce military expenditures by the full extent of Vietnam war costs. Forces will be deployed to other areas, such as the Middle East, to counter new threats to peace that will undoubtedly develop. Reequipment with new weapons systems will have to go on, to maintain a defense posture of readiness for new emergencies. The budget presented in January 1972 called for an increase rather than a decrease in military expenditure.

Thus, ending the hostilities in Vietnam will make possible a reduction in military expenditures equal only to part of Vietnam war costs. At the same time various welfare programs are waiting in the wings to expand their outlays by amounts equal to or greater than whatever may be saved in Vietnam. It is possible an end to Vietnam may bring on a recession; but it is unlikely this will be a direct result of any reduction in federal government expenditures.

Consumer economics.

In large part this field of study and activity is devoted to providing consumers with information so they can make more intelligent choices. On every hand we are today beset with advertising, often consisting largely of inflated claims that particular products will make us healthy, popular, and irresistible. Much of advertising seems calculated to mislead, as when the smallest olives offered are called large, or the giant economy package is in reality more expensive per ounce than the regular package, or when something is 12 cents off an unstated price.

One approach to informing consumers is through private organizations that objectively test products and report the results, such as Consumers Union. Such organizations perform a valuable service for their members by concluding, as a result of impartial tests, whether brand X is really better than brand Y; but being membership organizations their influence is limited. Often the consumers who need them most have no knowledge of or access to their services.

On the other hand, we have some legislation designed to protect consumers, although usually not from foolish choices. We have pure food and drug laws under which harmful additives, such as cyclamates, can be identified and sometimes banned. We also have standards, frequently developed by industry and government in cooperation, which provide some assurance that products will be at least minimally functional for the purpose intended. These standards are often voluntary; where they are compulsory, enforcement consists chiefly of sanctions applied by the industry itself.

Other general legislation is designed merely to inform consumers rather than to protect them. We have, for example, a Federal truth-in-lending law, which requires that charges for credit and on installment accounts be stated in annual rates of simple interest. This was passed on the theory that many consumers did not know they were paying from 18 percent to 36 percent rates for such credit. A similar truth-in-packaging bill, which has not yet become law, would require labeling packages in prices per ounce or per pound of contents. The theory of both these efforts is that, if consumers know what they are buying, they can make more intelligent choices.

The consumer movement has been gathering strength lately, on the theory that the consumer interest has been neglected and unrepresented for a long time, whereas other interests—of labor, of manufacturers, have been represented by lobbyists and others who have succeeded in obtaining special advantages for them. We are all consumers, in addition to whatever other interests we may have in the economic system, as bricklayers, or bankers, or merchants. As is well known, housewives do the bulk of the buying and disperse the largest part of family income. Efforts by or on behalf of consumers have thus been largely directed by or at housewives. To date, consumer advisers to the President of the United States have all been women.

Other efforts to protect consumers have taken the form of federal standards against flammable fabrics and requirements that actual fabric contents of clothes, blankets, etc., be stated on the label. Safety standards for automobiles have also been prompted, at least in part, by the consumer movement.

It is probable that other steps to inform and protect consumers will be taken in the next few years; at this time, however, it is impossible to predict what these steps will be. Sentiment for consumer protection is growing; federal agencies lose few opportunities to protect an interest group; sometimes it seems they become overprotected, as the farmers are. Thus we can expect more of both legislation and regulation, supposedly dictated by the consumer interest.

Location of industry.

To date the location of industry has been decided almost exclusively by economic factors; but the time may be coming, and soon, when this will no longer be the case. With the current interest in antipollution and in preserving the environment, industry may no longer be permitted to locate where it wishes. Already the British have adopted some rigid controls over the location process; other countries may soon follow suit.

Location to date has been a matter of picking the site where costs would be cheapest and where the market could best be served. Factors in location have been access to good and cheap transportation, nearness to suppliers and customers, access to materials and cheap power, nearness to labor of the proper skill, and similar factors that determine costs per unit of product. Proper location has been a strong factor in competitiveness; a poor location has often caused businesses to fail.

The British approach to controlled location has been two-pronged. On the one hand, plants have been encouraged by subsidies to locate in distressed areas where unemployment is high and growth slow. On the other hand, plants have been barred from certain areas near cities where the plan is to recreate open spaces with parks and other amenities. When controls over location of industry come in this country, it is probable they will be based on a similar blend of incentives and prohibitions.

We already have a program of incentives to draw industry to distressed areas. To date the incentives offered have generally not been powerful enough to offset the cost disadvantages which these distressed regions already have. The disadvantages may be poor transportation, high cost power, or distance from markets, or perhaps some combination of all three. At any rate it is these disadvantages which caused the region to become distressed in the first place, and not to participate fully in the growth process.

Unless the incentives offered by the government are of sufficient magnitude to offset these cost disadvantages, the incentive program alone will be a failure. We are learning, in our distressed area program, that quite powerful incentives are needed to be effective.

Preservation of the environment.

Since this issue has become a national concern, it has been discovered to have all sorts of economic overtones. One still unresolved question is how the costs of the program that finally evolves will be distributed: Should fines and special taxes be levied on the polluters? Should the program be financed from general tax revenue? Or should tax incentives be given to firms and agencies that reduce pollution?

Tax concessions are a way of sharing the cost between general revenue and the polluters who modify their polluting activities. To date the tendency seems to be toward a combination of special fines and taxes and general revenue financing. Whether this policy will continue or not is still an open question.

Apart from pollution in the generally understood sense, there are many other environmental questions with economic implications. For example, there is the question of maintaining coastal wetlands, such as the Florida everglades, in their natural state. These regions are threatened by the encroachment of industrial plants, by use of water for other purposes, by airport building, and other land uses that disturb the balance of nature.

So far the policy that has evolved for preserving these areas is a combination of creating new national parks and discouraging unwanted activities by both tax incentives and disincentives. This latter combination has yet to become law (in 1971) but may well be enacted before long. The theory of this approach is merely to discourage land uses that are inconsistent with preservation of the environment in its natural state.

In preserving the environment, new techniques of federal, state, and local government cooperation may well prove necessary and have to be worked out. To date this cooperation has come mostly through grants in aid, and through federally set standards which are left to the local governments to enforce. We now have the possibility of revenue sharing, which in the first instance will probably weaken established techniques of cooperation. Over the long run, however, cooperation may improve under revenue sharing, since all levels of government will meet as more nearly equal partners.

Until now, since the federal government has been the source of most of the money, it has exercised a disproportionate influence in planning, standard setting, and fixing priorities. We hear much these days about the new federalism, but have few examples of how it is actually to function in practice. No doubt time will tell whether the new federalism is more than a slogan.

It seems clear that, as population continues to increase, the cost of preserving the environment will rise more than proportionately; much of this cost will doubtless have to be met from general revenues, regardless of how the fine and fee structure evolves. The real question is therefore what priority environmental programs will command in the federal budget.

If this priority is too low, the needs will not be met; if it is too high, we shall waste resources in pursuit of what is admittedly a worthwhile national objective. Already the voice of the environmental lobby can be heard in the land. It will grow stronger as time passes, unless some other crusade comes along. It is to be hoped that ecology will prove neither a momentary enthusiasm nor a ruling passion. Economists can best cooperate with the ecology movement by carefully assessing both its costs and its benefits.

Literary vs. mathematical method.

This is an old question in economics and one where fashions change. From time to time mathematical methods will be in the ascendancy only to lose popularity in favor of old-fashioned or literary statements of principles and conclusions. At the moment we are going through one of those phases where mathematical techniques are again popular. The current professional economic journals are replete with equations and statements of inequality, all expressed in mathematical notation.

Mathematics, particularly the calculus, differential equations, and the theory of functions has always played a role in scientific economics. Since mathematics is a language, it has long appealed to some economists as an elegant way of stating theorems which could only be expressed more laboriously in ordinary language.

Much of economic analysis consists of deductive logic from stated premises. Reasoning of this type is considerably assisted by the use of mathematics, although at the risk of some loss of comprehension by the average reader. But many economists are not concerned about the average reader. They write solely for their professional colleagues, for on these colleagues their reputations depend. It seems unnecessary to add that scholasticism lies in being obscure, and that economics is not an esoteric but a vital subject.

The great economists, from Smith to Keynes, were never obscure; they always wrote for the general reader and hoped he would follow their efforts; only the petty economists find it necessary to conceal their thought behind mountains of technical terms and masses of mathematical equations.

The idea that scientific economics can only be propounded with the aid of mathematics is on a par with saying it can only be expressed in Arabic or Chinese. To the best of my knowledge no reputable economist maintains this latter proposition. It would seem, therefore, that mathematics should be regarded as a tool subject, like statistics or accounting, both of which are useful but not absolutely essential to the explanation of economic principles.

The pendulum will undoubtedly swing again, as it has so often in the past, toward economics as a humanistic rather than a scientific subject. Although forecasting techniques are becoming more elaborate and mathematical, policy is still discussed mainly in the old framework of ordinary language. One hopes it will remain so. When economics becomes so technical that only the professional economists can understand it, it will become like medieval theology, highly refined but quite useless. Much better that it should remain a useful, if inexact, art.

Chapter **18**

FOR WANT OF A POLICY–Economic Policies

Max Weber, a German economist and sociologist, wrote in 1922 that the function of social science is to provide "concepts and judgements which are not empirical reality, nor pictures of it; but which allow us to arrange it intellectually in a valid manner." From this arrangement can be drawn policy implications and policy prescriptions.

Considerably earlier, in 1848, John Stuart Mill, a thoroughly classical English economist, wrote that "in the particular circumstances of a given age or nation, there is scarcely anything really important to the general interest which it may not be desirable, or even necessary, that the government should take upon itself, not because private individuals cannot perform it, but because they will not."

The White House has become the center for economic policy making in this country. Once policy may have been made in the board rooms of large corporations or banks, but now the Government has become too large and too intertwined in economic affairs. Presidents today receive economic advice regularly from a number of sources and translate that advice into policies and programs of an economic nature, such as wage or price stabilization programs, programs for the reduction of unemployment, and the like.

Economic policy often, but not always, involves government intervention. As problems become more complex, the functions of government proliferate, as we have already noticed in an earlier chapter. Since economics is always concerned with "the particular circumstances of a given age," the concerns of policy are contemporary, immediate problems.

Economic policy is, in a very real sense, the cutting edge of economic analysis. The chief reason for studying economics, apart from intellectual curiosity and general understanding, is to formulate or appraise policies under which the economy will perform better, or more equitably, or more efficiently. This chapter will be concerned primarily with national economic policies, although we cannot neglect both regional and international policies as well.

National economic policy is primarily the province of the President and his advisors; also the Congress which must implement policies by legislation and appropriations. Thus national economic policy is both formulated and implemented in a political setting, but that does not change its essence. It is still subject to economic laws and to economic limitations.

It is manifestly impossible in this short book to discuss all elements of national economic policy. Instead, we shall limit ourselves primarily to macroeconomic policies concerning the level of economic activity and the general functioning of the economy. This does not mean that microeconomic policies are unimportant; they may be of the essence for efficient economic performance; they are simply less in the foreground at the present time.

Employment policy.

Let us turn first to full employment policy. It is now the objective of all national administrations, Republican as well as Democratic, to keep the economy at all times functioning as close to the full employment level as possible. Generally, "full employment" is taken to mean employment of about 96 percent of the labor force, with no more than 4 percent unemployed.

A certain volume of unemployment is necessary to provide for shifts and transitions in the labor force, people moving from industry to industry, from locality to locality, and from job to job. If no more than 4 percent of the work force is unemployed, jobs can usually be found for nearly all who want them, and labor shortages do not severely restrict production. Below that level, say at 3 percent unemployment, labor shortages in some industries and localities will be a common occurrence.

The objective is not only to maintain full employment, but to do this without serious inflation. We can always reach full employment by overspending, by running a big budget deficit, and by stimulating the economy through special incentives, such as tax concessions or government grants. The object is not to do this, not to spend ourselves rich as the saying goes, but to achieve a balanced posture in which the economy will be operating at close to normal capacity without serious inflation.

This policy objective is a comparatively recent one, which has been generally accepted only since World War II. Before that time it was felt that the business cycle was inevitable—that prosperity and depression would follow one another regardless of what a government did. To be sure it was possible to mitigate the swings somewhat—to curtail prosperity a little and to fill in a depression somewhat—but it was not considered practical to eliminate business cycles altogether.

Today some economists take the position that, with all the power and resources governments have, there are no longer any fundamental reasons for depressions. So-called new economists, who were chiefly Democratic advisors with Keynesian leanings, were perhaps the most extreme in claiming the business cycle need no longer exist. More conservative economists, while conceding that the government's tools for controlling or fine tuning the economy are stronger than ever before, doubt that the necessary foresight is in hand to keep cyclical swings from recurring, much as the amplitude of these swings may be dampened by contracyclical measures.

The tools for maintaining full employment have been primarily monetary and fiscal policies. Monetary policy is the province of the independent Federal Reserve Board. Fiscal policy, which means primarily tax policy, has to do in its macroeconomic sense with whether the Federal Government is operating to expand or to contract the private sector. Tax policy is closely related to budget policy in the sense that the economy may be stimulated either by reducing taxes or by increasing government expenditures. The private sector may be restrained by reducing expenditures, by increasing taxes, or perhaps by a combination of both.

Lately it has become increasingly apparent to many that fiscal and monetary policies, as we know them, are not enough and that another weapon, *incomes policy,* is necessary in the policy arsenal if we are to achieve full employment without inflation. An incomes policy is a policy of restraint on prices and wages, so that these do not rise too rapidly before full employment is actually reached. An incomes policy may range in force all the way from mild restraint by moral suasion, with little or no power actually to make it effective, to outright control over wages and prices such as we have had during World War II.

In the Johnson administration, incomes policy was mainly a matter of "jawboning" in the more flagrant cases of wage and price increase. It is difficult to measure the impact of such a policy since the real measure is what happened with jawboning compared to what would have happened without it. Students of the question have concluded that the jawbone policy did have some effect, although it is difficult if not impossible to quantify this effect.

In contrast, the Nixon administration, at least for its first 2 years, failed to embrace any incomes policy, feeling this was not necessary in the economic environment in which it was operating. However, as unemployment climbed to 6 percent, and as monetary policy was eased in late 1970, both without any tendency for prices to stop rising, more and more talk was heard about the desirability of an incomes policy, presumably one not very different from that used by the previous administration. It is curious that new administrations, after being vigorously critical of their predecessors, often wind up doing practically the same things that these predecessors did. This proves, if anything, that economics is no respecter of political parties. On August 15, 1971 there was instituted a Republican incomes policy, implemented by a *Pay Board* and a *Price Commission.*

Monetary policy can be adapted very quickly to changing economic circumstances. The Federal Reserve can change, within a few days or weeks at most, from a stance of restriction to one of ease. It is all a matter of supplying more reserves to the commercial banks. As we have seen in the discussion of banking, this is done mainly by purchasing United States Government securities in the open market. The Federal Reserve is in the market for government securities almost daily, so it is a simple matter to change objectives and buy on net balance instead of selling.

Often it will be some time before the dealers in government securities and the banks themselves know what is happening. The simplest way to keep abreast of Federal Reserve policy is to watch the weekly Federal statement which shows the size of commercial bank reserves and whether they are *free* or *borrowed.*

A position of net borrowed reserves, where borrowings at the Federal banks exceed the amount of excess reserves, is synonymous with tight money. When excess reserves exceed borrowed reserves, the difference is described as free. This is the best indication we have that an easy credit policy is being followed.

In contrast to monetary policy, which can be changed or reversed very quickly, tax policy requires much longer to change. It now takes a year or longer to get a tax bill legislated; thus if tax reduction is being used as the vehicle to stimulate the economy, in preparing a program one must forecast that the economy will still need stimulating a year hence.

One reason tax bills take so long to become law is that they accumulate amendments in their passage through the legislative mill. This happens more in the Senate than it does in the House, which tends to pass whatever bill the Ways and Means Committee brings out. Floor amendments are prohibited. In the Senate, on the other hand, floor amendments are frequent. Often these have very little to do with the main purpose of the tax bill, which is to reduce rates in order to stimulate the economy.

Budget policy, like tax policy, is also relatively slow to change. The President sends up a federal budget only once a year, in January. Thereafter it may be nearly a year before all the appropriation bills are passed, even though the fiscal year to which these bills apply is nearly half finished. Budgets also have to be prepared long in advance of presentation. Very often a Department will be preparing a budget for the next fiscal year, even before it has had hearings on the one for this year. In these circumstances not only must forecasts be made, but also assumptions are required at nearly every step of the budgetary process.

A budget concept now coming into vogue is that of the balanced budget at full employment. President Nixon advanced such a budget in January 1971 to cover the fiscal year 1972. Although this budget projected an actual deficit of more than $18 billion, it maintained that, if the economy were operating at the full employment level, the budget would be balanced because revenues would be $18 billion larger. The actual deficit was described as an expansionary force that would push the economy nearer the full employment level.

Most of the large budget deficits of recent years, apart from wartime, have arisen from revenue shortfall. When personal income declines, income tax yield declines more than proportionately. Even more importantly, when corporate profits decline, as they did in 1970, yield from the corporate profits tax falls off disproportionately. These declines in income tax yields produce the revenue shortfall because it is almost always assumed, in the revenue estimates included in the budget, that the economy will continue to grow and that income tax yield will be higher than the year before.

This annual growth in income tax yield is sometimes called the "fiscal dividend," that can be relied on to finance new expenditure programs, or to permit tax reduction. Unfortunately the fiscal dividend does not always work out as expected, just as corporations sometimes have trouble making their dividends. Fiscal dividend is a concept of the new economics. It is sometimes known as spending your money before you get it, a characteristic that is becoming all too common.

Full employment policy, to be successful, is extraordinarily dependent on correct forecasting. Both tax and budgetary policy are slow to turn around if restraint rather than expansion is wanted or vice versa. Only monetary policy can be quickly changed. For this reason it often bears the brunt of efforts to fine tune the economy or to maintain it precisely at the full employment level. Even this ability to alter policy swiftly is illusory since the effects of monetary policy often take a long time, up to 18 months, to work their way through the economy. The policy may be changed quickly, but the effects, which are what is wanted, may not be felt for some time.

In part this stems from our avoidance in this country of selective credit controls. We prefer only to restrict credit generally, leaving it to the market to work out which types of credit will actually be restricted and by how much. One thing that happens with general credit restraint is that housing always feels a tight monetary policy worse than any other sector. Mortgage loan rates are set for long periods, and a change of 1/2 percent on a mortgage makes a substantial difference over a 20- or 30-year period.

It may be said, by way of general appraisal concerning full employment policy, that it is by no means 100 percent efficient! Despite the best efforts of intelligent and dedicated men, unemployment does fluctuate above and below the 4 percent level, often by fairly substantial amounts. The situation is undoubtedly better than before we had a national full employment policy, and it will undoubtedly get still better as we gain additional experience. It is becoming clear that all elements of full employment policy must be coordinated—that budget policy, tax policy, monetary policy, and incomes policy must all be consistent and pointed toward a common objective.

Also it is plain that forecasting techniques and forecasting results must be improved. More and more elaborate econometric models are being developed for this forecasting function; as yet, however, more elaborate techniques have not contributed much to noticeably greater accuracy. The more elaborate the model, the greater seems the possibility of error. While some errors are self-canceling; others are systematic and tend to bias the entire result.

President Nixon announced in a televised speech on August 14, 1971, his new economic policy. It is the latest development in full employment and anti-inflation policy. As is now well known, this policy embraced four elements, namely: (1) a 90-day wage and price freeze, to be followed by a less comprehensive and less compulsory system of wage and price restraint; (2) a 10 percent import surcharge on dutiable products imported from abroad, designed to improve the United States balance of payments; (3) a limited tax reduction designed to stimulate both business investment and consumer expenditure; and (4) *de facto* devaluation of the dollar by embargoing the export of gold and allowing the dollar to float against other currencies in the foreign exchange market.

As this is written it is too soon to evaluate the effects of this policy upon the economy. Some of the price rise has been stopped but may well resume when the freeze is lifted. Other countries, particularly Japan, Canada, and the members of the European Common Market, are disturbed by the trade restriction and by the new uncertain status of the dollar. The retaliatory measures these foreign countries may take have yet to emerge. The tax reduction bill made its way through Congress, emerging in only a slightly different form than the President proposed. While we have yet to fix a new parity in the International Monetary Fund for the dollar, it would seem that a decision cannot be long delayed, if the dollar is to retain its position as the principal reserve currency of the world. When the pending bill passes Congress, the dollar will be officially redefined as 1/38 of an ounce of gold.

This new policy points up the fact that economics is clearly central to domestic political policy, and that United States economic policy is necessarily closely linked with the economic policies of other countries. Past is the time when we could be isolationist in economics, just as we can no longer pursue that course in diplomacy or environmental management. We

Loading goods for export at San Francisco. Exports of merchandise are a main pillar in the United States balance of payments. Normally an export surplus has helped to pay our deficit on travel account and for the support of military forces abroad. With the disappearance of an export surplus in 1971, the United States was forced to resort to emergency measures including devaluation and the 10 per-cent import surcharge.

live in an interdependent world, whether we like it or not.

As the effects and implications of this new economic policy unfold, you will have a case study in macroeconomic policy that will enable you to apply many of the principles this book has sought to present.

The welfare state.

Closely related to full employment policy are other policies for improving the living conditions and the opportunities of people. We already have a Department of Health, Education, and Welfare, which President Nixon proposes to rename the Department of Human Resources. A society which attempts many programs to improve the welfare of people is sometimes known as a "welfare state." Some years ago conservatives deplored the growth of welfare programs as making people less self-reliant and encouraging them to lean on a sheltering government, whose functions would inevitably proliferate. Today it appears the welfare state is here to stay. Let us examine briefly some of the implications of this broadening of the functions of government.

The welfare state is a state in which a substantial part of the revenue and much of the concern of government is with improving the lot of human beings who are disadvantaged or distressed in some way. Some manifestations of the welfare state to date are social security, unemployment compensation, aid to veterans and the handicapped, and, of course, outright relief to the needy.

As our society has grown richer, welfare outlays have grown correspondingly, not because poverty and human misery have grown, but because social consciousness has advanced. The Bible says the poor are always with us. In the 19th century it was rather blithely assumed that people were poor because they were lazy or slovenly, or because they had too many children. Now we recognize the root causes of poverty to be more complex, and to include unpromising family background, lack of education and training, and a general feeling of inability to surmount the very real obstacles that surround impoverished groups, in urban slums and elsewhere.

Human rights, once seen rather narrowly in a context of equality before the law, and freedom to worship, are now seen also to have an economic dimension, such as the right to a job, and a reasonable opportunity to advance by one's own efforts. In 1946 the United States Congress passed the Employment Act which set full employment as a continuing goal of national policy. In pursuit of that goal, certain procedural steps are required—an annual economic report to the Congress, continual surveillance of the economy by the Council of Economic Advisers, and recommendations for legislation deemed necessary to achieve and maintain full employment—a condition nowhere defined in the law but now generally interpreted as being employment of at least 96 percent of the labor force, those persons willing to work and either doing so or actively seeking work.

The labor force is an elastic magnitude; married women frequently move into and out of it as do students, older workers, and new entrants who have little or no job experience. Four percent unemployment is commonly regarded as normal, in view of the ebb and flow of different occupations, movements from one area to another, and other shifts in occupational attachment.

Some of those who deplore the growth in the welfare state, and many conservatives do, are not guilty of lack of humanity, or inadequate concern for their fellow men, but rather are troubled because in all sincerity they believe that the provision of welfare services erodes incentives to work, and robs people of responsibility for their own condition, a responsibility they may feel but be unable to carry. Instead of the poor being humble, they are today often militant. Their attention is fixed on the immediate present; long-range programs for their benefit have little appeal to them.

There is now more general acceptance of elements of the welfare state once considered radical or controversial. In the 1930's social security was considered by many to be a radical idea; it was called financially unsound, a deterrent to thrift, and many other things. Thirty-five years later few would question its utility or its contribution to the general welfare, whatever that may be.

The "general welfare," however vague its meaning, is a concept that recurs constantly in government and in economic prescription. "Economic prescription" is that part of economics which presumes to tell groups or nations what they should do—to avoid or to cure well-recognized problems.

There is a body of economics called "welfare economics;" it claims to analyze scientifically some propositions that relate to the well being of groups of people. This is a very difficult field of study because it is well recognized that satisfactions realized by different people are not comparable. We each place different subjective valuations on fast autos, symphonic music, thick steaks, vacations and travel, and all the other things, tangible and intangible, that we consume if our means allow.

Nor do tastes differ only with regard to objects of consumption. There are trade-offs between work and leisure, and between today and tomorrow. In a poor society the number of these choices is limited and the range of choice narrow; as we become affluent, the range broadens although our options may not increase correspondingly. Few individuals, for example, can decide whether they want to work 6, 7 or 8 hours a day; hours are generally prescribed and dictated by the rhythms of the business in which they are employed.

The general welfare, then, is now a vague entity that may be recognized but cannot easily be described. Efforts to describe it generally turn out to be slogans such as "better housing for all," "a guaranteed annual wage," or the like. These may initially be mere verbalizations of a common aspiration; sometimes such verbalizations can be translated into practical programs for progress toward that aspiration. These programs are the very essence of the welfare state.

Presently there is great concern for pollution of the environment. It is inevitable that an affluent society will have more waste products—more wrappings, more containers, more smoke, more heat dissipated, and more noise. It is also true that polluters of the environment cannot expect indefinitely to throw the burden of their actions upon the society at large. A dirty chemical plant, for example, cannot continue to dump more and more waste into a stream, to the detriment and expense of thousands of individuals and installations located miles downstream. Yet, generally, we lack legislation, consensus policies, and even agreement on principles for coping with this kind of situation. We do, however, have certain approaches to these basic principles.

If a steel mill pollutes a stream, we say that the private cost of steelmaking is less than its social cost, which includes the cost of overcoming or clearing up the pollution. If by legislation we forced all steelmakers to install waste disposal systems so they did not pollute streams, the price of steel would probably rise to cover the cost of installing and maintaining these systems. We would then say that the private and social costs of steelmaking had been more nearly equalized.

Much of welfare economics is a search for areas and for ways and means whereby private and social costs can be brought more nearly together. This by no means exhausts the subject matter staked out by the welfare economists. They have much to say, for example, about the relative usefulness of different types of public expenditure.

Economic growth policy.

Much of economic policy today is concerned with promoting economic growth, preferably without inflation. Growth refers to increasing output in constant or stabilized prices and is commonly measured by deflated gross national product. Often growth is measured by "per capita deflated GNP." An economy in which output is not growing faster than population is not really progressing in a fundamental sense.

Growth is attributable to a number of factors. One is increasing the intensity of use of existing resources. If labor and capital are unemployed, additional product can be secured by bringing the economy up to a full employment level. Policy to achieve full employment is often regarded primarily as contracyclical policy rather than growth policy *per se.*

Some economists think growth should be measured only over fairly long periods, such as 25 years or more, and that the measurements should be based on the trend from corresponding points in successive cycles, i.e., from full employment points only.

Another source of growth is increased input into the productive process, such as more people at work, more land under cultivation, and more machinery in factories. Economic inputs have both quantitative and qualitative dimensions. Improvements in the education and skill of the labor force are essentially a qualitative increase in labor input. Some economists feel this factor of skill has been a primary source of economic growth in advanced economies during recent decades. Lack of education and skill has certainly been a strong reason why many less developed countries have been unable to achieve satisfactory growth rates, in spite of both capital and technical assistance from outside.

Another source of growth has been the expansion of output per unit of input. This is often called "productivity." It stems largely from technological advance, from better organization of productive processes, and from new and

Testing a solar battery. This device converts the sun's rays into electrical energy. New technology is constantly giving us new and better products, but the development period is often quite long. That solar energy could be used has been known for a long time; but most applications are too expensive to compete with conventional energy sources.

better methods of doing things. Whereas coal was mined formerly by men armed with picks and shovels, it is done today by complex machines that undercut a seam of coal, break it loose, and load it by mechanical conveyers. One man with such a machine can mine far more coal in a day than could a crew of 20 with their picks and shovels; moreover, the cost per ton is less, despite the fact that the machine is very expensive.

Technological progress consists largely in mechanizing processes that were formerly done by hand. An electric company until recently needed a large roomful of clerks to calculate and send out monthly bills. Now this is done by a computer operated by only two or three people.

A fourth source of economic growth is increasing specialization and subdivision of labor. Formerly an automobile factory fabricated virtually all the parts in a car—the wheels, the engines, the body, the upholstery, everything. Rolls Royces and Ferraris are still made this way. Today's typical automobile factory, however, is primarily an assembly point for components made by many different plants scattered over a wide area. One plant may make only carburetors, another only mufflers, a third only wind-

Alexander Graham Bell, inventor of the telephone, talking on one of his first instruments. The telephone is a prime example of a seminal invention that has given rise to a large industry. Bell, who suffered from deafness, spent many years studying the transmission of sound through various media. The telephone was his only significant invention.

shields. By specializing in a single product the advantages of mass production methods can be realized to the fullest extent.

Technological progress also arises from inventions and discoveries and their adaptation into functioning productive practices. Economists call such adaptations "innovations." Some innovations may be extremely simple in conception—for example, the self-service retail store or supermarket. Thirty years ago such establishments were virtually nonexistent; today most retail establishments operate on this basis. Fewer clerks are needed, the customer gets a better exposure to the range of products available, and costs are lower.

Similarly, the invention of the transistor or semi-conductor during World War II has resulted in the general redesign of radios, television sets, and electronic gear of all types. These products can now be made smaller, more durable, and cheaper than when vacuum tubes were standard. Aircraft can carry more complex navigation and communication equipment with greater safety and effectiveness.

As our economy becomes more complex and technological, the emphasis of work will necessarily change. More and more of a premium is being placed on knowledge, skill, and the capacity for independent thought. The demand for common labor is steadily diminishing, while the demand for electronic engineers, computer programmers, and ecologists is steadily increasing. Some pundits even go so far as to see the economy of the future as one in which machines will work and people will think.

There is a grain of truth in this proverb except for the fact that thinking is work, and hard work too; but it is of a different character than shoveling coal. The economy of the future will want more thinkers and fewer coal shovelers. This means the incomes of thinkers will increase and those of coal shovelers will diminish.

Invention and innovation.

New products and new processes are a potent source of economic growth. It is a source of pride with many technologically oriented companies that a substantial share of their output consists of products unknown ten years ago. During your lifetime such new products as transistor radios, teflon coatings, and indoor-outdoor carpet have appeared on the market. Those of us who are a little older can remember many more products, like television, that once were totally new.

New products come into being because of *inventions.* Invention is encouraged in this and other countries by a patent system. In the United States, if you invent something you believe is new, you file an application for a patent with the United States Patent Office. There your application

Searching patents at the United States Patent Office. Prior to filing a patent application, it is customary to have a search of existing patents to determine whether a possible invention is really new. If the search discloses that similar patents have not been issued, the application can be filed with a reasonable expectation that a patent will be granted. Examiners in the Patent Office conduct a second and more thorough search after the application has been filed and before the patent is granted. These men are probably patent attorneys or patent agents.

will be carefully examined by technically trained people to determine whether it is actually novel or is comprehended in the prior art. If the examiner finds it is indeed novel and is something more than a mere detailed improvement such as could be expected of a skilled mechanic, you will be granted a patent giving you the exclusive right to make, use, or sell your invention for a period of 17 years.

You can make the product yourself if you have a factory and sufficient capital, or you can license the patent to an established manufacturer, usually for a *royalty,* that is, a contract under which the manufacturer will pay you, say, 5 percent of the income from the sale of the patented product. You may assign or sell him the patent outright for a fixed sum, or on a royalty basis. You may license only one maker with an exclusive license or several with nonexclusive licenses.

Usually a fairly long and expensive amount of development work will be involved before an invention can be translated into a commercial product. Machinery may have to be redesigned; the product market tested; people trained to produce, package, and sell it. All this development work may be quite expensive, so the manufacturer may want an exclusive license in order to undertake it.

If you are employed by a company as an engineer or research worker, you will probably be required under your employment contract to assign any patents you may acquire in the course of your work to your employer, who may or may not pay you special compensation for any such inventions.

Once a newly patented product or process has been engineered and put into use we have what economists call an "innovation"—something new to be sold or some improvement in business practice. This will give the company with the innovation a competitive advantage in the way of increased sales or lower costs. Other companies will attempt to follow suit. Some may copy your new product without obtaining a license. This is called "infringing" a patent. The owner of a patent is entitled to sue infringers and to obtain damages from them if the infringement can be proved.

Other companies will not infringe a patent but attempt to invent around it, come up with some product or process that is similar but not the same as the one you have invented. They may find it difficult or impossible to obtain a patent on their variation, since your patent is already on file.

Because of the importance of new technology, many companies maintain research laboratories staffed with technically trained people just to work out new products and processes. This company financed research and development work is especially important in such industries as ethical drugs, chemicals, sophisticated machinery such as computers, and electronics. Companies with the capability for advanced technology may also do research work on contract for the United States Government, in such fields as military hardware, space travel, and atomic energy.

Sometimes military or other government work will have spin-offs in the way of civilian applications. For example, making heat shields for space vehicles may develop coatings and make more durable mufflers for cars. Government expenditures for research and development, or "R and D" as it is called, are several times as large as company-financed R and D for their own purposes; but fewer patents result per $1 million of outlay by the government. In part this is because the work is highly specialized and may have no civilian counterpart.

When a patent expires after 17 years, the technology involved moves into the "public domain" and may be used by anyone without payment of royalties. Thus Edison's original patents on the electric light bulb, the phonograph, etc., have all now expired. However, improvements on an original idea may be patentable and may run for some time after the original patent has expired. Color television circuits, for example, are covered by a large number of patents, some of them still in force.

If you obtain a patent in the United States, it is good only in this country. If you wish to market your invention in Germany or Japan, you must obtain separate patents from those countries. Other countries have patent systems that are generally similar to ours, although the details may be a bit different. Some countries, for instance, grant a patent to the first to file; we give it to the first to invent, even though he is not the first to file.

Closely related to the patent system are the laws governing *trademark* and *copyright.* A trademark is a business symbol, such as "Kodak" or "Coca Cola," that is registered with the United States Patent Office. Once registered and found not confusingly similar to some other registered mark, the registrant has the exclusive right to use it and to sue others for infringement. The registrant must take care, however, to protect his mark and to prevent its being used as a common term. Such words as cellophane, thermos bottle, and nylon were once registered marks that have become generic words and are no longer exclusive property.

Once a business registers a trademark, it is advertised and used to promote sales. The trademark "Kodak," for example, is an extremely valuable asset of the Eastman Kodak Co. Coined words like "Kodak" are easy to maintain because they have no ordinary meaning. Trademark registrations may be renewed indefinitely as long as they are used and remain distinctive.

Copyright protection is granted to literary, artistic, or musical compositions, which are original and are filed with the Copyright Office, which is a part of the Library of Congress. Should you compose a popular song, for example, you need only deposit it with the Copyright Office, pay a small fee, and receive in turn control over the right to make copies for 28 years. You could then license this copyright to a music publisher, or a manufacturer of records, for a royalty. Books, magazine articles, newspapers, and even sermons are commonly protected by copyright. Similarly, performances by singers, bands, etc., are protected by copyright, even television commercials.

The theory behind patents, trademarks, and copyrights is that individuals, by scientific or intellectual effort, have created unique properties which they own and for which they deserve to be rewarded. Only by marketing the fruit of their effort in some fashion will this reward be obtained. Usually it comes in the form of a royalty. An author, for example, gets a royalty from his publisher based on the number of books sold; an inventor may be similarly compensated.

Human Resources policy.

Closely related to policies for promoting economic growth are policies to improve our *human resources.* The relation is close not only because people who are better fed, housed, and educated make better workers, but also because many problems such as crime, drug addiction, etc., which cost tax dollars are, in part at least, attributable to lack of economic opportunity. We are all aware that unemployment, crime, and other social ills are much higher in urban ghettos than in other areas. All these problems are complex and do not yield to any single remedy; but better education, better housing, and access to jobs are at least part of the answer.

An important component of the welfare state is programs for improving human resources. Thus we now have antipoverty programs, economic opportunity programs, programs to promote minority business enterprises, head start programs for underprivileged children, adult education programs, student loan and assistance programs, low rent housing programs, and many others of this general nature. For those unable to work we have "medicare" and "medicaid," and for those without income we have "welfare," formerly called "relief." These programs are all concerned with basic human needs such as food, shelter, medical care, education, and jobs. Welfare programs of all kinds are now the largest civilian expenditure in the federal budget, being second only to military outlays.

Human resources programs all recognize that people are the nation's most important resource, and that the stable fabric of society, as we know it, rests on all the people being decently fed and housed, and having reasonable access to methods of earning their own living. It is deplorable that in an affluent society—the most affluent the world has seen—we should have so many pockets of poverty, and that they should be so resistant to cleaning up as they seem to be.

We are coming to see that those who are deprived may have their own culture and this is not necessarily to be changed merely by changing one aspect of it such as housing or job opportunity. The culture of the deprived also has racial overtones, although poverty is by no means a Negro problem. The American Indian is perhaps the most deprived minority still to be found in the United States. Theirs is not an urban but a rural poverty; it is no less real because they have been the wards of the United States Government for some time. If one looks closely at the Indian, it is hard to be optimistic about other federal programs to help the disadvantaged.

Housing has been a special concern of the federal government for some time. Besides low rent public housing for the poor we have many forms of assistance to home ownership, such as FHA, veterans housing, the model cities program, and others. Government guarantees home mortgages, subsidizes home ownership by allowing interest and property taxes as income tax deductions, and gives grants to local governments for schools, highways, and other necessary conveniences.

Whereas 50 years ago home ownership was a luxury for the well-to-do, today it is within the reach of nearly every family. Nevertheless, a significant fraction of the population is still ill housed. Although we are building in excess of 1.5 million new dwelling units per year, the backlog of housing needs will not be worked off for a long period.

One aspect of the housing problem that is just beginning to get the attention it should have had for some time is the problem of "suburban sprawl." The bulk of housing around cities has been built in suburban areas, with the central cities decaying and declining as desirable places to live. This has meant the city tax bases have eroded, and consequently the revenue needed to provide essential services within the cities—police, fire protection, street maintenance, trash removal, etc.—has been lagging behind. While most noticeable in large cities such as New York or Chicago, this has been happening in smaller cities as well. Suburban living has raised mass transportation problems, clogged highways, and created severe parking problems within the central city business districts.

We can expect housing to continue to be a major preoccupation of the federal government, and housing programs to continue to expand and grow more expensive. The latest wrinkle is rent subsidies to low income families, who are unable to be accommodated in subsidized public housing. The only subsidy to home ownership is a small one to veterans who buy houses with the assistance of government-guaranteed mortgages.

The oldest and still the largest government program for the improvement of human resources is public education. Through high school this is still primarily a local concern, although there are programs, such as the school lunch program, in which the federal government assists localities. At the college and university level, many institutions are basically state supported while others are private, being supported by churches, endowments, and in other ways. Many state colleges originally received land grants from the federal government in return for teaching agriculture, engineering, and other subjects then considered particularly useful. Basically, however, most state schools are supported by appropriations which are generally unrestricted, from the state legislatures. Private colleges have to be constantly passing the hat to friends and alumni, and raising tuition, virtually on an annual basis. The lot of the private college, in this era of soaring costs, is by no means an easy one.

Education is increasingly necessary as our society grows more complex. One needs to know more, not only to earn a living, but to cope with more complex devices, to live in an urban society, and to utilize the increasing leisure that is one of the by-products of economic advance. It is no longer necessary to work from sunup to sundown as our forefathers did, whether on farms, in factories, or in stores. Today the 8-hour day and the 5-day week are standard. More and more, talk is being heard about the 7- or 6-hour day and the 4-day week. Both these objectives will doubtless be realized in your lifetime.

Education is manifestly one of the most important programs in human resources development, but what is needed is a balanced program. Academic training is not for everyone; one of the greatest needs at present is for good vocational high schools in sufficient numbers to train those whose *formal* education will stop at the high school level. In colleges much training is being given in the wrong subjects because students too seldom forecast accurately the knowledge they will need 10 and 15 years hence. Too many courses are selected for momentary appeal or because they appear germane to enthusiasms of the moment.

This is not to imply that college studies should be guided solely by vocational plans and interests. On the contrary, liberal arts training, divorced from vocational plans, is often the best training for careers where breadth is required. Rather, the plea is for acquiring knowledge systematically, in whatever field is followed, than for studying smatterings of many different subjects, as though sampling hors d'oeuvres at a buffet table.

Policy regarding human resources is clearly a broad field, the dimensions of which are as yet imperfectly laid out. We can be certain that government activity in this area will increase and that new and broader programs will appear as time goes on. What maybe the eventual shape of these programs is anyone's guess at this time.

This brief survey of the rudiments of economics is now complete. It has touched only the high points and omitted most of the subtleties and intricacies. These will be found in deeper and more specialized books. As a subject economics has neither beginning nor end. Its origins are lost in antiquity, while its end will come only if the world ceases to be a complex, interdependent society.

In 1790 Edmund Burke, English lawyer and politician, wrote that "the age of chivalry is gone. That of sophisters, economists, and calculators has succeeded." Burke's lament, his remembrance of things past, is the longing of many for a bygone age. But life does not stand still. So long as man must struggle for a living, and so long as the institutions of commerce and government grow more complex, the economist will be with us. In his curious way he will continue to study men, money, and markets.

INDEX

A

Acceleration principle, 237
Accounting, 13-15
Ad Valorem duty, 255
Affluence, 2
AF of L, 219, 222-3, 255-6
Agricultural development, 274
Alger, Horatio, 216
Alice in Wonderland, 20
American Civil War, 42, 197
Annuities, 152
Appropriations, 165-7
  deficiency or supplemental, 172
Appropriations committees, 165-6
Aristotle, 148
Auction, 58

B

Balance of trade, 249
Balance sheet, 14, 16-17
Bank acceptance rate, 135
Bank deposits, 149-50
Banking, 119-21
  central, 124-7
Bank of England, 128
Barter, 115
Batting average, 26
Bears, 139
Beggar your neighbor policies, 47
Bill of exchange, 145
Bonds, 34
Bond yields, 145
Book-of-the-Month Club, 131
Break even point, 23
Brokers vs. dealers, 141
Budgets, 163-82
  current and capital, 171-2
Bulls, 139
Burma, 9
Business cycles, 234-40
Business, great variety of, 20
Business, location, 21
Business, repair, 21-3
Business, similarity to war, 31

C

Cantillon, Richard, 214
Capital budgets, 171-2
Capital, meanings, 8
Capital requirements, 22
Central banking, 124-7
Chancellor of the Exchequer, 163
Cheap money, 40
Checking accounts, 150
Chicago Board of Trade, 58
Choices, 111
Churchill, Winston, 267
Classical school, 51
Collective bargaining, 219-20
Commercial paper, 34, 135
  rate, 135
Committee for Economic Development, 180
Competition, 28-32
  fair and unfair, 30-2
  pure, 29
  regulator of business profits, 30
Consumer economics, 278-9
Contracyclical policy, 240-5
Convertible bonds, 36
Copyright, 298
Corporate securities, 154-6
Corporation, 33
  bonds, 155
  income tax, 187-9
Cost, 63-6
  fixed, 65
  overhead, 65-6
  variable, 65
  of service principle, 87
Costa Rica, 174, 249
Council of Economic Advisers, 41, 169, 239
Craft unions, 219
Credit, 131-5
  and confidence, 147
  open book type, 132
Credits, 13
Crusoe, Robinson, 52
Cyclical turning points, 234

D

Dartmouth College Case, 33
Death taxes, 189-90
Debentures, 34

Debits, 13
Debs, Eugene, 222
Debt management, 175-6
Deficiency appropriations, 172
Demand, 58-60
  elasticity of, 61-3
  schedule of, 59-60
Demand charge, 89
Depreciation, 15, 94-5, 101
De Tocqueville, A., 247
Discount rate, 133
Discretionary income, 5
Disraeli, B., 147
Diversification, of investments, 161
Dollar, U.S., 115
  Hong Kong, 115
Dow Jones averages, 140

E

East India Company, 85
Econometric models, 246
Economic
  decisions, 5
  growth, 292-5
  inputs, 293
  policy, 110-13
  planning, 269-70
  theory, 11
Education, 300-1
Efficiency, 53
Egypt, 265
Employment policy, 284-90
Endowment policy, 151
Entrepreneur, 6
Epictetus, 98
Equation of Exchange, 123
Equilibrium, 18
Equity capital, 35, 202-3
Estate tax, 189-90
European Common Market, 258
Exchange controls, 261-2
Excise taxes, 190-1

F

Factors of production, 20-1, 200-12
  optimum combination of, 23
Fallacies, 20, 43-4
Federal Reserve System, 127-30, 144
Feudal system, 216
Fine tuning, 244
Fiscal dividend, 287
Fiscal incentives, 186
Fixed cost, 65
Floating exchange rates, 262-3
Ford Foundation, 81
Ford, H., 35
Forecasting, 245-7
Foreign aid, 178
Foreign exchange, 249-51
  crises, 274
France, 269
Franchise contracts, 160
Free enterprise system, 6
Free trade, 49
Friedman, M., 123
Fringe benefits, 217
Full employment, 284
Functional distribution of income, 199-204

G

Galbraith, J. K., 1
Gardner, John, 11
GATT, 254, 265
Geographic location of industry, 36-8
General Motors, 7, 80
German historical school, 51
Germany, 42
Gift taxes, 189-90
Goldsmith principle, 120
Gompers, S., 219
Government securities market, 141-2

H

Haggling, 58
Harding, W. G., 13
Heckshel, E., 268
Hemlines, 19
Heraclitus, 43
History and economics, 40
Hitler, A., 117
Hoover, H., 241
Hope Natural Gas Case, 97-8
House Appropriations Committee, 80
Housewifery, 182
Hull, C., 254
Human resources policy, 299-301

I

Import taxes, 192
Income distribution, 199-213
Incomes policy, 285-6
Income tax, 185-7
Increasing returns, 75
Indianapolis, 204
Industrial revolution, 2, 45-6
Industrial unions, 219
Inflation, 116
Innovation, 73
Innovation theory, 236
Interest, 208-9
    rates, 202
Intermediate products, 78, 100
International
    Labor Organization, 227-8
    Monetary Fund, 116, 122
    Payments, balance of 249-50
Interstate Commerce Commission, 87, 91
Invention, 295-7
I.W.W., 223

J

Jawboning, 285
Jefferson, T., 198

K

Keynes, J. M., 42, 46, 180, 239
Knights of Labor, 221-2

L

Labor, Department of, 220
Labor force, 228
Labor mobility, 206-7
Labor theory of value, 233
Laissez-faire, 51
Land values, 200-2
Leading indicators, 236
League of Nations, 227
Leverage, 35
Life insurance, 150-2
Liquidity, 121-2
Location of industry, 279
Locke, Jr., 198
London Metal Exchange, 52
Loss leaders, 31

M

Macaulay, T., 267
Macro and micro economics, 12-13
Malthus, T. R., 2-3
Management and Budget, Office of, 165, 168
Marginal concept, 25-7
    cost, 25
    product, 26
    revenue, 25
Markets, 53
Marshall, A., 18
Marshall, J., 33
Marx, K., 199, 237
Mathematical method, 281-2
McCulloch vs. Maryland, 198
Mercantilists, 41
Microeconomics, 57
Middle Ages, 216
Mill, J. S., 211, 283
Mississippi River, 41
Mitchell, W. C., 236
Molly Maguires, 221
Money, 115-21
    forms of, 118-19
    functions of, 115-18
    quantity theory of, 123
Monopolist, 83
Most favored nation principle, 254
Multinational business, 266
Mutual funds, 157

N

National Labor Union, 221
National income, 105-7
National product, 99-105
Nature of economics, 4
New economics, 50
New York Stock Exchange, 135-9, 143
Nixon, R., 179
Norris LaGuardia Act, 224
Nuclear physics, 46

O

Off-peak rates, 89
Open Market Committee, 129-30
Overhead costs, 63

P

Pakistan, 178
Partnership, 32
Patents, 296-7
Pay Board, 286
Pensions, 230-2
Perry, Admiral, 45
Personal exemptions, 187
Petty, Sir W., 19, 99
Physiocrats, 50
Piecework, 205
Piggy-back income taxes, 196-7
Property taxes, 196-7
Plato, 148
Plutarch, 56
Policy formulation, 55
Pollution, 292
Polo, M., 248
Pound sterling, 117
Preferred stock, 35
Preservation of environment, 280-1
Price Commission, 286
Price-earnings ratio, 154-5
Price flexibility, 71
Price system, 3, 66-8
Pricing in a socialist economy, 68
Prime rate, 133
Product differentiation, 28
Profit, 21, 23, 25, 203-4
Profit maximization, 79
Property taxes, 196
Proprietorship, 32
Prospectus, 34
Proudhon, M., 213
Public borrowing, 197-8
Public utilities, 85-98
Public utility valuation, 93-4, 98
Pure competition, 29
Puts and calls, 157
Pyramids, 24

R

Rate base, 91-2
Rate setting, 86
Real estate, 158-9
Regulation of credit and capital markets, 143-4
Rent, theory of, 210-11
Reparations, 42-3
Retail credit, 145
Revenue earmarking, 173-4
Revenue flexibility, 186
Revenue sharing, 195
Ricardo, D., 183, 210-11
Robertson, D. H., 8
Rockefeller, J., 31
Royalty, 296
Russia, 212

S

Sales tax, 193-4
Savings accounts, 150
Savings bonds, 153
Say, J. B., 233
Schumpeter, J. 236
Securities and Exchange Commission, 34
Shaw, G. B., 1
Silent partner, 33
Small Business Administration, 143
Smith, Adam, 21, 50, 51, 84, 212
Smyth vs Ames, 97
Social cost, 292
Social Security Act, 225
Social security trust fund, 173
Special drawing rights, 122
Specific duty, 255
Standard deduction, 187
Stationary state, 211-2
Steel production, 36-7
Sterling silver, 117
Steuart, Sir J., 46
Stock exchanges, 135-9
Stock market, 48
Substitution, 76
Switzerland, 253

T

Tariffs, 254-6
Tawney, R. H., 1
Taxable income, 187
Taxation, 183-97
Technology, 22
Term insurance, 152
Textile industry, 38
Tolstoi, L., 114
Tom Jones, 57
Trade barriers, 253-6
Trademark, 298
Transfer payments, 107

U

Underconsumption theories, 238
Underwriters, 34-5
United States
  Customs Service, 255
  Employment Service, 204
  foreign trade, 259-61
  Government securities, 68-9, 153-4

V

Value added, 108
Value added tax, 191-2
Value of service principle, 87
Variable costs, 65
Variables, 54
Voltaire, M., 217

W

Wages, iron law of, 3, 214
Wampum, 118
Warburg, P. 130
War finance, 275-6
Warrants, 35, 156-7
Wealth, 8-10
Weber, M. 283
Welfare state, 290-2
Wells, H. G., 1
Wheat farming, Canadian, 24
Work, motivation for, 215-17

Y - Z

Yap, island of, 118
Yardstick competition, 96
Yellow dog contract, 224
Zero base program review, 177